ART *of*
McSWEENEY'S

by THE EDITORS OF McSWEENEY'S

CHRONICLE BOOKS

SAN FRANCISCO

IMPOSSIBLE, YOU SAY?

*Nothing is impossible
when you work for the circus.*

Subject:
Date: Mon, 13 Jul 1998 16:28:25 -0400
From: deggers@hearst.com (David Eggers)
To: brent@pivtech.com

Here are both emails, which I originally sent a few weeks apart. Bear in mind that the quarterly will not be all laughs and levity, though this implies, I guess, it will be just that.

#1.

Hi you people. This is about that quarterly I'm starting later this summer. This might be the first you've heard of it. It might not. Does it matter? Nah, you're hooked already!

I think it will be called McSweeney's, after a man named
Timothy McSweeney, who, when I was growing up, used to write long, tortured, often incomprehensible letters to my family, claiming to be a long-forgotten member of my mother's side (she was Adelaide McSweeney), and outlining when and where he would be in the coming months, should we need to reach him and bring him back into the fold.

If it's not called McSweeney's, I'll find an obscure but appropriate word in the dictionary -- or, better yet, a word in another language! -- and call it that. Whatever its name, it will be about 160 pages, perfect-bound, and will in many ways look like most literary quarterlies. (I mention this to clarify that it will not be what is known, among the youth, as a "zine.")

Related conversation with ████████ :

████ : I think I have a thing for your little zine.
Me: What little what?
████ : That zine you said you were putting out.
Me: It's not a "zine." And it's not "little."
████ : Whatever it is.
Me: It's not a zine.
████ : Well, what is it?
Me: It's a quarterly.
████ : Will it actually be published quarterly?
Me: No, probably not.
████ : Okay, so I have an idea.
Me: And it's not little.
████ : Do you want to hear the idea or not?
Me: Fine.
████ : Okay, so;
Me: Asshole.

The hope is that this will be a place where odd things that one could never shoehorn into a mainstream periodical, and might be too quirky for other journals, might find a home. I do not expect everyone, or anyone, to produce brand-new stuff. I am relying on everyone who gets this letter, or who passes it on to a friend (feel free), will have things sitting in a closet that they had long ago abandoned hope of publishing.

There will be an emphasis on experimentation. If you have a story that's good, but conventional, you'd probably be better off sending it somewhere legitimate. This thing will be more about trying new, and almost certainly misguided, ideas.

So far I have: an unstageable play, by genius/bon vivant Mark O'Donnell, about alien invaders with exceptionally good taste who rid the earth of bad architecture; a short story, by O. Henry winner Arthur Bradford, about a giant mollusk; a treatise about artistic senility by conceptual artists Komar & Melamid; a lot of little things by former Might people; and a lot of (thus far) empty promises from legions of other "writers," "friends," and "friends" who are "writers."

In answer to your silly question, no, there is no pay and no, I do not have specific guidelines for contributions. Essays, fiction, journalism, that sort of thing. Cartoons might be okay. Diagrams are good. Two-sentence stories are fine. Stories written in rhyme are good. Poetry? No, probably not.

Other ideas for those of you without any good ones of your own:

Unfinished stories
At McSweeney's, it does not matter if the story is what you or convention would normally consider "finished." We like stories that have not been finished because the author got stuck and quit. We also like stories that have not been finished because they did not need to be finished ¦ stories that ran their course before reaching a neat conclusion. Maybe, by publishing unfinished work, we're making a much-needed point. Then again, maybe we're not.

Character sketches
Similar to the unfinished stories in that there need not be any great attention paid to plot or structure or state of completion. Let's let the world read about your long-languishing Charlie Muckenbottom, even though he isn't given much to do, plot-wise. Be free, Charlie!

The Magic of Editing
There will be a regular feature that will reveal, using a "Before and After" sort of structure, the glorious process of editing for what is known, in parlance, as "space," "tone" or "clarity." Open to particularly to writers recently touched by the wizardry of magazine editing, who are encouraged to submit 500 or so words (or much less -- but not much more) of their original text, along with the published piece, after it was much improved by an editor. The editor's and magazine's names will be removed or included, as requested.

Unaccepted pitches
Again, in an attempt to peak behind the scenes of publishing, here writers are encouraged to publish the pitches -- for magazine stories, books, whatever -- that failed to interest those who know best.

Essays that you'd write if you had the time
Here, free those ideas that you know you'll never actually flesh out. Summarize the main points, outline how you might have written the thing up, letting everyone know that if you had more time, you'd be a goddamn genius.

Short reviews of wars and skirmishes
All historical periods and opinions welcome. Reviews can be up to 2500 words, but should end with a judgment of "thumbs up" or "thumbs down."

One-question interviews with semi-famous people.
This is an interview recently conducted with Jim Cantelupe, a new linebacker for the Chicago Bears:
McSweeney : Your name is Jim Cantelupe?
Jim Cantelupe: Yes.

I suppose it sounds sort of zine-y. Maybe in some respects it is. But bear in mind that your contributions needn't be at all funny, or even all that odd, and that the quarterly won't be ziney-looking. It will look beautiful, actually, with a restrained, antiquey sort of feel. It's being designed by Elizabeth Kairys, art director of Salon. She good.

Call me with questions. 649-4291. Send me stuff, via email or c/o Esquire, by July 8. It will be out in August. Note: Anyone who wants to "wait and see," who says they'll send stuff for the "second issue" will be considered sort of finky.

C'mon everyone! It'll be fun, and if we're not careful, we might make publishing history!

#2.

You people have been so good. I have gotten so many nice things. Please keep them coming. So far, though, I have a shortage of the following:

- fiction
- essays
- reviews of wars

Please help me remedy this situation. I could also use interviews. Jason Zengerle, friend and former coworker of Stephen Glass, is doing an interview with a man who stands outside the White House with a sign that says "I WAS MOLESTED BY A PEDOPHILE PRIEST." But we're thinking that maybe in the interview he doesn't ask the man any questions about molestation or priests. That might be fun.

Other news:
My last email made its way to Ana Marie Cox, who owes me money and to whom I was once engaged, and who wrote a thing about the premise of McSweeney's in Feed.com. Take a look. An expanded and, ideally, clarified version of it will appear in the inaugural issue.

I've thought of a few other things that could become regular features:

1) Cartoons without pictures

If you cannot draw, but fancy yourself something of a cartoonist, here's your forum. Simply *describe* the picture, and provide the caption or dialogue. The following example, and the idea in general, were provided by Greg Beato:

PICTURE: The set of an infomercial called "Hair Today!" Bigfoot, suffering from male pattern baldness, sits on stage next to the infomercial's host.

caption:
BIGFOOT: The big feet I can live with. The hair loss is another story.

2) EXPLANATIONS OF NEWSPAPER AND MAGAZINE HEADLINES
This will provide a service which is long overdue. How often have you been reading a popular magazine or newspaper, and will see a clever and catchy headline, but become confused as to what pop culture or literary source it is referencing? This will elucidate those often arcane but important connections. For example:

Headline (NYT, June 13, Main Section, p.3):
IN ANDORRA, SEX, LIES AND UNEMPLOYMENT

Explanation:
This is a play on the title of a 1989 film by Steven Soderbergh entitled "Sex, Lies and Videotape," starring Andie McDowell (in a breakthrough performance), James Spader and Laura San Giacomo, now of television's smash hit "Just Shoot Me." The headline is using the movie title as a springboard to note that in Andorra, a small country bordering Spain, they are having difficulties with prostitution ("Sex"), government coruption ("Lies") and unemployment ("Unemployment"). Using a play on the title of this popular movie, of which most readers are familiar ¦ because most readers also enjoy movies and television shows ¦ helps readers get the "gist" of the article quickly, while perhaps making them smile in appreciation of the editor's thoughtful literary marriage of the politics of a small European country and a small American film, which also starred Peter Gallagher.

3) OVERLY-ANGRY REVIEWS OF TELEVISION ADS

This one I don't have time to flesh out, but you get the idea. Describe the ad, then write a passionate review, ideally using words like "pernicious," "derivative," "tired," "unconvincing," and "lamely Bergmanian."

4) ESSAYS NOT WRITTEN BY WHO WE SAY WROTE THEM
This is Zev Borow's idea. He's writing a spirited and very bitter essay about a certain demographic, and will be crediting a well-known writer other than himself with it. We're not sure why we're doing this, but are hoping the reason might become clear soon.

Deadline for everything is rapidly closing in. A week or so. Please get things to me soon. If you've sent me something but have not heard back, you will soon; I'm a little backed up. And feel free, as always, to send this to friends, as long as they are nice people to whom I was not once engaged.

I leave you with three short interviews conducted by Jill Stoddard:

Me: You have to pay for that over where it says "cash register."
Al Gore: Oh. Thank you.

Me: You know, I didn't think the doll thing was scary at all.
Stephen King: Really.

Me: Would you like one of our discount cards?
John Tesh: Heh heh. No thank you. I'm not from around here.

Art of McSweeney's

Copyright © 2010 by McSweeney's

Library of Congress Cataloging-in-Publication
Data available.

ISBN: 978-0-8118-6623-1

Manufactured in China
10 9 8 7 6 5 4 3 2
Chronicle Books LLC
680 Second Street
San Francisco, CA 94107
www.chroniclebooks.com

7/13/9   44 PM

This book is being published at a time when there are some rumblings about the dire future of the book, and of the printed book in particular.

There are various rumors that people read less now, and that people will read still less in the future. And that, even if they do read at all, it will be on screens, and not on paper. In fact, there are business people who spend their days crowing about a future where physical books are no more.

McSweeney's is a small company dedicated to these physical books that purportedly have no future. We spend a good deal of time editing books, and producing books of the highest quality we're capable of, in the hopes that in doing so, we'll keep people mindful of the pleasures of the book-as-object. We believe, in fact, that the attention paid to the book-as-object has a role in ensuring the survival of the words within that book's covers.

The average novel we publish, for example, takes three or so years to write. Another year to edit and polish. Four years of work and worry and craft. To honor all that work, and to try to get that book into as many hands as possible, we pay a lot of attention to the production of that book. To its cover, its paper, its endpapers and spine, to the package as a whole. Because if we're to ensure the survival of physical books, these books have to be things you want to buy, hold, bring to bed or the tub or the beach. Things you want to keep.

This book is dedicated to readers who love books as physical objects, and also to showing young publishers-to-be how much fun can be had while making books, and how available the means of production is to them. Throughout the book we'll talk about and show the process of publishing, and will reveal all we can, in hopes new and probably—happily—small publishing houses will continue to appear and even thrive, albeit in their admittedly and perpetually modest ways.

It should be noted that no one at McSweeney's has any formal training in book design or production. Pretty much everyone in our small company was first a volunteer or intern, and everyone considers themselves a perpetual student of the craft. We came together and remain together only out of a mutual love of words, of the neverending process of reinventing language to best help us understand the world and ourselves, and are committed to the neverending process of reinventing bookmaking to best guarantee those words live and last.

—DE, fall, 2009

What's in the Quarterly?

1
Fiction
Non-Fiction
Letters
Other

2
Fiction
Non-Fiction
Art
Other
Letters

3
Fiction
Non-Fiction
Art
Letters
Other

4
Fiction
Art
Letters
Non-Fiction
Other

5
Non-Fiction
Art
Letters
Other
Fiction

6
Art
Fiction
Non-Fiction
Other

7
Fiction
Non-Fiction

8
Fact or
Fiction
Art
Letters
Other

9
Fiction
Other

10
Fiction
Non-Fiction
Art
Letters
Other

11
Fiction
Art
Other

12
Fiction
Letters
Art
Non-Fiction
Other

13
Comics
Commentary

14
Fiction
Letters
Art
Other

15
Fiction
Letters
Art
Non-Fiction
Other

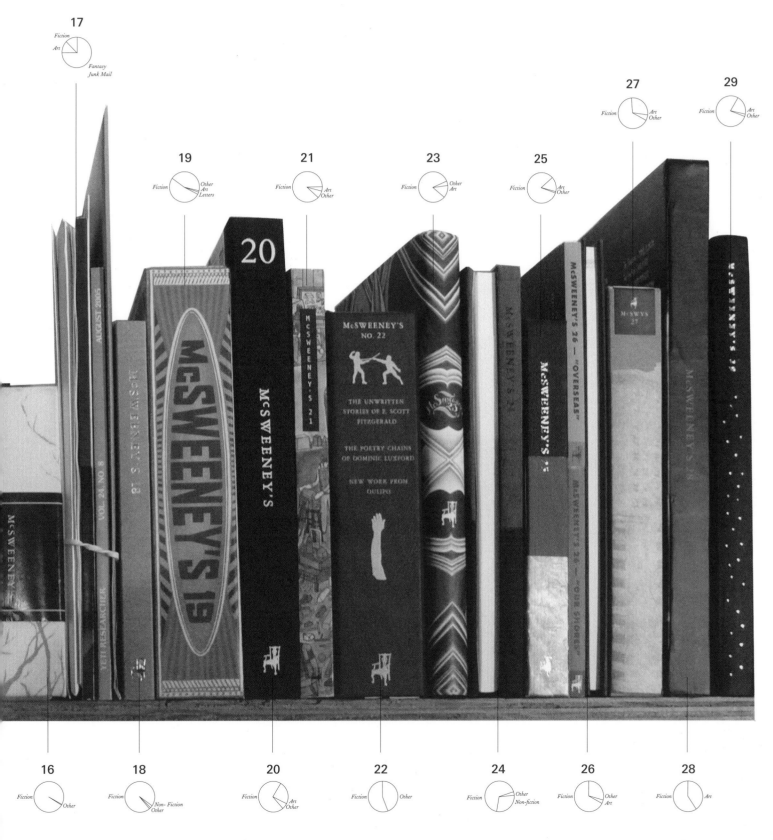

17
Fiction
Art
Fantasy
Junk Mail

19
Fiction *Other* *Art* *Letters*

21
Fiction *Art* *Other*

23
Fiction *Other* *Art*

25
Fiction *Art* *Other*

27
Fiction *Art* *Other*

29
Fiction *Art* *Other*

16
Fiction *Other*

18
Fiction *Non-Fiction* *Other*

20
Fiction *Art* *Other*

22
Fiction *Other*

24
Fiction *Other* *Non-fiction*

26
Fiction *Other* *Art*

28
Fiction *Art*

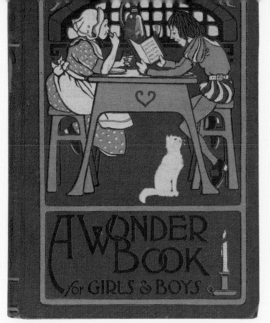

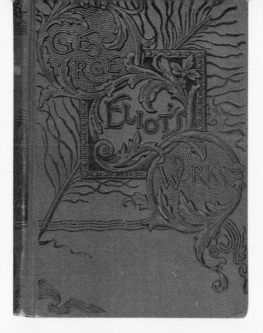

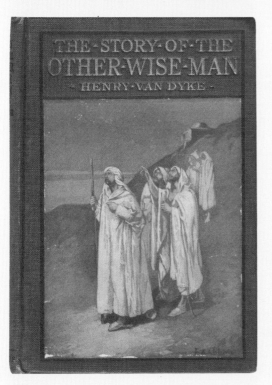

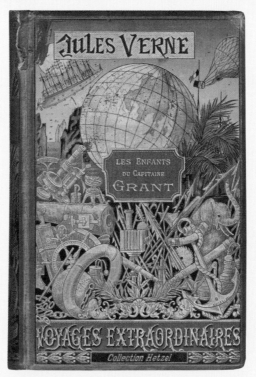

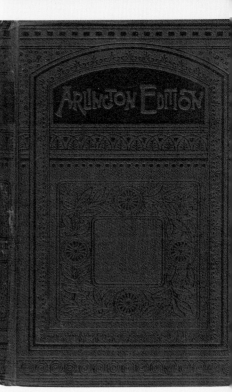

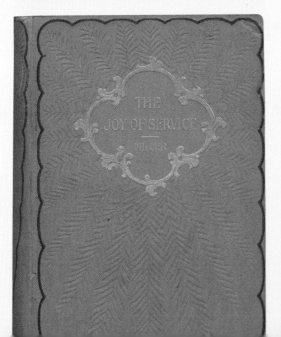

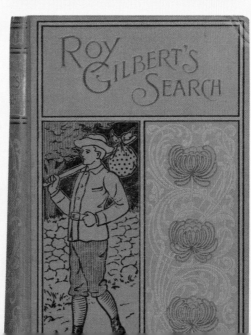

McSweeney's has always learned a lot from, and has always been inspired by, the design of older books. These examples were selected at random from the McSweeney's reference shelf. Whenever we think we've seen it all, we stumble upon (or someone shows us) something we've never seen. Several other old books from the McSweeney's collection appear throughout this book.

BECAUSE THERE IS STILL SO MUCH MISUNDERSTANDING, THERE IS:

TIMOTHY

MCSWEENEY'S

QUARTERLY CONCERN.

(FOR SHORT SAY "MCSWEENEY'S.")

KNOWN ALSO AS

"GEGENSHEIN."

Also answering to the names:

"THE STARRED REVIEW";
"THE MIXED REVIEW";
"THE GRIM FERRYMAN";
"THE PRIMITIVE";
"MCSWEENEY'S: DIAMONDS ARE FOREVER";
and
"CONDÉ NAST MCSWEENEY'S FOR WOMEN."

To you we say:

WELCOME TO OUR BUNKER!

LIGHT A CANDLE, WATCH YOUR HEAD AND— WHO, US? WELL, OKAY... AHEM:

Believing in: INDULGENCE AS ITS OWN STICKY, STRONG-SMELLING REWARD;
Trusting in: THE TIME-HONORED BREAD SAUCE OF THE HAPPY ENDING;
Eschewing: THE RECENT WORK OF SAUL BELLOW;
Waiting for: THE LIKELY SECOND COMING OF OLAF PALME;
Still thinking about: HOW THE LOCKOUT WILL AFFECT THE NBA'S LONG-TERM FAN BASE;
Relying on: STRENGTH IN NUMBERS, PROVIDED THOSE NUMBERS ARE VERY, VERY SMALL;
Hoping for: REDEMPTION THROUGH FUTILITY;
Dedicated to: STAMPING OUT SANS SERIF FONTS; *and*
CREATED *in honor of and named for*

Mr. T. Mc.

a troubled fellow, an outsider, a probable genius of indeterminate age, who wrote endlessly, recklessly to the editor's dear mother, born ADELAIDE MCSWEENEY, *pleading, in tortured notes in the margins of postal brochures, for help with his medical bills, transportation costs — put simply, he wanted attention, some consideration, an attentive ear and also, perhaps — perchance, to dream! — re-admittance into the* MCSWEENEY FAMILY, *prominent in Boston, the members of which, however — however! — did then and do now, to this day, blithely deny any knowledge of* TIMOTHY's *existence. Well!*

FOR HIM AND FOR YOU WE PRESENT THIS, WHICH INCLUDES STORIES INVOLVING THE FOLLOWING SUBJECT MATTERS: SOLDIERS DYING; GOLD MINING; SPIDERS; HAWAII; KISSING; ROMANIA; TELEVISION; SUNKEN TREASURE; FIRE.

OUR MOTTO:

"WE MEAN NO HARM."

CREATED IN DARKNESS BY TROUBLED AMERICANS.
PRINTED IN ICELAND.
1998

McSweeney's 1

(1998)

SARAH VOWELL:
I remember getting these hopeful, purposeful emails from Eggers about how we were all supposed to band together and start a journal. It was not, he emphasized, going to be a "'zine." I approved of his terminology. At the time, I didn't think there could be a less dignified name for a publication than *'zine*. Of course, that was back before I ever heard the word *blog*.

ELIZABETH KAIRYS:
I met Dave while working as an art director at Salon.com in 1997. He told me about a new publication he was developing, which spawned from the mysterious letters he had been receiving from Timothy McSweeney, and asked if I could come up with some mock-ups for the prototype.

SARAH VOWELL: At that time I was mostly earning a living writing about popular music. But I had this secret life as a person with a sparkly kitchen sink. My other writing outlets at the time, *Spin* magazine say, didn't offer me much of a forum to discuss my passion for cleaning products. They only wanted to know what I thought of the new Slayer record or whatever. But then *McSweeney's* came along and I finally had a platform to talk about antibacterial sponges.

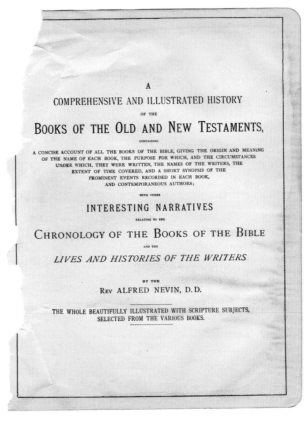

A
COMPREHENSIVE AND ILLUSTRATED HISTORY
OF THE
BOOKS OF THE OLD AND NEW TESTAMENTS,
CONTAINING
A CONCISE ACCOUNT OF ALL THE BOOKS OF THE BIBLE, GIVING THE ORIGIN AND MEANING
OF THE NAME OF EACH BOOK, THE PURPOSE FOR WHICH, AND THE CIRCUMSTANCES
UNDER WHICH, THEY WERE WRITTEN, THE NAMES OF THE WRITERS, THE
EXTENT OF TIME COVERED, AND A SHORT SYNOPSIS OF THE
PROMINENT EVENTS RECORDED IN EACH BOOK,
AND CONTEMPORANEOUS AUTHORS;
WITH OTHER
INTERESTING NARRATIVES
RELATING TO THE
CHRONOLOGY OF THE BOOKS OF THE BIBLE
AND THE
LIVES AND HISTORIES OF THE WRITERS
BY THE
REV ALFRED NEVIN, D.D.
THE WHOLE BEAUTIFULLY ILLUSTRATED WITH SCRIPTURE SUBJECTS,
SELECTED FROM THE VARIOUS BOOKS.

One of several old text designs that inspired the text-heavy design of the earliest McSweeney's *covers.*

RICK MOODY: I can't really remember when all this happened, maybe '95 or '96 or so. My good friend Courtney Eldridge, the excellent short story writer, told me she'd met this guy who was trying to make a magazine that was going to include nothing but writing that had been rejected from other magazines. She said she thought she might sort of try to help him out with it a little bit. She wanted to know if I might have something that cohered with the guidelines, that had been rejected elsewhere. Well, of course, I always had stuff around that had been rejected. It is perhaps my fate as a writer to always get a lot of rejection letters, to attract and repel in equal measure. Courtney said it could be really short, didn't matter how short.

JOHN HODGMAN: Here is what happened. In 1997, I was working as an assistant at a literary agency, reading and rejecting manuscripts and feeling pretty awful about it. Then I received an email. This felt like a kind of magic, for in 1997 I suspect I had written about ten emails in my whole life. The email was from Dave Eggers looking for contributions to a new print journal. This email was not intended for me. It

11

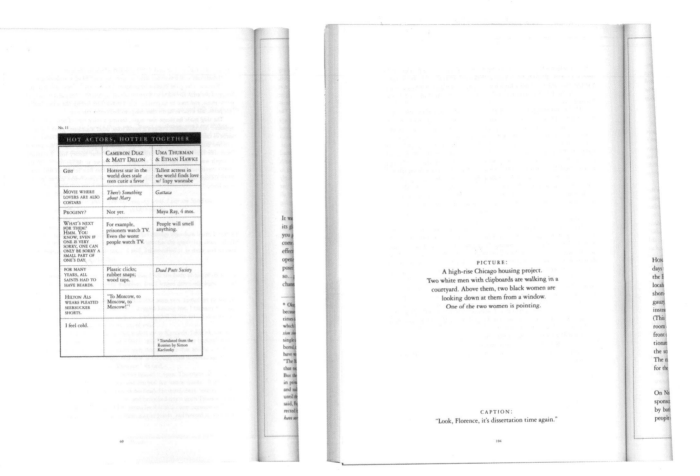

Left: An informational chart plotting hot celebrities against bearded saints and feeling cold.
Right: A cartoon featuring a brief description of a picture in lieu of a picture.

was forwarded along by my friend, Sam Potts (who is now a famous book designer and creator of all the products at the superhero supply store at 826NYC), who himself had received it as a forward. Dave's email asked for pieces that had been rejected from other magazines, as well as unfinished short stories. Given my current job of rejecting writers, I admired the first mission; and given my side job of starting but not finishing earnest short stories, I was cheered by the second. So I quickly sent him an unfinished short story about a middle-aged Argentine journalist. Dave wrote back immediately. "Who are you?" he wrote. "And how did you get my email?"

RICK MOODY: As it turned out, I had been approached not long before by the *New York Times Magazine*, a periodical I truly detest, to write something about television. For an issue they were doing on that subject. I admitted that I hated television and didn't have one, but that there was one show that I thought was truly revolutionary, that program being *The Yule Log*, a film loop of a gaily lit fire in a suburban fireplace that used to run on Xmas Day in the greater New York metropolitan area. I had been told in no uncertain terms that this was *not* in the spirit of their issue on television. I think I was supposed to write about my love for *Fantasy Island*. Anyway, I gave the piece to Courtney, who gave it to the guy with the magazine of rejected things. Then she came back a while later and said that the guy liked "The Yule Log" and was going to run it, and by the way the magazine was going to be called *McSweeney's*. Which I thought was about the worst name for a magazine I had ever heard. And I told her so.

JOHN HODGMAN: At that time I did not know Dave, though I had seen a cartoon he had drawn for a paper in San Francisco, and I presumed that made us best friends. He did not seem convinced by this logic. Nor did he want to publish my short story. However, he asked, would I have anything that might fit in their letters column? I considered this, and eventually ended up sending him pretty much the only other email I had written that year. My old friend Josh Sadow had written from Seattle asking me how I liked my new job. And since I didn't like my job and couldn't admit it, even to myself, I wrote him back pretending to be deranged. I pretended to be a high-powered publishing insider offering him all sorts of unasked-for advice on how to get published. This advice included telling Josh to insert a tiny troll into his own head, at which point in the letter it was to become clear that the high-powered publishing insider was actually crazy, and probably not very high powered, and probably, in his own way, as sad and powerless and desperate as I was feeling myself at the time. I named this character "John Hodgman." I think Dave published the letter because he enjoyed my suffering, as I know he does still. Josh, meanwhile, still lives in Seattle. He never wrote back.

ARTHUR BRADFORD: I was sending my short stories out to various magazines and getting rejected everywhere. Dave, whom I'd been in touch with back when he was at *Might*, began working at *Esquire*, so I sent him this story "Mollusks" about two guys who find a giant slug in a glove compartment. Dave wrote back and said there was no way they could ever publish a story like that, but he liked it. A little while later Dave contacted me and said he was starting this new literary journal and asked if he could print the slug story. I said sure.

SARAH VOWELL: To me, Arthur Bradford's "Mollusk" will always be *the* McSweeney's story. Besides the fact that it's funny and strange and suspenseful in its way, it was always the greatest hit of the early readings. Arthur was so tall and charming and lanky, and he accompanied himself on acoustic guitar. He had this kind of wicked innocence about him, if that makes sense.

ARTHUR BRADFORD: When *McSweeney's* first came out I was living without electricity in a handmade cabin in northern Vermont. Dave told me they were having a release party, and I was eager for social interaction so I decided to go. I had worked up this

Arthur Bradford in New York City, 1998. He has just smashed his guitar after reading a story about a mollusk in a glove compartment.

act where I would read my stories and play guitar at the same time, and Dave said, "Oh yeah, you should do that." So I did and it was well received, but I think that's because the reading was in a bar where people were drinking.

DAVE EGGERS: When I got to New York in 1997, I was pretty amazed at how expensive the nightlife could be in Manhattan. I remember the first time I ever went to a bar in New York. It was just after I'd moved there, and I went out with a few friends from college—all of us from Champaign-Urbana. And I thought I'd be a big man and buy everyone a round. I ordered three drinks and the bartender told me it was $24. For three drinks. In 1997. I had $20—enough, I thought, for a week of socializing. Anyway, thus started my strained relationship with New York nightlife. I wasn't so excited about the waiting-in-line-to-get-in sorts of bars and clubs, so for all the early McSweeney's parties we set out to find the uncoolest places in Manhattan. The Issue 1 release party was at a cowboy-themed bar-restaurant, where honestly no one had ever been. It was great, with hay on the floor and everything. Anyway, we needed to find an equally uncool place for the first McSweeney's reading. I spent a lot of time trying to get T.G.I. Friday's to let us have the restaurant for free, but they wouldn't do it.

TODD PRUZAN: The first reading was at Burp Castle, on East Seventh Street. The place was staffed by mute Ukrainian monks. The owner sounded wary over the phone. He said he'd given the magazine a shot, but that he was really more of a Carl Hiaasen man. Fair enough. I don't recall much from the evening, but there was a lecture by Komar & Melamid on "the new senility."

DAVE EGGERS: David Rakoff and Colleen Werthmann came with Randy Cohen; they helped act out a play written by Oliver North. Randy had gotten hold of it and it was amazing. That's where we first met Rakoff and Werthmann, actually.

TODD PRUZAN: What I do remember clearly of that reading was presenting the "results" of our alleged "Five Under Five" competition—five short works ("The Big Truck," "I Have a Stomachache!") by five very young "authors." "The writers couldn't make it tonight," I told the crowd. "Apparently, they're booked to read at some place called KGB."

ARTHUR BRADFORD: The next reading was in a big Chinese banquet hall. About a thousand people showed up. I wrote this story that had a moment where the narrator slammed a big snake into the ground repeatedly. The idea was I would smash my guitar all over the place during that part. I bought this cheap pawnshop guitar and told John Hodgman, the MC, about my plan. He said "I don't think you should do that." But I did it anyway, and although the effect was somewhat jarring, I sensed people enjoyed it. There were bits of guitar all over the audience. At least they shut the fuck up for a minute! I'm kidding! After that I made friends with a pawnshop owner and arranged to buy defective but operational guitars from him at a discounted price. For several years I would make a point of smashing guitars at readings, especially the McSweeney's readings. Sometimes I'd find an excuse to smash two of them. It was a lot of fun, but it's been a while since I've pulled that particular stunt. I guess I'm more mature and docile, plus I lost touch with that pawnshop guy.

SARAH VOWELL: Arthur would smash his guitar out of nowhere. Showmanship! Once I got a splinter in my eye.

TODD PRUZAN: The last page of the first issue happened like this: one night my roommate came in with a note she'd found on her windshield—*I watched you bump my car, I saw it from my kitchen window*, blah blah blah. "And it's signed!" she shouted. "Meg McGillicuddy!" We sat down at our kitchen table, and I began scribbling furiously: *The Adventures of Meg McGillicuddy*." I drew a ten-year-old sleuth with a missing tooth and a magnifying glass. Pretty soon, we had forty titles. The next year we turned this into an order form ("Have You Read Them All?"). After the issue came out, a buyer from Quimby's in Chicago sent an email requesting more information about the series. A week later, we received a torn-out order form from David Foster Wallace. He'd circled three Meg McGillicuddy titles in red ink.

ALSO AVAILABLE FROM MCSWEENEY'S PUBLISHING CONCERN,

THE "MEG McGILLICUDDY" SERIES.

Meg McGillicuddy's the name, and -- just as soon as she's done with soccer practice, piano lessons, pre-algebra homework, and talking on the phone about boys -- fighting crime's the game! Meg's had lots of adventures! Have you read them all?

MM15568	MEG McGILLICUDDY AND THE SECRET DOOR	$2.95
MM15264	MEG McGILLICUDDY AND THE PURPLE DOG	$2.95
MM13560	MEG McGILLICUDDY AND THE HIDDEN ISLAND	$2.95
MM15563	MEG McGILLICUDDY AND THE STOLEN HOUSE	$2.95
MM23522	MEG McGILLICUDDY AND THE HIDDEN ENTRANCE	$2.95
MM17889	MEG McGILLICUDDY AND THE HIDDEN TREASURE	$2.95
MM25436	MEG McGILLICUDDY AND THE STOLEN TREASURE	$2.95
MM90867	MEG McGILLICUDDY AND THE HIDDEN DOG	$2.95
MM12463	MEG McGILLICUDDY AND THE MYSTERY IN THE ATTIC	$2.95
MM19844	MEG McGILLICUDDY AND THE FAULTY LIGHTSWITCH	$2.95
MM10988	MEG McGILLICUDDY AND THE WHISPERING WIND	$2.95
MM17867	MEG McGILLICUDDY AND THE BURIED TREASURE	$2.95
MM10009	MEG McGILLICUDDY AND THE GLOWING CAVERN	$2.95
MM11178	MEG McGILLICUDDY AND THE PURLOINED COW	$2.95
MM23338	MEG McGILLICUDDY AND THE FRIVOLOUS LAWSUIT	$2.95
MM90887	MEG McGILLICUDDY AND THE RUSTY NAIL	$2.95
MM11001	MEG McGILLICUDDY AND THE BROKEN KEY	$2.95
MM15523	MEG McGILLICUDDY AND THE BOOTLEG T-SHIRT	$2.95
MM44566	MEG McGILLICUDDY AND THE STOLEN DRUGS	$2.95
MM98889	MEG McGILLICUDDY AND THE DAY OF THE BIG TEST	$2.95
MM11000	MEG McGILLICUDDY AND THE WATER CLOSET	$2.95
MM11324	MEG McGILLICUDDY AND THE BAD BUTTER	$2.95
MM11672	MEG McGILLICUDDY AND THE WEEPING WINDOW	$2.95
MM11908	MEG McGILLICUDDY AND THE TERRIBLE ODOR	$2.95
MM11002	MEG McGILLICUDDY AND THE MUDDY GALOSHES	$2.95
MM15533	MEG McGILLICUDDY AND THE CRACKED VALISE	$2.95
MM11034	MEG McGILLICUDDY AND THE CURIOUSLY STRONG MINTS	$2.95
MM15220	MEG McGILLICUDDY AND THE SECRET OF THE MUSTACHIOED POLICEMAN	$2.95
MM11342	MEG McGILLICUDDY AND THE GYM TEACHER	$7.95
MM10088	MEG McGILLICUDDY AND THE BURNING POND	$2.95
MM10091	MEG McGILLICUDDY AND THE FURRY POCKETBOOK	$2.95
MM11172	MEG McGILLICUDDY AND THE STAINED STOCKINGS	$2.95
MM32452	MEG McGILLICUDDY AND THE MEDDLESOME CROSSING GUARD	$2.95
MM19987	MEG McGILLICUDDY AND THE DELICIOUS CHICKEN DINNER	$2.95
MM11498	MEG McGILLICUDDY AND THE REALISTIC TOUPÉE	$2.95
MM00119	MEG McGILLICUDDY AND THE STONE BUCKET	$2.95
MM00120	MEG McGILLICUDDY AND MRS. JOHNSTON AT THE BEACH	$2.95
MM00212	MEG McGILLICUDDY: DIAMONDS ARE FOREVER	$2.95
MM00982	MEG McGILLICUDDY AND THE STOLEN, HIDDEN TREASURE	$2.95
MM00001	MEG McGILLICUDDY AND THE LITTLE DOG	$2.95

ORDER FORM

NAME _____

ADDRESS _____

CITY, STATE, ZIP _____

TITLES REQUESTED _____

Volume discounts available.

Please send cash to:
Martin McGillicuddy
292 Honolulu Avenue
Baltimore, MD 94117

A clip-and-mail order form for books in the McSweeney's "Meg McGillicuddy" series.

THE McSWEENEY'S
STORE
at 429 SEVENTH AVENUE

FOR: SMALL RUBBER CUBES
LUMBERJACK SUPPLY
CUSTOMIZED TROPHIES
RODEO SUPPLY
PEWTER CAST BIRD FEET
PUZZLE PIECES
DENTISTRY SUPPLY
INDOOR BADMINTON
TAXIDERMY SUPPLY
DIRT
ANIMAL TRAPS
BOOKS BY THE PAGE .....

{1999–2003}

429 7TH AVE
BROOKLYN, NY
11215

SARAH MIN: Building the Store in Park Slope, Brooklyn was a lot of fun. Scott Seeley, who would become the manager, and Ted Thompson, an early and extremely intrepid McSweeney's intern, were like contractors. They would wear these little masks while they were painting and building, because of the dust.

TED THOMPSON: It took about five months, I think, to build the Store. Lots of late nights in that tiny space with drills and Mountain Dew.

SARAH MIN: Sometimes they would find a piece of furniture from I don't know where and drag it in.

TED THOMPSON: Scott and I spent weekends driving around to yard sales in the tri-state area buying old furniture and strapping it to the roof of his car.

SARAH MIN: My brother and his friend did a tin-tile ceiling. It was a tiny, tiny space, and it became our

makeshift headquarters. It had a front retail zone with a cool old cash register and then a little office with a tiny bathroom in the back. We'd all go in the back for meetings. Max Fenton worked the cash register regularly for a couple years.

MAX FENTON: Everything we sold was labeled accurately. We sold books by the page, paintings by elephants, collected snow, hog slappers, ferret-cleaning supplies, and small rubber cubes.

SARAH MIN: We'd get the weirdest invoices from random vendors of, say, steel wool. We also sold T-shirts for which Dave wrote random sayings. "I Like It Here." was my favorite. And the McSweeney's books and quarterlies. We sold those, too.

TED THOMPSON: To keep the Store financially viable, we started running a reading series out of it in 2001, which I organized and ran. The money made on book

sales and the $5 cover charge went to the Store's rent. Eventually, the reading series outgrew the Store, and we'd host readings in venues all around New York City.

SARAH MIN: I don't think the Store ever made much of a profit, but our rent was really cheap.

MAX FENTON: Among the other dry goods, we sold single gloves. Like a glove lost and found, but each glove was for sale. In all the time I worked, I don't remember anyone buying a glove, until the very last sale of the store, on Christmas Eve, 2003.

It was in the works that the Store would close just before Christmas and then simply never open again. The 826NYC tutoring center was being planned and the core people—Scott and Joan and Sam and the architects—were ready to start working in January.

It was bitter cold out and the restaurants and tattoo shop next door and even the bodega at the end of the block were dark. Mostly men had trickled in throughout the day, favoring the cast metal bird feet and, of course, books. A year before had been about the same, but tonight it looked like it would snow and the stragglers were no doubt sitting down to meals, so it had been quiet about an hour.

The cowbell tied to the glass door rang and a guy in full cyclist gear walked in. Helmet, spandex shorts, the works. He walked in, looked left and right and asked, "Do you have a glove?"

"Yes, sir. In the glove box below the squirrel."

He looked in, rooted around, pulled one out. "This one?"

"Well, it's Christmas Eve, so... two bucks."

SARAH MIN: The one thing I really regretted was that Marcel Dzama did these colored drawings and the Store was selling them for $50 a pop. At the time, I didn't think I could afford one and I still beat myself up over it!

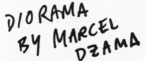

DIORAMA BY MARCEL DZAMA

PEOPLE, PEOPLE—STOP BLAMING YOURSELVES! HAVE YOU FORGOTTEN:

TIMOTHY
McSWEENEY'S

BLUES/JAZZ ODYSSEY?

(FOR SHORT SAY "McSWEENEY'S.")

KNOWN ALSO AS:

"POLLYANNA'S
BOOTLESS ERRAND."

NOW FIX YOUR COLLAR—TODAY COULD BE YOUR DAY!

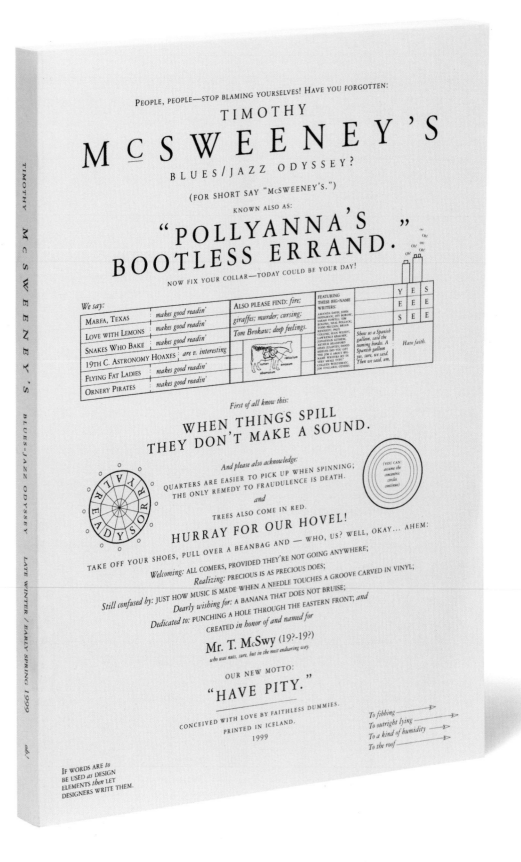

We say:		Also please find: fire;		FEATURING THESE BIG-NAME WRITERS:		Y E S	E E	S E
Marfa, Texas	makes good readin'	giraffes; murder; cursing;		AMANDA DAVIS, JOHN HODGMAN, ZEV BOROW, SARAH VOWELL, TIM ROGERS, NEAL POLLACK, TODD PRUZAN, BRIAN KENNEDY, PAUL COLLINS, SEAN WILSEY, LAWRENCE KRAUSE, JONATHAN LETHEM, ARTHUR BRADFORD, HEIDI JULAVITS, DAVID BERLIN, DID YOU GET THE JOB ABOUT BIG NAME WRITERS SET IN VERY SMALL TYPE? COLLEEN WERTHMAN, JIM STALLARD, OTHERS.				
Love with Lemons	makes good readin'	Tom Brokaw; deep feelings.						
Snakes Who Bake	makes good readin'				Show us a Spanish galleon, said the teeming hordes. A Spanish galleon yes, sure, we said. Then we said, um.		Have faith.	
19th C. Astronomy Hoaxes	are v. interesting							
Flying Fat Ladies	makes good readin'							
Ornery Pirates	makes good readin'							

First of all know this:

WHEN THINGS SPILL
THEY DON'T MAKE A SOUND.

And please also acknowledge:

QUARTERS ARE EASIER TO PICK UP WHEN SPINNING;
THE ONLY REMEDY TO FRAUDULENCE IS DEATH.

and

TREES ALSO COME IN RED.

HURRAY FOR OUR HOVEL!

WHO, US? WELL, OKAY... AHEM:

TAKE OFF YOUR SHOES, PULL OVER A BEANBAG AND —

Welcoming: ALL COMERS, PROVIDED THEY'RE NOT GOING ANYWHERE;

Realizing: PRECIOUS IS AS PRECIOUS DOES;

Still confused by: JUST HOW MUSIC IS MADE WHEN A NEEDLE TOUCHES A GROOVE CARVED IN VINYL;

Dearly wishing for: A BANANA THAT DOES NOT BRUISE;

Dedicated to: PUNCHING A HOLE THROUGH THE EASTERN FRONT; *and*

CREATED *in honor of and named for*

Mr. T. McSwy (19?-19?)

who was nuts, sure, but in the most endearing way,

OUR NEW MOTTO:

"HAVE PITY."

CONCEIVED WITH LOVE BY FAITHLESS DUMMIES.
PRINTED IN ICELAND.
1999

To fibbing ⟶
To outright lying ⟶
To a kind of humidity ⟶
To the roof ⟶

IF WORDS ARE *to* BE USED *as* DESIGN ELEMENTS *then* LET DESIGNERS WRITE THEM.

McSweeney's 2

JONATHAN AMES: Through the cultural-zeitgeist psychic network, I started hearing about some new magazine that was going to publish stories that had been rejected by other magazines. This sounded like a great premise to me. Then one day I was in my local bookstore talking to Jonathan Lethem, who lives a few blocks from me, and he held up an issue of *McSweeney's* and said something like, "If I can, I'm going to contribute to every issue of this magazine."

JONATHAN LETHEM: Back in 1999 I was still a frothy young man spilling over with foolish extra writings, and delighted to have another dumping ground—I figured the Jerry Lewis piece could find its natural resting place in *McSweeney's*, with an audience of the other contributors and their parents. You'd be right to guess I wouldn't have expected to be answering eleventh-anniversary questions about it.

JONATHAN AMES: I was impressed by Lethem's immediate loyalty to this new start-up, and thought I should try to contribute something. But I think I was scared of being rejected by a magazine that was looking for rejects. I mean, if such a magazine rejected me, it would be like a double rejection.

DAVE EGGERS: It was hard at the beginning, because we did turn down submissions, and we actually did get some people pretty angry. I think people might have been confused, thinking that we were an automatic home for anything and everything that hadn't been accepted elsewhere.

PAUL COLLINS: I wrote to Dave the day after buying Issue 1. I'd been sending this piece about Victorian astronomer Thomas Dick all over the place, and getting rejected everywhere. I was a total unknown who'd never published anything, and the piece had absolutely no news hook. It had unhookedness of biblical proportions. So I sent Dave the article with a cover letter that read, in its entirety: "Everybody hates this. Maybe you will too." About a week later I got an email from him asking me to send him everything I had. For the next couple years, every new piece I wrote went straight to him and into *McSweeney's*.

DAVE EGGERS: This was when we were still sort of figuring out what the focus, if anything, would be. At the time, I was just opening the mail and reading everything. The MO hasn't changed much over the years, I guess. My advice to any aspiring writer is to do some research and write about something other than relationships and living in New York. Those are worthy subjects, sure, but journals get a massive amount of similar material. When, like Paul, you send a series of stories about history's most peculiar inventors and explorers, then the work stands out markedly. Wilsey's work was like that. I had just been to Marfa, Texas, this fascinating place, and then a few months later, Wilsey sent in this piece about the town.

SEAN WILSEY: I first wrote the "Republic of Marfa" as a Talk of the Town story for the *New Yorker*. It got killed, so I sent it to the address listed in the journal. After I sent it Dave said, "This is good, just make it longer." When I sent in the next draft, at about five thousand words, he told me to write more, that it wasn't complete yet. Thus, a thousand-word piece expanded into a ten-thousand-word essay. When I came in to show illustrations for the piece—Dave wanted maps—he asked me, "Can you help me edit some of this stuff? Write some decks and subheads." And so I became an editor. Or editor-at-large.

DAVE EGGERS: Sean and I shared a sort of autodidactic education, I think. We both felt kind of out of place among the magazine folks in New York, and he was a natural fit for *McSweeney's*. He also seemed to have a lot of time on his hands. He started helping to bring in and edit fiction, and I focused on the journalism and the interviews with scientists.

BRENT HOFF: I sent in this interview with a mathematician, Paul Duchateau, not really sure if it had a place in a literary journal. I had known him for years. Soon after the issue came out, the interview was reprinted in the *Chronicle of Higher Education*, which sort of surprised and briefly worried Dr. Duchateau, as such wry candor as his is not the most prized attribute among academic professors, it turns out.

NEAL POLLACK: I'd been reading these little spoken-word pieces at open-mike nights around Chicago. My friend Todd Pruzan forwarded me an email from Eggers saying that he was looking for contributions, so I sent along a little gift pack. Eggers said something to Pruzan like, "I didn't know Neal was funny." Much to my amazement, he made four of the pieces the lead bit in the first issue of *McSweeney's*. Then he published my "Letter From Paris" in Issue 2.

DAVE EGGERS: I met Neal when he and Todd were at Northwestern. I was at U of I, in Champaign-Urbana, and used to drive up there every so often. We all met outside a Kurt Vonnegut reading one night. I didn't get to know Neal well at the time, but then so many years later this very astute satirical stuff came through the mail. His stories became a mainstay of the magazine for a while. It was a strange mix, really: the scientist interviews, Neal's stuff, the heavy journalism of Wilsey and others, and then a bunch of fragments and experiments. I was just writing to anyone I'd met, asking if they had anything in their drawers that couldn't be published in any respectable journal.

HEIDI JULAVITS: "The Mineral Palace: The Lost Chapters" are snippets, or "shrapnel," as I think Dave called them, from the buried-in-the-drawer prequel to another book I wrote. I'm an inefficient writer who

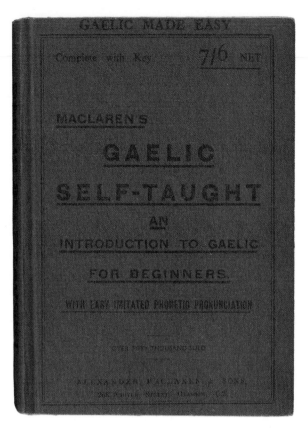

An informational booklet from the early 20th century.

writes two books for every book published—in an attempt to dignify the loser twins in each pair, I've started to think of them as "prequels." As books they suck. But there are moments of interest in them— they're like mapping exercises that trace how I got from the sucky book to the less-sucky book. It was Dave's idea to publish them. They show pretty clearly my writerly angst at that time—what kind of writer am I? What's just a gimmick, and what's essential to the story I'm telling?

TODD PRUZAN: We decided we should have a Meg McGillicuddy–type order form in the back of each issue, like we had for Issue 1. I'm looking at the second installment, Willi Nilli, about a Bavarian brown bear and his friends. We also made a Choose Your Own Adventure story for the issue, "Hooper's Bathhouse." We tried to make it as dull as possible.

CHRIS GAGE: I am not a designer, nor am I a writer, so instead I annoyed Dave by copyediting my copy of

GAELIC SELF-TAUGHT: SICILY'S HUGE CAPYBARAS: MOHAIR, MOHAIR.

NOTE: to be read left to right. Bracketed words in SMALL CAPS indicate illustrative direction. Narrator's voice in *itals*.

by MARY GALLAGHER

This particular area of northern Sicily, just north of the volcanoes and a bit west of the projects, was known for its beautiful, lushly yellow—ochre, more like—hills. It was not known for its capybaras, because capybaras, the largest of the animal kingdom's rodents—known to reach four feet long and 100 lbs—are not native to northern Sicily, or any part of Sicily, for that matter. They are usually found in Central or South America. Also: they are vegetarians. The point is that for the longest time, the capybaras lived in Central or South America, and there were lush ochre hills in northern Sicily.

Birds hover.   Sun.   Sky faded-blue-construction-paper blue.

Hills of yellow mohair, rising and falling with uneven but smooth, smooth curves. [STIPPLED W/ DRY BRUSH]

A small elm.   Small village at base. A road weaves through.

But one day the hills came alive. It started with a stirring, a wide and deep vibration that felt to the villagers like an earthquake, or worse, the awakening of a volcano. What was happening?

Sky as bright as ever.

Same hills, same view, though shown blurring.

Village woman, with child on hip, looking up to hills, covering eyes with hand.

The hills were alive! The hills were growing! The hills grew, the hills bursted upward from their moorings, rising 50, 100, 200 feet in the air. And just when it looked like these hills—gigantic!—would fly into space, it became clear: The hills were capybaras!

Birds [LITTLE V'S] scattering like bats.

Two capybaras, 200 ft. tall, standing on all fours.

Another capybara, kneeling, rising.

Dirt falling from their backs, legs, huge boulders, like.

Villagers run, run out of panel.

Yes, the hills had been capybaras. They were sleeping all along. Now, there are no hills. There are only capybaras.

The horizon, now flat.

Six gaping holes, each the size of a shopping mall. Layers of earth show, the various colors and textures—like a vast stripmining site.

137

Excerpt of a short story written and designed in the style of a comic book without pictures.

Issue 2. I wrote up about fifteen single-spaced pages of corrections (e.g., page 20, line 10: change "which" to "that"; page 20, line 11: comma after "example") and mailed them to Brooklyn. Because I didn't know who I was writing to, I took the approach of presenting myself as a necessary savior: "For Issue 3, you need my copyediting expertise to do justice to your venture." Dave wrote "Call me" on the inside of an envelope—no note, just on the inside of the flap. I thought: kind of terse for all my effort. Much later, Dave told me he hated me for my letter, which was understandable.

DAVE EGGERS: I honestly don't know why we liked having parties at the time. Now, thinking back on it, I can't muster the energy to even think about putting on parties like that; it was so much work and so stressful. But after the first parties went well, we thought it would be good to have a bigger one, and so we rented a huge dim-sum place in Chinatown. We were again looking for a cheap and very uncool place to have a party. I think Wilsey found the place; it was near the room he was renting to write in.

DIANE VADINO: I drove Dave and Brent to the Chinatown party for Issue 2, in my parents' Jeep Cherokee. It was so stuffed with boxes that—if memory serves—both guys had to sit in the way back, with their legs hanging out. Every time we went over a pothole I was convinced that (a) they were going to fall out and be run over by a cab or (b) the raised back door was going to somehow slam shut on them, and I was going to be responsible for killing them.

BRENT HOFF: That was one of those nights where Dave was like "Hey, come by, I got a thing tonight" and then next thing you know I'm drenched in sweat, lugging fifty book boxes across town dressed as a ninja or something. Maybe I was dressed as a mime that night. But either way, the food was delicious.

DAVE EGGERS: We had charged people five dollars to get in, and I think about six hundred people came. So I had about three thousand dollars in my backpack at the end of the night, and got in a cab, heading home.

But my head was all over the place, and when I got home I left the backpack in the cab. I never got it back. Between that and the stress of putting on these big events, we decided to pull back a bit. I think that was the last big party we did.

NEAL POLLACK: I went to New York for a release party, and was stunned at the hundreds of people, many of them quite attractive, in attendance. I got stars in my eyes. When the website started, I continued along with my "Neal Pollack" character, still developing. I wrote "I Am Friends with a Working-Class Black Woman" and "It Is Easy To Take a Lover in Cuba," which I still think are the best pieces I wrote in that voice. I posted regularly and started getting fan mail. Previously, I'd receive maybe one letter a month at the newspaper where I was working, so fan mail—*fan mail, for me*—was addictive. Meanwhile I started doing readings with Dave in Chicago and New York. He actually flew me to Pittsburgh and Toronto to entertain the people. The crowds grew larger, the events grew wilder, and my ego grew bigger.

DAVE EGGERS: Neal became our Bluto. He was really prone to saying the most awful things on stage and in print, and he got everyone, and me in particular, in trouble. He was so loud and obnoxious, and we were so closely linked, that it was causing me ulcers. So eventually, as much as we loved him as a human, we had to create a little distance. But speaking of fan mail, around this time, Neal fell in love with a fictional woman, to whom he sent much embarrassing fan mail himself. I had been writing some stuff in the journal and on the website under the name Lucy Thomas—some short and severe prose-poems—and Neal took to it. He would write to me, wondering who she was, all this, and I didn't know Neal so well, so I didn't immediately tell him that I was Lucy. I let him write three or four letters to her before I let him in on it.

Opposite: Diagram of the names of God in Athanasius Kircher's Oedipus Aegyptiacus, *c. 1652—one of a handful of indirect inspirations for the cover of Issue 3 (next page).*

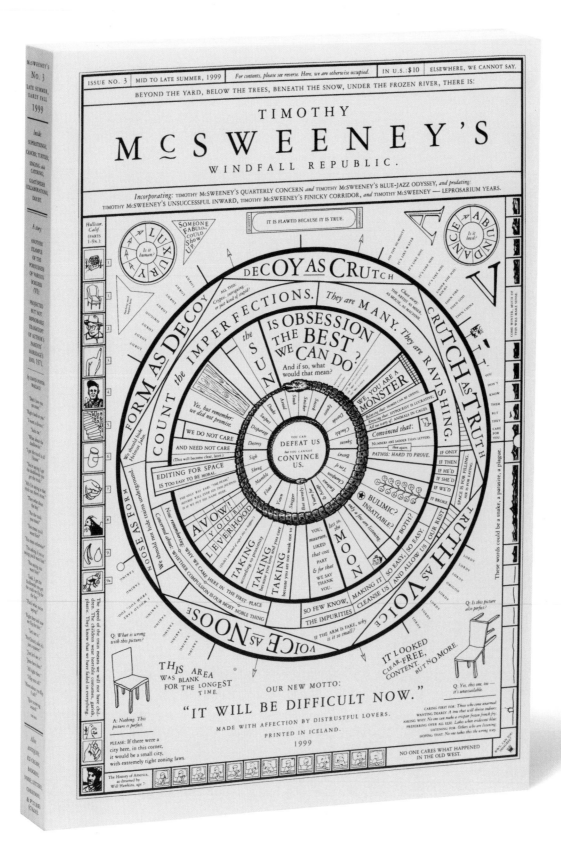

McSweeney's 3

TODD PRUZAN: There was this story that really should have been in a major magazine. I now understand the logistical problems of publishing it, but at the time we were keen to shed some light on Gary Greenberg's Unabomber interview.

GARY GREENBERG: I wandered into McSweeney's without a plan or even an excuse. I had no idea who this McSweeney guy was, but for some reason, I thought he would want to read the twenty-five thousand words I'd written about my attempt to become a famous writer—by convincing the Unabomber to anoint me as his official biographer. I didn't yet grasp just how appalling my story of trying to toady up to a serial killer was, how feckless and callow its would-be hero. That ignorance is in itself a little appalling, but it's also fortunate, because without it, I might not have put the pages in the mail.

TODD PRUZAN: The draft kept all the scaffolding intact, all the anguished backstory about Gary being in touch with the Unabomber.

GARY GREENBERG: Turned out that McSweeney was at that very moment appalled enough with his own authorial hubris to overlook mine. By then, I'd learned that his real name was Dave, that he had something going on about Iceland, stayed up really late at night (I pictured him as a pasty-faced techno-geek living in his mom's basement), and edited in

An early sketch for Issue 3.

capital letters: No! No! THEY'LL CRUCIFY YOU! THIS WHOLE SENTENCE IS TOO BLITHELY TOSSED TO CONTAIN SO MUCH EXPLOSIVENESS. / WHO SAYS CHILDHOOD IS "VICIOUSLY AMORAL"? / DO YOU HAVE TO PUSH EVERY METAPHOR TO ITS ABSOLUTE LIMIT?

TODD PRUZAN: One night Dave handed me a few loose-leaf sheets that had come to Gary from Florence, Colorado. The Unabomber's penmanship was clinical, rational, methodical— the antithesis of my idea of insanity. It was the closest thing to an unholy relic, a supernatural artifact, I'd ever held. I ran my index finger over the text to feel the penciled impressions. This would work for a typeface, I said, but Dave briskly shook his head at my perverse idea. I had nightmares for a week.

GARY GREENBERG: The notes were a little hard to take. But then Dave passed along the comments of one of his editors, who wondered if he should spend so much time calming me down—maybe they should just let me twist on my own rope, he suggested. Suddenly, Dave's warning didn't seem so bad.

BRENT HOFF: A lot of people were disturbed by Gary's Unabomber piece, but if there's one thing on my bookshelf right now that I most fear my kid finding and reading, it's Rodney Rothman's "Fresh Step" letters. That was probably the most deeply disturbing, bowel-evacuating *McSweeney's* piece I've ever read.

MᶜSWEENEY'S
No. 3
LATE SUMMER,
EARLY FALL
1999

Inside:
SUPERSTRINGS;
CANCER; TURTLES;
SINGING *while*
CATERING;
GOAT/SPIDER
COLLABORATIONS;
DOUBT.

A story:
ANOTHER
EXAMPLE
OF THE
POROUSNESS
OF VARIOUS
BORDERS
(VI):

PROJECTED
BUT NOT
IMPROBABLE
TRANSCRIPT
OF AUTHOR'S
PARENTS'
MARRIAGE'S
END, 1971.

by DAVID FOSTER
WALLACE

"Don't love you
no more."
"Right back at you."
"I want a divorce."
"Suits me."
"What about the
doublewide."
"I get the truck is all
I know."
"You're saying I get
the doublewide you
get the truck."
"Alls I'm saying is that
truck out there's mine."
"Then what about
the boy."
"For the truck
you mean?"
"You mean you'd
want him?"
"You mean otherwise?"
"I'm asking if you're
saying you'd want him."
"You saying you
want him?"
"Look, I get the
doublewide you get
the truck we flip for
the boy."
"That's what you're
saying?"
"Right here and now
we flip for him."
"Let's see it."
"For Christ's sake it's
just a quarter."
"Just let's see it."
"Jesus here then."
"All right then."
"I flip you call."
"Hows about you flip
I call?"
"Quit screwing
around."
THE END.

Also:
ANTIQUES;
ICE CREAM;
BADGERS;
NOISE; LETTERS;
CHRISTMAS;
& PICTURES
(COLOR).

*The spine of Issue 3,
featuring a story by
David Foster Wallace.*

RODNEY ROTHMAN: The publication of some of the "Fresh Step" emails in Issue 3 was the rare—perhaps only—case of a piece of television comedy getting adapted into a letter-to-the-editor of a small Brooklyn literary journal. It was the winter of 1998–99. Three writers from "The Late Show with David Letterman" and I created a "boy band" called Fresh Step. Fresh Step looked just liked the Backstreet Boys and sounded just like *NSYNC. We stole their name from a popular brand of kitty litter and wrote a song for them called "You Gotta Be Fresh (To Fresh with the Fresh Step)." Paul Shaffer wrote the music. The band appeared on the Letterman show, and then we somehow convinced MTV to bring them on "Total Request Live." Hours later, Fresh Step's email box—we'd made a website for the band—began to fill up with emails from fourteen-year-old girls who thought the band was for real. Eventually, the band received in excess of ten thousand emails.

SEAN WILSEY: Issue 3 was also the one where Lawrence Weschler's "Convergences" came in for the first time.

LAWRENCE WESCHLER: I'd been trying to launch a regular series of Convergence-type pieces everywhere (I had a whole backfile of prior instances all saved up), offering the idea to numerous publications, and everywhere encountering the same confounded, perplexed, defeated shrugs—impossible, would never work, couldn't sustain interest. Sean and I were both at the *New Yorker* at the time. He and I went out for coffee with Dave who, without batting an eye, declared, "Of course. Let's just do it." And we were off. I'm glad to see that from the very start, that first paragraph in the introduction, we were referencing the true father of this series, the great English critic John Berger. And wasn't that the issue with David Foster Wallace's great little short story, the one you would tell your friends to make sure to read and they'd come back to you complaining that they couldn't find it, it wasn't there, and you'd have to refer them to the volume's spine? And wasn't that the first issue, as well, where we included poetry (Rick Moody's "Confessional Poem")? I do wish we'd do more poetry.

RICK MOODY: I had all these found poems lying around, because I have made found poems for almost twenty years. It's just something I do to relieve stress from having to narrate all the time. I thought that because the magazine had this collage-oriented look to it—like it would swallow up almost any kind of text, any voice or alternative structure—that maybe Dave would go for a found poem or two. But I also sent along to him this "actual" poem, even though I don't think of myself as an "actual" poet. For reasons that I have never understood Dave accepted that one, the "actual" one, which is really just a list of product names. I

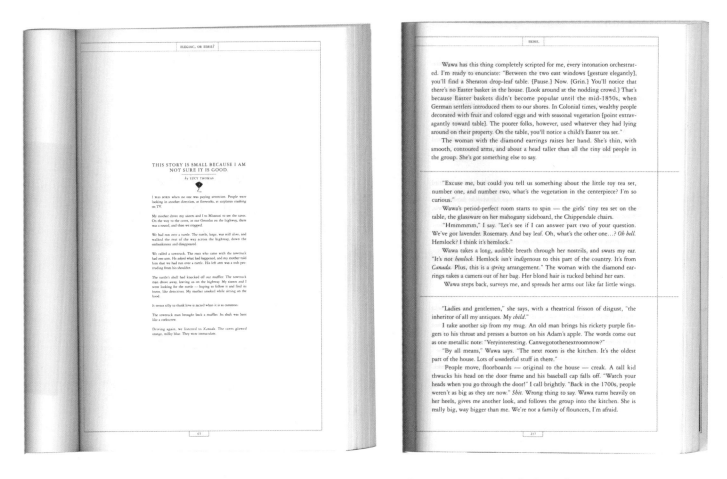

Left: "This Story Is Small Because I Am Not Sure It Is Good," a short-short story printed smaller than usual.
Right: Excerpt from a short story by Adrienne Miller that invites the reader to cut its pages along the dotted lines to reveal new narratives.

mean, I can understand why he didn't take the found poems, because they are recondite and hard to understand. But it was kind of touching that he took the real one. It might have been my first-ever published poem.

TODD PRUZAN: There were probably about a thousand copies that needed to get sealed, stamped, labeled, and crammed down the gullet of every mailbox we could find. A handful of people volunteered to help with the mailing of this issue, so we should have only needed a couple of hours to get it all done. But the hours began to snag, and after the pizzas were gone the Samaritans left. By the time somebody noticed the label bearing a Tenth Street address, just around the corner from us, it was already ten o'clock. I said, "Let's hand deliver it," and Dave said, "Oh,

yeah, set that one aside. We'll bring it over to them, that'll be amazing." We all agreed, because none of us had kids or jobs that required us to show up in Midtown wearing suits eight hours later. And because, I mean, honestly, who wouldn't want a magazine staff to assemble on their doorstep like a bunch of apple-cheeked Christmas carolers, proudly handing over a sharp-edged copy of their new issue, fresh off the boat from Reykjavik, in the dead of a February night? Who would feel threatened enough by our delightful surprise that they'd call the cops? I have no idea. But when I recall those two squad cars flying down Seventh Avenue, lights ablaze, and us all ducking around the corner, I wish I could remember that subscriber's name so I could tell him what McSweeney's had already become so adept at saying, at almost every turn: We're sorry.

What Are Convergences?

LAWRENCE WESCHLER: Convergences are simply unlikely alignments. What I do is, I put disparate images together and say, "Look at this, now look at this," inviting the reader to enjoy the beguiling resonance. The first installments appeared in *McSweeney's* Issue 3. More followed in later issues.

Eventually, a few publishers expressed interest in doing a book version of the series, but every single one of them backed down when they realized that we had not been securing ironclad permissions on the images we had been deploying. And with good reason! Our usage of the images was a classic instance of Fair Use, and we were adamant that we did not need any such permission. The various book publishing editors would all agree but then cower, noting that their legal departments would never let them get away with such an assertion—and that beyond that, going back now and trying to secure all of those permissions would prove so onerous (both in terms of money and the bureaucratic man-hours required) as to render the prospect impossible. I raised this question with Dave and Eli, and true to form, they just said, "Let's do it ourselves."

And in fact nobody did bother us. (But nor did any foreign publishers end up hazarding any overseas editions.)

"FOUND TRIPTYCH" ISSUE 3
Left to right: Georges de la Tour, The Newborn Child *(detail); Henry Matisse,* Study of a Woman (Sirene); *Hannah Wilke (© Estate of Hannah Wilke).*

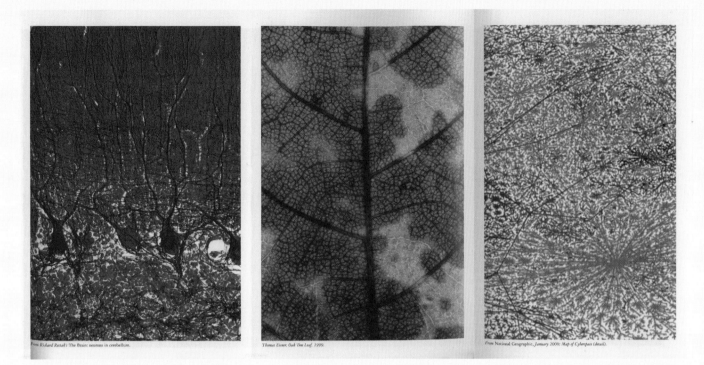

"BRANCHING OUT FURTHER" ISSUE 5
Left to right: From Richard Restak's The Brain: neurons in cerebellum; *Thomas Eisner,* Oak Tree Leaf, *1999; From* National Geographic, *January 2000: Map of Cyberspace (detail).*

"EXPRESSIONS OF AN ABSOLUTE" ISSUE 3
Left to right: Artist's rendering of two colliding galaxies, Life *magazine, 1954; Jackson Pollock,* Autumn Rhythm; *Lunar landscape; Mark Rothko,* Untitled, *1971.*

Why Iceland?

DAVE EGGERS: In 1998, I was living in New York City and going to a lot of shows at galleries downtown, thinking vaguely about writing an article about artists who went to great lengths to produce their work. I greatly admired the work of Christo, and wanted to highlight others like him, who worked well beyond the canvas, as it were. One day I walked into a gallery on, I think, 8th Avenue, and saw some startling work. Huge photos of houses falling through the sky. They were astounding images, of ranch houses and other small homes plummeting from thousands of feet, as if thrown by God from the heavens. I bought the catalog for the show, and inside there was a fairly in-depth explanation of how the artist, Peter Garfield, achieved the photographs. Apparently he would buy damaged pre-fab houses and hook them up to huge military helicopters, which would then lift the houses a few thousand feet, at which point they would be dropped onto a hillside, with Garfield capturing the fall with his camera. In the catalog, there were pictures of Garfield and his assistants wearing hardhats, watching the action, examining blueprints, and in every way

PETER GARFIELD

Above: The cover of Peter Garfield's Harsh Reality, *an art catalog printed in 1998 at Oddi Printing in Reykjavik, Iceland.*

Right: One of the artworks in the Harsh Reality show catalog: "Mobile Home (Communique)," 1996.

Opposite: Peter Garfield's team of house droppers, as seen in Harsh Reality.

looking very official and capable. I thought Garfield was that very brave and visionary sort of artist who, like Christo and Jeanne-Claude and Richard Serra and Andy Goldsworthy, would not let laws of physics and budgets and municipalities get in the way of making their visions real. So I contacted him, in hopes of doing some sort of story about him, perhaps watching the next home-drop. We set up an appointment. On the way to his Brooklyn studio, I paged through the catalog again, again marveling at the ambition of Garfield, and it was then that I noticed something strange about the catalog. On the copyright page, there was this line: "Printed in Iceland by Oddi Printing." I'd never heard of anyone printing anything in Iceland, and I thought this was some kind of small joke. When I showed up at Garfield's studio, my first question was about Christo, about that scale of artmaking, which I'd always admired as an art student myself, and blah blah blah. I don't know how long I blathered about how inspiring it was that Garfield would go to such lengths for an image, before Garfield interrupted me. "You know that was all a hoax, right?" I don't know if these were his exact words, but the point was made. The catalog was a hoax. There were no actual homes,

no helicopters, no hillsides. He eyed me curiously, as if I was kidding about being so gullible. He brought me to a table in the studio and showed me the homes that had been photographed: they were model-train homes, about two inches high. I had been hood-winked! It turns out that the only true line in the entire catalog was the one that had given me pause: "Printed in Iceland by Oddi Printing." I went home, chastened and dejected. But the name Oddi stayed with me. And so about a year later, when the idea of McSweeney's was bubbling up, I called Peter Garfield again, looking for a contact name for this Oddi company. I'd always been intrigued by Iceland, and I called, knowing as the phone rang that if Oddi was real, and if their prices were competitive, McSweeney's would be printed in Reykjavik. Turns out their prices were fine, the quality of their work was unparalleled, and so we got started. The first thirty or so McSweeney's journals and books were printed there at Oddi, and I visited there many times, and even spent a summer on a fjord north of the city. Anyway, they're excellent printers and artisans, from the top salespeople to the youngest pressmen, and you really should visit Oddi sometime, if you're ever in Iceland. Try to go in the summer.

BJÖSSI VÍÐISSON: When you're a printer who works with artists, you have to be optimistic about turning good ideas into actual books. Sometimes the incredible design ideas don't work out, but we always give it our best. For some of the McSweeney's projects, like Issue 8—with the birds on the cover—we did many tests before we figured out the solution. Hours of meetings with the people from the bindery and the press department helped me find the way to make it look how Dave and the designer wanted it to look.

ARNI SIGGURDSON: I can't pick out one McSweeney's project as the most memorable, but *McSweeney's* 15 is somewhat special to me for two reasons. First, it presents the work of Icelandic writers and has

wonderful Icelandic art on the cover. Also, it was the last book I did with you guys before I quit working for Oddi and moved back to Iceland.

BJÖSSI VÍÐISSON: *McSweeney's* Issue 7 is without a doubt the most memorable book I have printed. This is the issue with the rubber band, the loose booklets, and the wraparound hardcover piece. We were working on this issue a few weeks after September 11, 2001. The production schedule was tight, but everything was working out. Arni found a company in New York to make the rubber bands and send them to Iceland. Meanwhile, I finished the printing and binding of the books so everything would be ready when the rubber bands arrived. When the rubber bands finally arrived, we only had a day or two to finish the books and send them to the shipping company. When we opened the boxes with the rubber bands, they were covered with white powder. Aware of the situation in the U.S. at that time—this was during the anthrax scare, when terrorists were supposedly sending anthrax powder through the mail—I decided I couldn't ship thousands of books wrapped in powder-coated rubber bands. What could we do? We couldn't afford an extra day in the schedule, let alone the weeks or months the books might lose if they were held up in U.S. Customs. I called a dry cleaner here in Reykjavik to see if he could wash the rubber bands. It turned out he could, so he got started immediately. This was in the afternoon. The cleaning company had people up all the night, washing the rubber bands. We got them back the next morning. Of course we finished the books in time to send out on schedule.

In addition to Issue 7, I'm most proud of the book with the die-cut "I" [*I* by Stephen Dixon] on the cover. We spent a lot of time figuring out how to do that one, and when it was done, we had a unique book. As far as we know, nobody in Iceland had done anything like that before.

The key to the success of McSweeney's projects is that Dave and his designers were always very positive about changing the design if we absolutely did have to make some adjustments. A can-do attitude helps everybody.

Those press guys below are on a lunch break, believe it or not. "No better nourishment than a satisfied customer," I just heard them say. And hey, here's Bjössi fighting with Roy over whose turn it is to play with the six-color Heidelberg. Go home, men. Time for fresh air.

ARNI SIGGURDSON: The formula was always like this: Dave Eggers comes with strange idea for design and Bjössi says: "It is possible." From there it is creativity and hard work. This attitude is not too common anymore, but has taken McSweeney's and Oddi Printing a long way. The few that work by this recipe will make good things in life.

BJÖSSI VÍÐISSON: The covers of the first three *McSweeney's* issues are my favorites. They look quite plain, but that's the type of design I like. Classic. If I were to play around with the design of a *McSweeney's* cover, I'd go for an elegant, simple design and nice materials. Fish skin would present an interesting challenge.

A BASIC BOOK (NO BELLS & WHISTLES) — PRINTING SPECS & APPROXIMATE COST

FORMAT .... paperback

SIZE .... 6″ wide, 9″ tall

NUMBER OF PAGES 176

PAPER .... *cover:* basic white cover stock
interior: basic white text stock

INK .... *cover:* one-color (black)
interior: one-color (black)

QUANTITY .... 5,000 copies

PRINTING COST .... $7,550 (1.51 per copy)

DOMESTIC FREIGHT .... $800 (0.13 per copy)

TOTAL COST .... $8,350 (1.67 per copy)

WHERE WOULD MCSWEENEY'S
PRINT A BASIC BOOK LIKE THIS? .... We'd probably print this at one of our North American printers—Westcan
in Winnipeg, Canada, or Worzalla in Stevens Point, Wisconsin.

WHY? .... North American printers offer competitive prices on no-frills books. Because they're
nearby, they're able to offer cheaper shipping and faster turnaround than an overseas
printer like TWP in Singapore, another printer we often use. For some reason,
it's also easier to get natural/textured paper stock at North American printers.

WHEN DOES MCSWEENEY'S
PRINT IN SINGAPORE? .... We print in Singapore when we need full-color printing, handwork, unusual
sizes, and unusual bindings.

DOESN'T MCSWEENEY'S
PRINT IN ICELAND, TOO? .... Yes. Our earliest publications were all printed in Iceland, before the value of the U.S.
dollar did a tremendous belly flop.

BELLS & WHISTLES — ADDED COSTS (PER COPY)*

INTERIOR

ONE-COLOR PRINTING, NOT BLACK $0.00
Many printers will print your one-color book in a different color—e.g., brown ink instead of black ink—at little or no additional cost.

+ 16 PAGES $0.12
Books are usually printed 16 (or 32) pages at a time. Thus, it's helpful to think in multiples of 16 when determining the page count of your book. A 192-page book will cost the same to print as a 178-page book.

TINTED PAGES $0.26
Colored paper is very expensive, so we don't use it. Instead, we achieve the effect of colored paper by printing the color on white paper. McSweeney's Issue 12 was the first of many to print with tinted pages.

TWO-COLOR PRINTING $0.26
Also called a "adding a spot color." All the illustrations in McSweeney's Issue 14 were printed in a blue spot color. Black text + blue illustrations = two colors.

RIBBON BOOKMARK $0.34
like in The Neal Pollack Anthology of American Literature. A ribbon bookmark can be built into the spine of the book.

FULL-COLOR (CMYK) PRINTING $0.84
Also called "four-color," "4c," and "full-color process." McSweeney's Issue 6 and Issue 13 were our first to be printed with full-color interiors.

COVER

TWO-COLOR PRINTING $0.04

FULL-COLOR PRINTING $0.11

BROWN KRAFT BOARD $0.02
A cheap alternative to basic white cover stock; like the cover of Dear New Girl.

ONE-COLOR PRINTING ON INSIDE COVERS $0.05
In a paperback book, the inside front cover and inside back cover can be printed at the same time, for one price. If you print something on the inside front cover, you might as well print something on the inside back cover.

FULL-COLOR PRINTING ON INSIDE COVERS ...$0.12

LAYFLAT COVER LAMINATE $0.12
A laminate is a thin layer of transparent plastic that protects a cover against damage—especially moisture damage. Laminates are available in glossy and matte finishes. When we use laminates, we always use matte laminates.

ROUNDED CORNERS $0.13
like on Dear New Girl.

DIE CUT (SIMPLE SHAPE) $0.22
like the circular hole in the cover of McSweeney's 29.

FOIL STAMP....................................$0.27
like the red flowers on the cover of The People of Paper and the silver birds on the spine of McSweeney's Issue 8.

FRENCH FLAPS $0.29
French flaps on a paperback book cover look and function like the dustjacket flaps on a hardcover book. McSweeney's Issue 12 was our first paperback with French flaps. Some of the Believer books have them, too.

DIE CUT (SPECIAL SHAPE) $0.36
like the "I"-shaped hole on the cover of Dixon's I.

HARDCOVER ....
There are countless ways to "upgrade" your paperback to a hardcover (a.k.a. "case-bound") book. Here are some of our favorite configurations:

- RAW BOOKBOARD + CLOTH SPINE.............$2.03
  like You Shall Know Our Velocity. No cloth or paper wrap covers the gray-brown bookboard. The book is held together by a cloth spine.

- WIBALIN CASEWRAP $2.04
  like The Latke Who Couldn't Stop Screaming. This is a hardcover wrapped wholly in Wibalin, "Europe's leading non-woven cover material." In some ways we prefer Wibalin to cloth: it holds printers' ink exceptionally well and it doesn't fray like cloth can.

- PRINTED PAPER CASEWRAP $2.06
  like the cover of McSweeney's Issue 20.

- CLOTH CASEWRAP $2.25
  like the cover of I.

- LEATHERETTE CASEWRAP $2.30
  like the cover of McSweeney's Issue 11.

HARDCOVER EXTRAS

ENDPAPERS — FULL-COLOR PRINTING...........$0.05
Endpapers are the slightly thicker pages at the front and back of every hardcover book. We always print on them because it looks so good and costs so little. (Paperbacks almost never have endpapers.)

REMOVABLE BACK-COVER STICKER $0.07
We sometimes print a book's barcode and blurbs—the sales materials—on a one-color sticker that can be removed from the back of the book.

REMOVABLE BACK-COVER PAPER BAND $0.16
We sometimes print the barcode and blurbs on a one-color, removable paper band.

FULL-COLOR DUSTJACKET $0.17
Typically, a dustjacket is printed in full color on one side, then laminated on the printed side. The other side is unprinted.

ELASTIC STRAP CLOSURE $0.20
like on the cover of How We Are Hungry.

FULL-COLOR INSET $0.18
like on the cover of The Riddle of the Traveling Skull.

FOLD-OUT, POSTER-SIZE DUSTJACKET $0.27
Printed full-color both sides, like on McSweeney's Issue 13 or Issue 23.

OTHER

SHRINKWRAP $0.13
We try to avoid it, but shrinkwrap is often the best solution for holding together a multi-part publication.

8 X 10" SHEET OF FULL-COLOR
TEMPORARY TATTOOS $0.48

Z-BINDING $0.49
A hardcover with two spines, configured in a Z-like shape—like the cover of McSweeney's Issue 24.

SIMPLE MAGNETIC CLOSURE $0.61
a simplified version of the McSweeney's Issue 23 magnetic concept.

CD $0.71

DVD $0.77

PLASTIC STUD FOR HOLDING
CD OR DVD IN PLACE $0.03

* These prices reflect our experience with book printing, but we don't guarantee them. As the price of crab will vary from restaurant to restaurant (and from season to season), so too will the costs of printing services vary. There is no universal menu, and this is not our attempt to write one.

The goal here is to reveal—just roughly—the relative costs of some of the various "bells & whistles" we've used or have thought about using.

(Did you know, for example, that publishing a DVD and inserting a copy into a paperback book costs roughly half as much as adding a hardcover to that same book? And did you know that brown kraft board was such an afforable cover material?)

Every time we design a book, we run through a mental version of this chart, sort of.

TIMOTHY

McSWEENEY'S

TRYING, TRYING, TRYING, TRYING, TRYING.

ISSUE NO. 4

LATE WINTER, 2000

McSweeney's 4

(2 0 0 0)

SEAN WILSEY: Issue 4 was the first issue with a color cover. Explosive! It was an extremely ambitious issue.

DAVE EGGERS: We had no clue how to manufacture something like this. And definitely zero budget for a color cover. But we talked to a lot of people—designers, publishers—and got a lot of advice along the way.

SEAN WILSEY: I remember that when Dave and I were getting on the plane to fly to Iceland, in January 2000, there was a snowstorm. I said "Flying like this makes me nervous," and he replied, "What, are ya, yella?"

DAVE EGGERS: Most people don't know this, but Wilsey is scared of just about everything: loud noises, big fish, avocados. But to be fair, the plane ride was particularly harrowing.

SEAN WILSEY: Getting to Iceland in January was pretty cheap—about $300, if you stayed for a week. But everything was ridiculously expensive, and the days were really short. The sun would come up at 11 and set at 4. We'd get to Oddi at 6 in the morning and spend long days there because there was a ton of work to do. We had conversations about every detail. I remember saying in the editor's note that we were no longer going to use the word *tinseltown*. And that instead of *ringlets* we were going to say *profile cyclones*.

An early sketch of the cover of Issue 4.

DAVE EGGERS: I think we drove everyone crazy.

SEAN WILSEY: I didn't even totally understand the box idea. Dave said we'd do all these little booklets and that they'd all fit into a box, that the box would have a cover on it and be the cover of the issue. I thought he had it all sort of figured out, that we would just go to Iceland and be there at Oddi Printing to oversee it all. But in fact we got there and they were like, "We can't really do this." There was only one boxmaker in Iceland—Kassagerdin—and they said that we had to come up with another plan. But Dave had no interest in coming up with another plan. Meanwhile, Birna Anna Björnsdottír, a reporter at the daily paper in Reykjavik, wanted to interview us because it was so unusual for Americans to be over there printing anything. So we did this interview, and the next day the paper ran this big photo of us. The whole interview seemed to be just us complaining about the boxmaker and how they can't do the box and how it's really disappointing. This was in the national paper! We were walking around Reykjavik and people were recognizing us and waving to us. The next time we walked into Oddi, all the representatives from Kassagerdin were lined up along the table, suddenly taking us really seriously. And they had all these boxes—these mock-ups. They showed us a box for photocopy paper, and they said, "We can

The contents of the Issue 4 box:
fourteen booklets and an illustrated
subscription form offering lifetime
McSweeney's subscriptions for $120.
In all but one case ("Dabchick" by
Haruki Murakami), the cover art
for the booklets was selected by the
authors of the booklets.

On the cover of "Dar(e)apy," a ten-page
story by Ben Miller: a faithful reproduction
of the cover of a cookbook the author found
at a junk shop in Greenpoint, Brooklyn.

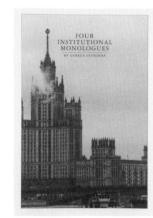

On the cover of "Four Institutional
Monologues" by George Saunders:
a "very institutional" picture the
author took in Moscow in 1982.

On the cover of "A Mown Lawn,"
a 215-word story by Lydia Davis:
a photograph of a lawn by
Lydia's son, Daniel Auster.

On the cover of "Threadworks of the
Seventeenth Century" by Lawrence
Weschler: a detail of Vermeer's "The
Lace-Maker," painted around 1669.

On the cover of "Hellhound on My Trail,"
a three-part play by Denis Johnson: a
drawing of a hellhound named Harold by
Matt Johnson, the author's son.

On the cover of "The Middle Tales"
by Sheila Heti: artwork by
Janet Bailey.

On the cover of "Paperback Nabokov," an
essay by Paul Maliszewski: a selection of
commemorative stamps featuring Lolita
cover designs from around the world.

On the cover of "K is for Fake,"
Jonathan Lethem's cover version
of Kafka's The Trial: a drawing
by William Amato.

On the cover of "Shorter Stories by
Various Authors": Men of the AAA
AW Battalion (MBL), c. 1952.

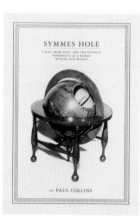

On the cover of "Symmes Hole," an
essay by Paul Collins: a globe John
Cleves Symmes modified to demon-
strate activity within the earth's core.

On the backside of the booklet-sized
subscription card: a diagram of
forgetting.

On the cover of "A Chance Meeting," an essay by Rachel Cohen: a 1926 photograph of Fifth Avenue and 42nd Street in New York City.

On the cover of "Notes and Background and Clarifying Charts and Some Complaining": a tiny drawing of a bullet, or a beak, or a fin.

On the cover of "The Double Zero," Rick Moody's cover version of Sherwood Anderson's "The Egg": an ostrich photograph taken by Rick Moody and digitally manipulated by Amy Osborn.

On the cover of "Dabchick" by Haruki Murakami: a completely unrelated photograph from the McSweeney's archives.

shrink this box down to the size that you want for the issue." And we were just like, "Okay, this is great."

BIRNA ANNA BJÖRNSDOTTÍR: I recall Dave and Sean complaining about Kassagerdin, the boxmaker, but I don't remember the piece revolving around that. Their fixation on such a detail made them even more eccentric. Also, it was one of those days where there was nothing in the news and so I got all the space I could fill. They ran the story prominently on page two. I don't think I fully realized how fascinated these guys were with Oddi until a few years later, when I was in California and went to Dave and Vendela's house for Dave's birthday. When the party started heating up Dave excused himself and then reappeared wearing a dark blue Oddi jumpsuit.

SEAN WILSEY: Because we were around the plant so much, eating in the cafeteria, using the computers, and I did some begging, we were given full Oddi uniforms, in royal blue. On the pants the word ODDI runs up one leg. Dave donned his immediately. All the printing guys wear them, and he fit in perfectly.

BJÖSSI VÍÐISSON: The legend that I wear a blue Oddi jumpsuit is unfortunately just a good story.

ARNI SIGGURDSON: I would like to say yes, we all wear the Oddi jumpsuit at all times. However, guys

like Bjössi, Eythor, Knutur, Grimur, not to mention Thorgeir and Baldur or Hanna Maria, Stina, Badda, and the other women at Oddi's upper floor would not be so excited about it. They're all wearing Armani.

BJÖSSI VÍÐISSON: But most of the printers and the people working at the bindery used to wear Oddi's blue jumpsuit. Now Oddi has a new suit but I can tell you we all miss the blue one.

GABE HUDSON: Issue 4 was one of the most exotic things I'd ever seen. Let alone been a part of. I had blindly sent in some short-short stories, and not long after Dave accepted my "The Size of My Heart." So there were a few words of mine there in print, included alongside some of my heroes: Haruki Murakami, George Saunders, and Lydia Davis.

LYDIA DAVIS: "A Mown Lawn," my first contribution to *McSweeney's*, appeared in Issue 4 after Dave wrote me a very long letter in tiny type. He introduced himself, explaining how he had tried to get one of my stories into *Esquire* and failed, and how he had recently approached my agent looking for a story for *McSweeney's* and been summarily turned away. His seriousness certainly got my attention. I happened to have a story I thought would fit nicely, since it combined absurdity and sincere passion, and he accepted it. For the cover illustration, I looked through the recent photos of my terrific photographer-son, Daniel (full disclosure—he's my son), and found just the thing—a mown lawn.

JONATHAN LETHEM: "K Is for Fake" was part of a cycle of Kafka stories written with Carter Scholz. It's still one of my favorites. The brilliant and meticulous Will Amato drew the Kafka postage stamp for the cover, according to my request to make Kafka look like a Keane baby. I know Will was unhappy with how it came out, and annoyed I went ahead and used it. I hope he's forgiven me.

SHEILA HETI: I was 22, studying art history and philosophy at the University of Toronto, living in my father's basement and writing stories. No one wanted to publish them, so I'd leave them in envelopes on the subway and mail them to random people from the phone book. I had read one issue of *McSweeney's* and knew they were interested in publishing fiction no one else wanted. I had a bad attitude and didn't believe it, so out of spite I sent them five stories through the mail, imagining I'd hear nothing and feel vindicated. One Sunday morning, playing Boggle with my dad and younger brother, an email arrived. Back then, one rarely got emails on a Sunday morning. The email was from Dave Eggers—just two sentences—saying I was a genius (he could tell!!) and that he wanted to publish all five stories. I returned to Boggle happy and safe, scooped up like a cat from the sea.

RICK MOODY: Dave had an idea that maybe people should write "cover versions" of famous short stories. So he told me. This seemed like a good idea. I like assignments, generally. And the more restraining and

The underside of the box. A story by Ben Greenman, "More Notes on Revising Last Night's Dream," runs around the perimeter of the box.

difficult the assignments seem, the better I like them. I think I was imagining I would volunteer to do a cover of something obvious, like maybe "The Fourth Alarm," by Cheever. Something that I knew inside and out. But Dave suggested a Sherwood Anderson story, "The Egg." I think it's one of those stories that just really struck him hard. Well, I'd recently been to a strange and awesome ranch in the Tucson area (the Rooster Cogburn Ranch, I think, is the name of it) where they farmed ostriches. These days, they have tiny little donkeys there too. Donkeys that are about as big as a golden retriever. Anyway, my wife and I went to this ranch, which is just off I-10, and nearly got pecked to death trying to feed these mammoth birds. There's just no room in that animal for a brain at all. Trust me. We bought an ostrich egg, too, which is gigantic and I think makes something like a half gallon's worth of french toast batter when you mix it up. So I set "The Double Zero" at an ostrich ranch, because I was, at the moment, preoccupied with ostriches. That's how it goes sometimes.

GABE HUDSON: When Dave was touring for his first book—he was also promoting Issue 4 at that time—I came out to meet him at his reading in Harvard Square. The first thing he said to me was, "I thought you'd be shorter." The next day he read at a huge bookstore in Boston, and we arranged for me to be in the audience, and act as a heckler. The crowd become so rightfully incensed that eventually he explained that I was a contributor to *McSweeney's*, and how about a round of applause for me.

Opposite: A couple letters from lifetime McSweeney's *subscribers, plus a drawing of an Alec Guinness–faced cloud by Dave Eggers. The lifetime subscription offer was canceled shortly after the release of Issue 4.*

Yes, yes, it is still available. It costs $120. For
$120 the Lifetime Subscriber will receive:

Every issue of McSweeney's, as long as we and you take breath
Copies of the first two McSwys mini-books, separate from the quarterly and
in the works, as we speak
A certificate indicating your new Lifetime Subscriber status, printed with
black ink on the finest laser paper
One McSweeney's T-shirt, in the size of your choice (please specify)
Two of the following (please choose two
and list them in your order):

A copy of issue #2, including, on its
first page, a drawing of a wheel
without spokes, sitting in a field,
above which hovers a cloud with the
face of Alec Guiness

A copy of issue #2, including, on its
first page, a drawing of a severed
hand

LARGE t-shirt please...

PLEASE SEND ME AN ISSUE #1 if you find one behind the radiator or some
such thing- if not, you don't have to say "no", just don't send it.

THANK YOU THANK YOU
-Nathan Abbot

email =

phone = (510)

Send monies to 122 Ambrogio Drive, Gurnee, IL 60031

Hi. I'd like a Lifetime Subscription. I'd like
my t-shirt to be size large, and any other free
gift to be a McS.'s issue, with or without drawing.

Missy Roser

Somerville, MA 02143

tel. 617.625.

(I tried using the form on the web, but I don't
think my browser was configured right. If by chance
it did get sent, w/ visa info, you can enjoy ripping
this check up. thanks.)

I FEEL PENSIVE.

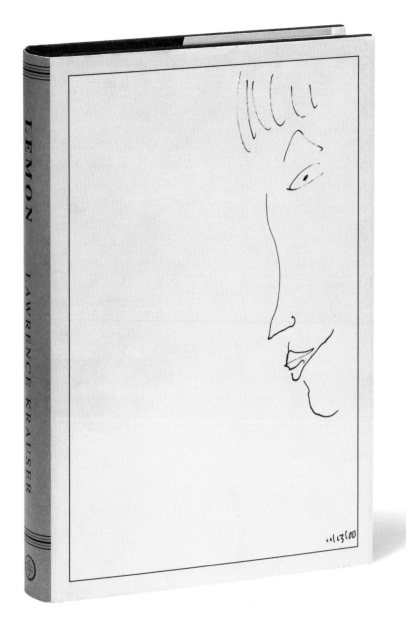

Lemon

by LAWRENCE KRAUSER (2000)

LAWRENCE KRAUSER: I showed a draft of this novel to an editor friend, who sent it to the literary agent Kyung Cho, who sent a portion of it to *McSweeney's*, who included the portion in Issue 2. A year went by during which the manuscript made no new friends—and then Dave Eggers contacted me about it again when McSweeney's began publishing books.

The "Oodles of Doodles" cover idea—to print the front of the dustjacket as a blank slate, so I could hand-finish each copy with a unique doodle—arose naturally in conversation when Dave, Larissa Tokmakova (my wife, whose painting is on the back jacket), and I met to discuss cover ideas. There were so many possibilities, as always—how to embrace/transcend the dilemma, for once? Well, maybe we weren't as detached as that. The idea was so enormously fun.

LARISSA TOKMAKOVA: The painting on the back of the jacket was made years before *Lemon* existed in novel form. Back then we played with the idea of making a film of the story, featuring a series of paintings of the protagonists, man and lemon. This painting was the first and last one to emerge from exploring that possibility. It became handy later, when we were trying to come up with a design for the book cover. The decision to put it on the back of the jacket came from realizing that the 10,000 covers plan had a lot of chaos in it, and could really benefit from a unifying image, something the reader could hold onto, no matter how Krauser might massacre the front of any particular copy.

LAWRENCE KRAUSER: Most of the covers were illustrated in public places, which proved a marvelous catalyst for meeting people, as well as a graceful way to

Opposite: Lawrence Krauser's hotel room in Chicago, where he holed up for several days with hundreds of just-off-the-boat copies of Lemon, *embellishing their blank covers with original drawings. The following pages present eighteen* Lemon *covers from various drawing sessions.*

recede from conversation when I wanted to. I drew them over a three-month period—about three hours' worth on a typical day. The drawing per se was usually swift doing, but once in a while I'd get wrapped up or bogged down in a particular cover. Or, if I ran out of books on a given day but was still jonesing, I'd ramp up the level of detail to prolong play. Most of the challenge lay in the avoidance of image repetition, and in negotiating the formidable physicality of books and boxes.

The maddest sprint was when I was holed up, then twice snowed in, in a motel room north of Chicago, where I did 2,776 covers in one week. We hauled them there from the warehouse in a minivan, and they colonized like kudzu. By the end I was sleeping on the floor in an aisle between heaps and towers of them. That was the second week of December, 2000. I watched Gore concede the election sitting on a sloppy divan built of books; it was a weird time-stopped week. I blogged about this and other adventures along the way in my "Cover Letters" page on the McSweeney's Web site.

I did a bunch of readings in and around Amsterdam when Vassalluci's Dutch translation came out the following year. They'd been so excited by the cover idea that when they gave me the books to draw, they held back a few hundred, which were then sold at the readings. People lined up with their purchased books, and often had very specific requests for what they wanted on their covers; it was very moving—the author/reader connection taken another step.

I confess to having drawn only 9,812 covers for the U.S. edition. I maintain a small hillock of unmarked books in a friend's garage; I do a few now and then when I visit, and give them as gifts. For the Dutch edition I did another thousand. So in all: 10,812 covers.

Occasionally I'll encounter a cover that strikes me as so sub-par that, with permission of the owner, I'll take another pass at it.

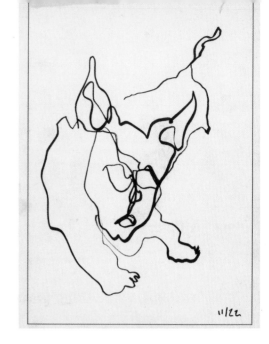

11/21

11/22

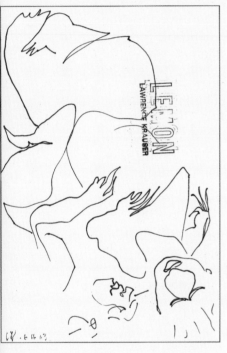

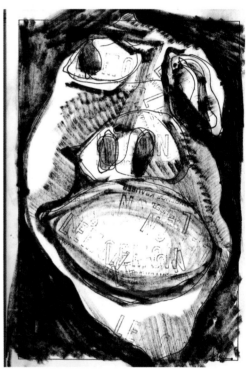

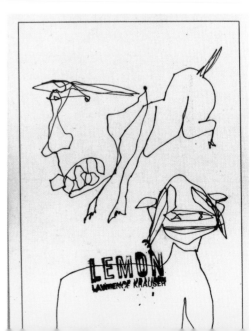

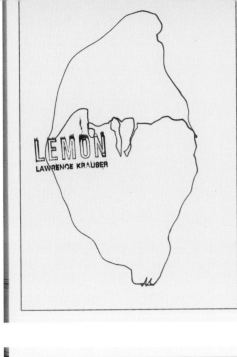
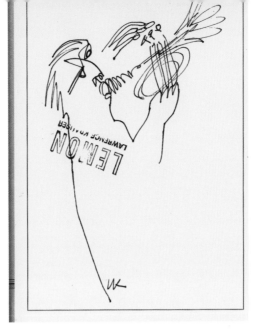
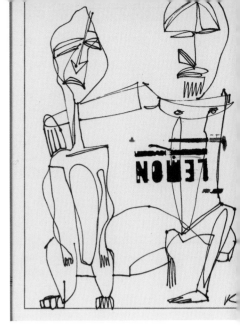
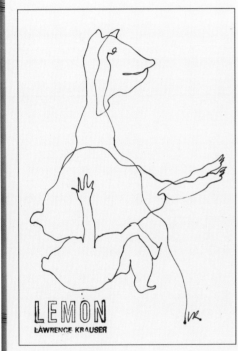
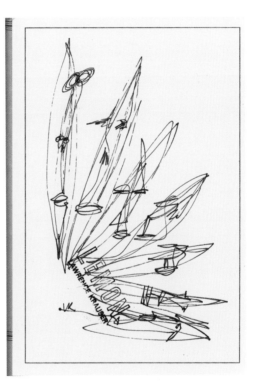

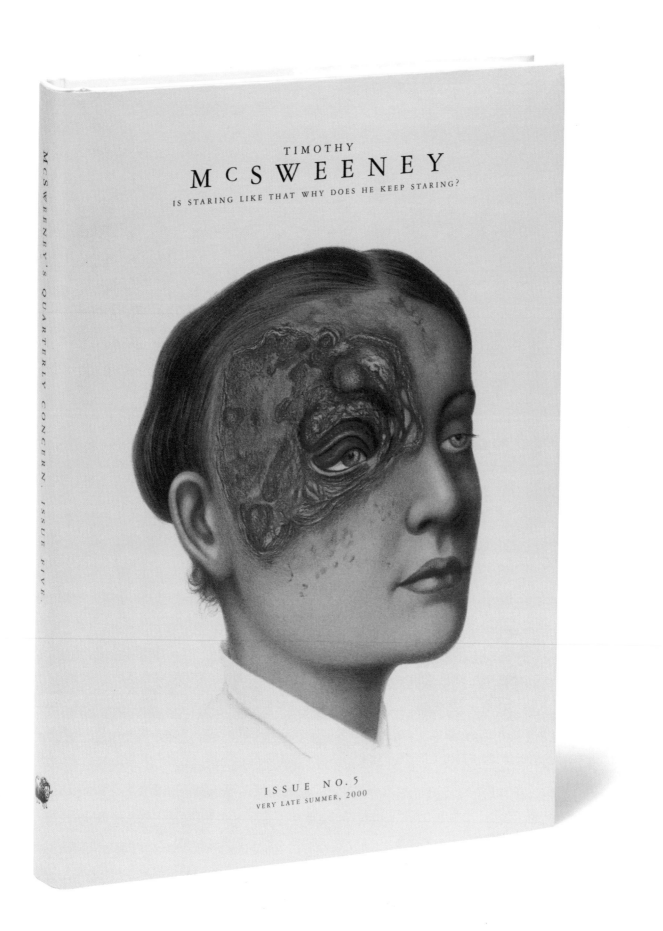

TIMOTHY
MCSWEENEY

IS STARING LIKE THAT WHY DOES HE KEEP STARING?

ISSUE NO. 5

VERY LATE SUMMER, 2000

MCSWEENEY'S QUARTERLY CONCERN. ISSUE FIVE.

McSweeney's 5

(2 0 0 0)

SARAH VOWELL: I had made the acquaintance of a *Nightline* producer, who let slip that Koppel had a thing for Marcus Aurelius. That actually explained a lot. Here was this cool customer who delved into the most terrifying topics—at bedtime. Of course the only way he could moderate discussions about every conceivable apocalyptic scenario night after night is if his hero is a Roman Stoic philosopher! My interviewing philosophy, though, is antithetical to Koppel's. He would get an expert to talk about his or her expertise. But I'm always more interested in a subject's off-topic enthusiasms. (Honestly, my favorite Bill Clinton interview of all time aired on VH1 and involved the former president just flipping through his record collection.) When the issue came in the mail and I saw Koppel's picture—in color—on the cover, I was thrilled. *McSweeney's* wasn't known for its colorful covers at the time. I loved that the most colorful cover to date was of a national-treasure newsman in a pinstripe suit.

DAVE EGGERS: Those Koppel shots turned out to be a little too small to print sharply at the size we printed them. You can see the pixels in his face. Oops.

RODNEY ROTHMAN: The Koppel cover gets all the hype, but Issue 5 had multiple covers. My copy had a cover illustration of a man with a grotesque facial lesion. It made for a lot of dirty looks while I read it on the subway. The piece I prepared for Issue 5 was called "My Glorious Publishing Empire." At the time of publication, there were a few fledgling publishing companies that claimed to be able to profitably print a handful of copies of any book you sent them. Ironically, that is pretty much what McSweeney's was, minus the claim to profitability. I sent a variety of manuscripts into these companies, and virtually all of them were turned down. Luckily

McSweeney's agreed to excerpt them. "Roller Coaster" (a proposed book consisting entirely of one extremely long "Wheeeeeeeeeeeeeeeeeeeeeeee eeeeeeeeeeeeeeeeeeeeeeeeeeeeeeeeeeeeeeeeeeeeeee- eeeeeeeeeeeeeeeeeeeeeeeeeeeeeeeeeeeeeeeeeeeeeee- eeeeeeeeeeeeeeeeeeeeeeeeeeeeeeeeeeeeeeeeeeeeeee- eeeeeeeeeeeeeeeeeeeeeeeeeeeeeeeeeeeeeeeeeeeeeee- eeeeeeeeeeeeeeeeeeeeeeeeeeeeeeeeeeeeeeeeeeeeeee- eeeeeeeeeeeeeeeeeeeeeeeeeeeeeeeeeeeeeeeeeeeeeeee…" printed over hundreds of pages) was a pretty dumb joke, but it made me laugh. I remember being very impressed by Dave's commitment to it. He really lavished some serious page count on the joke. Come to think of it, it would have been a funny follow-up joke to have McSweeney's publish the foreign translations of "Roller Coaster" in subsequent issues. I have never actually heard this, but I've always suspected that "Roller Coaster" is the one piece in *McSweeney's* that William Vollmann is most envious of.

LYDIA DAVIS: I submitted "Marie Curie: Honorable Woman," to Issue 5 under a slightly different title. The story is a bad literal translation of excerpts from a poorly written sentimental biography of Marie Curie. My English in the story is deliberately fractured. McSweeney's gave it to an intelligent and well-educated intern to read. He marked the English to death, attempting to correct it. Dave caught this and we had quite an email exchange figuring out how to make it clear to readers that the writing style was not a mistake. One possibility was some kind of explanatory note, but I thought that would make the story seem like an exercise. Finally I realized I could put the title in equally awkward English, and that would be enough. Then—the nicest part—we decided to print the whole of our email exchange—including a discussion of putting the exchange in the Letters section—in the Letters section of the mag.

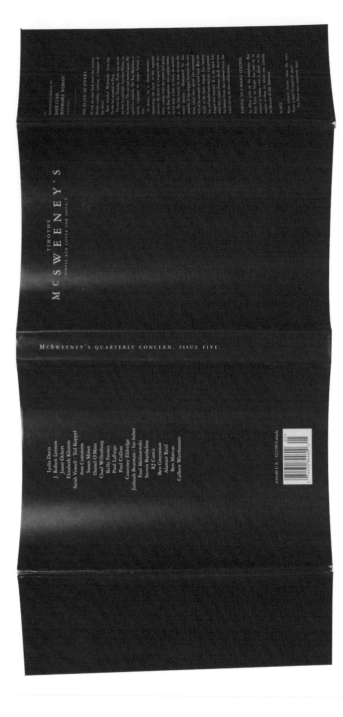

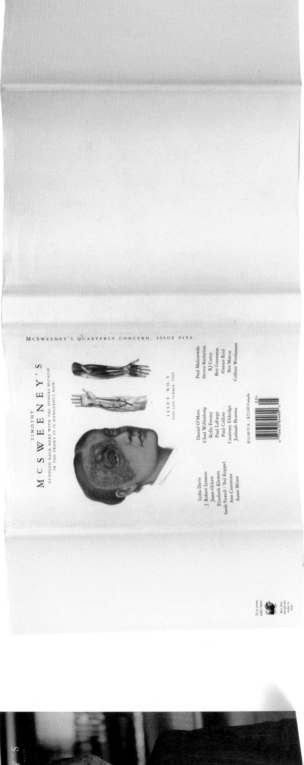

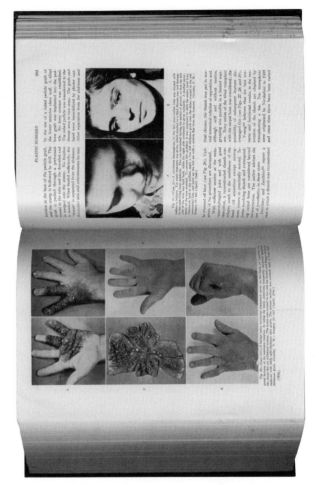

Above: The three alternate covers and three alternate dust jackets for Issue 5. Each jacket was paired with a specific cover, as shown. A full-scale, legible reproduction of the mirror-image cover (top) appears on the following page, now readable for the first time ever, anywhere.

Right: A spread from The Cyclopedia of Medicine, *an early 20th-century medical textbook with the kind of look and feel that, in part, inspired the design of the anatomy-themed covers and jackets.*

TIMOTHY
MᶜSWEENEY'S
YES PROJECTILE SHOT TOWARD THE NO PEOPLE

OOOOOOOOH!
IT'S ALL TOO MUCH TO GIVE UP!
It's just that:

Freedom says: THERE IS NOTHING THAT I DON'T WANT;

Despair says: THINGS HAVE BEEN TAKEN FROM ME;

Your God says: I HAVE THE GREATEST GIFTS OF ALL,

MONEY AND TREASURE AND CLOUDS, SO STOP SMILING AND OBEY.

And please also agree with this:
WHEN THE BUTTERCUPS BLUR, MILLIONS ON EITHER SIDE OF THE NARROW HIGH-GRASS
PATH, YOU KNOW THAT IT IS ONLY HERE AND WAS ALWAYS ONLY HERE
and
I WANT TO KISS YOU UNTIL YOU'VE BEEN WITH ME ALL ALONG

OOOOOOOH!
———————————
WHY CAN WE NOT MOVE ALL THE RELUCTANTS OUT OF THE WAY?
———————————

FOR TOMORROW:

Let's agree that: CHAOS IS ALL THAT WE KNOW.
And that: BREAKAGE IS ALL WE UNDERSTAND.
And that: FALLING DOWN IS ALL WE'VE EVER WANTED.
And that: WE ARE HAPPIEST WITH OUR FACE WET WITH TEARS.
Thus we believe strongly that: UNDERSTANDING IS A SOMETIME THING.

ooooooooooooooh!

this issue, as always, aims for the unhelmeted forehead of:
Mr. T. McSwy
to whom we gave everything and received this, only this.
OUR NEW MOTTO:

"WE ARE COMING TO GET YOU."

There were four before now,
all of which bow humbly, on trembling knee, before this:

ISSUE NO. 5

WHEN WE SEE YOU IN YOUR SOFT CLOTHES WE WANT ONLY TO WATCH YOU MOVE.
PRINTED IN ICELAND.
2000

Some Early Books

(2001–2003)

This Shape We're In
by Jonathan Lethem

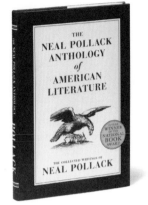

*The Neal Pollack Anthology
of American Literature*
by Neal Pollack

The Pharmacist's Mate
by Amy Fusselman

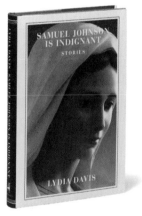

Samuel Johnson is Indignant
by Lydia Davis

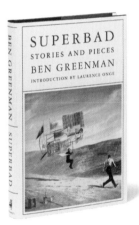

Superbad
by Ben Greenman

English as She Is Spoke
by Jose da Fonseca & Pedro Carolino
(Collins Library, volume 1)

*You Shall Know
Our Velocity*
by Dave Eggers

The Middle Stories
by Sheila Heti

Songbook
by Nick Hornby

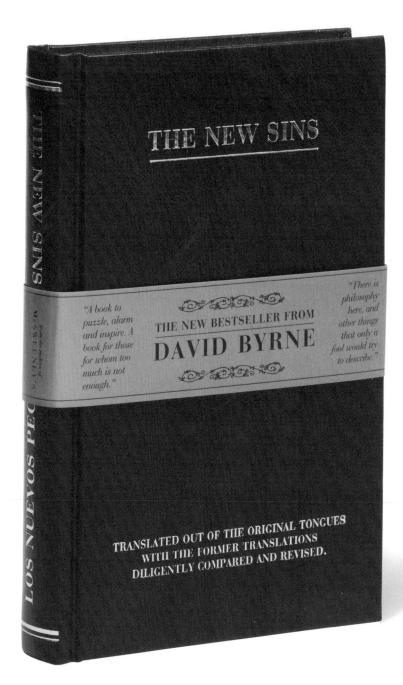

The New Sins & Arboretum

by DAVID BYRNE

(2 0 0 1 , 2 0 0 6)

DAVID BYRNE: It was the design that lured me into the McSweeney's world. I probably picked up an early issue at St. Mark's Bookshop and found it baffling (the letters sections) and seductive. The writing was unlike anything I'd encountered. I bought further issues as I stumbled on them, and realized that the journal implied that somewhere possibly close by there existed a whole scene or world that either I didn't know about or that was completely imaginary.

Around this time I was invited to participate in the Valencia (Spain) Biennial. I'd been there once before, and I agreed to participate and they said their theme would be Virtues and Vices. After some thought—I took their stupid theme seriously!—I proposed that I do a small book/tract on the theme of sins—given both their theme and that Spain is a Catholic country still. I figured doing a small book would cost about the same amount as crating and shipping art—but with a book the attendees would have something to take home besides mental pictures. I suggested that they place the books in hotel drawers in the hotels where the attendees would stay, essentially giving them all away.

I also suggested some nicely dressed young people might set up a table in one of the plazas and offer the book to passersby. That didn't happen. Well, I began writing the chapters about these New Sins, many of which we currently consider virtues, and I knew I would need a designer to help make the project look appropriately Bible-like. I remembered those *McSweeney's* journals I liked so much and contacted that organization and said I had a project and would like to hire/collabarate with your designer, whoever he or she is.

That designer turned out to be Dave and I was kind of shocked and flattered that not only did Eggers want to design the tome but he suggested

McSweeney's put it out here in North America. He meant in regular bookstores; the hotel drawer gag was only for Spain. I went out to the McSweeney's HQ in Brooklyn—the "store" that sold animal husbandry and taxidermy supplies. The store window was a kind of model-train art installation. Ah, here were the curious people who made those strange-looking journals! I bought a plastic bear tongue for the grizzly I hoped to place in my entrance foyer someday and some bird feet simply as curious objects. I may have also purchased a spray can of Hog NO, as the sows at my place were getting unruly.

DANIELLE SPENCER: Producing *The New Sins* involved many late-night phone calls with Dave (Eggers) from our studio in New York. David (Byrne) was polishing his treatise and selecting and editing photos and preparing to go on tour all at the same time, and Dave was designing the book out in San Francisco, and the art festival producers in Valencia who had commissioned the book were either radio silent or sending emails created by some random-message generator, and we were trying to fit all these pieces together. Dave speaks very softly, and these late-night calls were like a lulling burbling brook, musings over varieties of pleather binding and Bauer Bodoni font issues and his many brilliant design insights. One night we decided that I'd be the one to go on press to Iceland, so he told me what to expect: *You'll feel like you landed on Mars*, he explained. *Your flight will arrive in the morning, and you'll be exhausted, and you'll drive across this rocky landscape to Reykjavik, and it'll be like nothing you've ever seen before, and they'll make you go right to the printing plant—but it'll be okay. At the plant you'll meet Björn. He'll look after you. His name means Bear, and his nickname is Bjössi, which means Teddy Bear. A few*

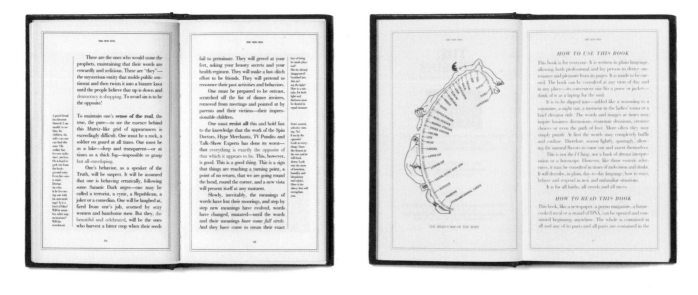

Left: The typography of a contemporary Bible: Red text indicates Jesus's speech. Narrow margins cross-reference the verses on the page with verses elsewhere in the Old and New Testaments.

Below: Four spreads from The New Sins, *designed to look biblical. This was the first and only* McSweeney's *publication intended for distribution through hotel drawers in Spain.*

Next pages: The cover of Arboretum *and a full-size reproduction—smudges and all—of one of its 92 tree drawings, "Hutcheson's Moral Senses."*

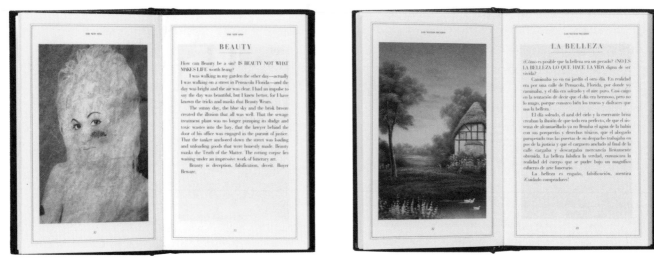

days later I flew to Iceland, and it was exactly as he said it would be.

DAVID BYRNE: In keeping with the spirit of the book I learned PowerPoint and participated in a number of McSweeney's events. I decided I would talk about these New Sins as if I were a motivational speaker, with slides and diagrams. These events were a lot of fun. And that was that.

Regarding *Arboretum*, my next McSweeney's book, Dave and I kept in touch and at one point he was visiting my studio and I showed him the "tree" drawings I'd been making for a few years. I myself was confused about how to present them, or if I should present them at all or keep them to myself. They were first drawn in some little sketchbooks and I'd redrawn a lot of them larger for exhibition—big or little? I didn't know.

Dave felt the experience of flipping through the original sketchbooks was important—that it brought you closer to my frame of mind when I jotted these diagrams down. A sketchbook or notebook or journal is, possibly, closer to the raw unpolished thought process of the artist or writer than the cleaned-up versions that might come after. Dave proposed that McSweeney's do a book of these. I was thrilled and after a while I went out to San Francisco, where a larger store—the Pirate Supply store and new McSweeney's HQ—had been established. Over the course of a few days Dave, Barb, Eli, Danielle, and I hammered out the look of the book, the title, the kraft paper, the cover treatment, and the massive fold-out at the end—an ingenious solution for captioning that wouldn't interfere with the visual experience. It was decided that some extra visual elements were needed so I got out my rapidograph pens and spent a morning at the nearby bed and breakfast carefully drawing vines and trees for submission to the McSweeney's art committee. Some of them passed muster and the elements of the book were set. The bed and breakfast featured only books about the great San Francisco fire—beautiful pictures of before and after scenes. It was decided that this book would be printed in Singapore so, to be safe, we asked the printer there to show us some samples. These were

just fine, but when the proof sheets began to arrive I noticed that the drawings had been "cleaned up." My pencil originals had erasure marks and smudges that we felt were integral to making the drawings seem like sketches—and to help reveal their pencil nature. At first we thought they weren't at high-enough resolution so these details were getting lost, but when we printed from copies of their digital files the smudges showed up. What was going on? It turned out that some well-meaning soul was carefully and painstakingly taking all the ghosty erasures and smudges out of the files. When it was made clear that we loved those, everything proceeded swiftly and smoothly. Ah, those inscrutable Westerners. I had approached cognitive scientists, philosophers, and psychologists to see what they thought of these mental maps—but all demurred, most saying they fell outside their area of expertise. I am still convinced that some of these wacky diagrams come (metaphorically) close to how we think, particularly how scientists and the like make connections and have insights. But maybe it only seems that way to me.

DANIELLE SPENCER: When David and I were sitting around the McProduction office, people were saying things like, "Let's make the cover out of bark!" Nothing was improbable; nobody was interested in why-you-can't-do-that. I think Dave had a very clear vision of the sketchbook facsimile approach since he first saw David's drawings. So the production and design was one of those processes that erases itself; it should look like the most natural thing in the world, the "presence of the hand" (as they say in art school) on the page. We had quite a time trying to keep the lovely smudges and half-erasures in the drawings which we'd so painstakingly preserved in the scans. We had the plant in Singapore print the files duotone—black and a slightly metallic silvery ink—to get as close to a graphite look as possible. Of course, despite that, they kept erasing the smudges from the proofs! Even up to the point when I was on press, at every shift change there would be worried faces, as they were concerned that the smudges were a mistake. In the end they did a really beautiful job, and I got to taste durian fruit, so it all worked out.

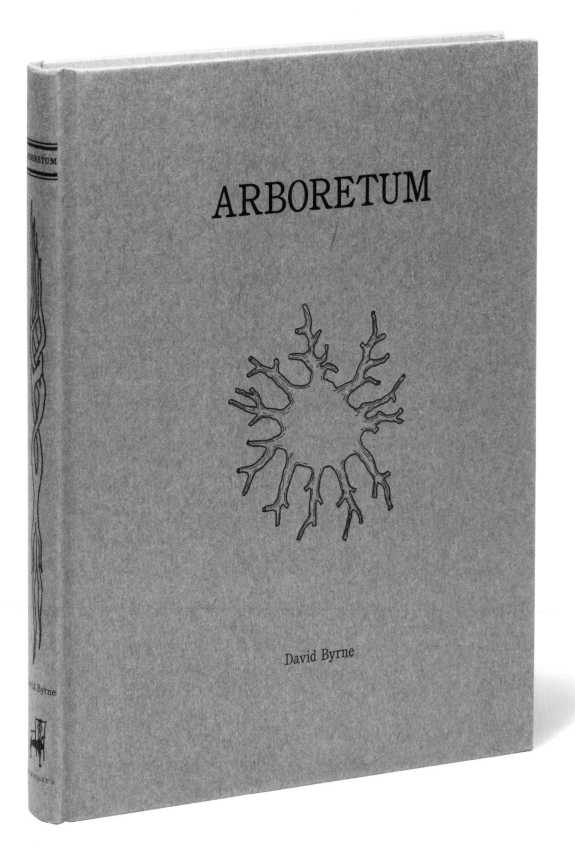

ARBORETUM

David Byrne

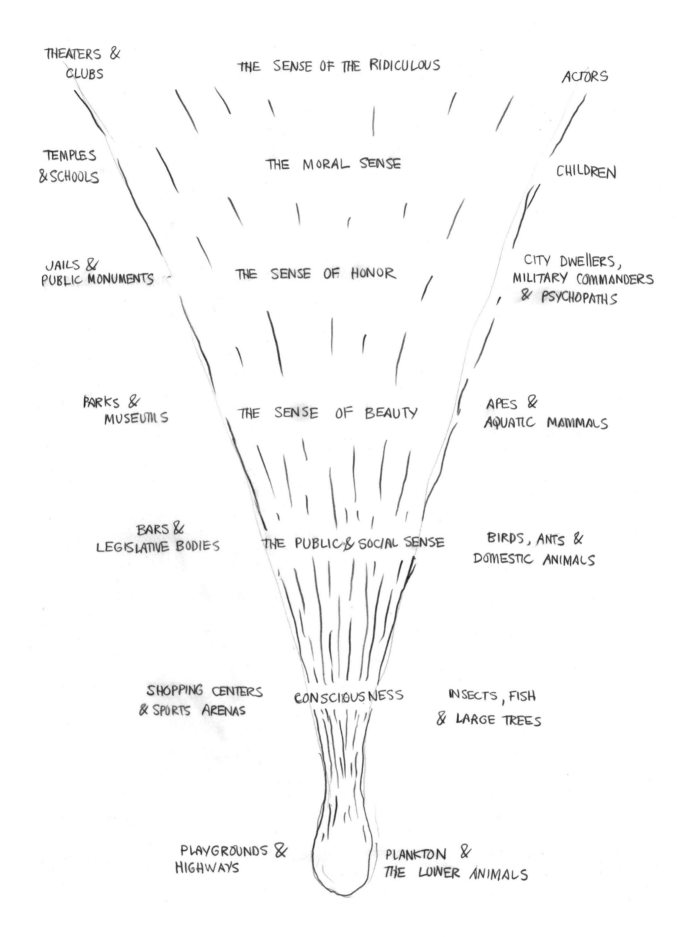

THEATERS & CLUBS

THE SENSE OF THE RIDICULOUS

ACTORS

TEMPLES & SCHOOLS

THE MORAL SENSE

CHILDREN

JAILS & PUBLIC MONUMENTS

THE SENSE OF HONOR

CITY DWELLERS, MILITARY COMMANDERS & PSYCHOPATHS

PARKS & MUSEUMS

THE SENSE OF BEAUTY

APES & AQUATIC MAMMALS

BARS & LEGISLATIVE BODIES

THE PUBLIC & SOCIAL SENSE

BIRDS, ANTS & DOMESTIC ANIMALS

SHOPPING CENTERS & SPORTS ARENAS

CONSCIOUSNESS

INSECTS, FISH & LARGE TREES

PLAYGROUNDS & HIGHWAYS

PLANKTON & THE LOWER ANIMALS

FINALLY,

UNEXPECTEDLY,

THE REAL
TIMOTHY McSWEENEY

—

{ from the introduction to McSweeney's *Issue 6 }*

(2001)

For two years now, you have known, to some degree, of a man named Timothy McSweeney. In each issue we have described, in various degrees of detail, the provenance of our journal's name. To sum up: Timothy McSweeney was the name of a man who wrote letters to this journal's editor when he was a child and teenager, living outside of Chicago. The letters were also directed to his mother, whose maiden name was McSweeney. So these letters would come periodically, and would be written in a strange and beautiful hand, and would insist that their author, Timothy McSweeney, was related to this Chicago family. Does this all make sense so far? Well, these letters were written on the backs of and inside various mailing vehicles—pamphlets, brochures, etc.—featuring prepaid postage of one kind or another. In many of these envelopes we would find train schedules recopied, plans and demands. The writer seemed intent on coming to visit and establish new roots.

Now, around the recipients' household, there was general agreement that the letters were written from an eccentric or prankster, and they were either discarded or kept in a drawer for amusement. But still, in the mind of the younger of the letters' two recipients, they held strong allure. First, they were very pretty, very much a kind of mail-art, a genre we all of course enjoy. The letters also offered, however remote, the possibility of a long-obscured and probably very dark secret. What if his mother really *had* another brother, named Timothy, who had for whatever reason been ostracized, or sent away, when young? This theory was supported,

eerily enough, by the postmark on all letters sent: Boston—a city very, very close to Milton, Mass., the hometown of his mother and her family.

But these letters ceased coming sometime around 1987. And then, more than ten years later, this journal came about, named for this Timothy for reasons easily enough inferred. We never expected to discover anything further about Timothy, though during the life of the journal, we have met many McSweeneys. First, we heard from a few dozen, from all over the land, who bought or subscribed to the journal for its name only. One such reader, whose name is, we think, Rob, actually showed up at the former 9th Street, Brooklyn, home office of *McSweeney's* just to say hello. He was in the Navy, was stationed in California and was out East visiting someone or other. He had a crewcut and he and his fiancée were both very nice. They were given a nice T-shirt for their trouble.

There were also, of course, the Massachusetts McSweeneys, they of www.mcsweeneys.com. We long had an involuntary association with them, having our home at www.mcsweeneys.net, and thus having confused many would-be visitors to either site. Eventually these McSweeneys—no relation to anyone relevant here—became our friends and we shared, for some time, responsibility for one combined web address, called the *Mega-McSweeney's Site*. It did not work out perfectly, but we parted as friends.

Recently, as one might have expected to happen at some point, we took on, as an intern, a bona fide McSweeney. His name is Ross McSweeney and he attends Columbia University, a college in New York City with a very good reputation. He started helping us, when time permitted, in the late summer of 2000. Sometime in mid-December, though, he, as the poet sings, "dropped a bomb on us."

It was at an impromptu gathering at a New York nightspot, a gathering where people who were helping McSweeney's in different capacities could meet each other and drink free drinks. This was the first time I— (I just ditched the third-person device)—met Ross, who, through some quirks of scheduling, I had missed a few times previously. Ross is a man of maybe twenty, who looks like he sang or should be singing in a choir. Or maybe a barbershop quartet. We do not know if he indeed sings, but he is clean-cut and kind. We sat on low soft stools and had this conversation:

"So you're Ross McSweeney."

"Yes."

"Where are you from?"

"Boston."

"Ha! Maybe we're related." (With small chuckle and dribble of beer on shirt.)

"Actually, we're not, I don't think, but I should tell you something. I think I'm related to Timothy."

It was that quick. Good god.

Then he related his story. You must trust that this is true:

One day, about a year and a half ago, Ross's sister, a student at the Iowa Writer's Project, encountered a copy of *McSweeney's*, this journal, at Iowa City's local independent bookstore, which is called Prairie Lights. She brought it home to Boston to show her family, amused by the journal's title. Her father looked it over with interest.

Ross's father is named David McSweeney. David McSweeney grew up with two older brothers and a younger sister, Kathleen. They were raised in the Dorchester section of Boston, which is close to Lower Mills, on the border of Milton, Mass. Their parents were Margaret (née Finn), who was born in Charlestown, Mass., to Irish immigrants, and David Philip, who was born in Ireland, came to the United States as a child, lived in Charlestown, as an adult

was very involved in the labor movement, and became fairly influential in local and national labor issues, as well as politics.

As we said, David McSweeney, Ross's dad, had two older brothers. Closest in age was Denis. The eldest was named Timothy.

Ross was telling me all of this in a bar, surrounded by people. Somewhere behind us, Kevin Shay was spilling his drink on someone. But what was at first unclear in Ross's telling was just how Timothy singled out my McSweeneys, given that there were surely hundreds if not thousands in the greater Boston area.

"Well," said Ross, "the thing started, we think, with your grandfather. He was an obstetrician, right?"

I told him yes, he was. My grandfather was indeed an obstetrician in Boston. He delivered some ridiculous number of babies over many decades, and was well-loved—our house was and is full of heavy lacquered plaques bearing his name. He even co-invented a precursor to the contemporary home-pregnancy test. His name was Daniel J. McSweeney.

"Well," said Ross, "we're pretty sure he delivered Timothy."

Oh Lord.

"And then my grandparents, my dad's parents, adopted him."

"So he wasn't a McSweeney by birth?"

"No."

"Oh god. Wow."

"And my dad recognized Timothy's handwriting from the sample you had in Issue 3. So the last time my dad went to visit him, he asked him to write down on a piece of paper the people he knew in the world. And this is what he

wrote." He handed me a piece of paper (opposite page).

As you can see, the handwriting displays a sharp intelligence and great artistic flair. After writing those names, he also drew a few quick sketches (this page).

Ross could not really explain the drawings, why and/or how. Eventually, I corresponded with Ross's dad, Mr. David McSweeney. Though Mr. McSweeney isn't sure that Timothy was delivered by my grandfather, he shed light on many of the questions. Why the drawings? Why the letters? Here is a portion of Mr. McSweeney's note:

Timothy was educated in Boston, at the Massachusetts School of Art, went on to Rutgers University and received an MFA. He taught at Rutgers in Douglas College while getting his MFA. He's had a very difficult and troubled life. He's sought peace, although never finding it. His art was his life and soul, and ultimately consumed him. He's had a long history of mental illness, alcohol abuse, and has been hospitalized many times.

The letter writing, and searching, has been an issue with Timothy for over 30 years. Timothy would often go through city and state records, find names and write to them. I'm not 100% sure but I believe there is a connection with your grandfather Dr. McSweeney and my mother, perhaps when she was trying to conceive. Timothy's life has been one of torment. It's difficult to accept, when you know the talent he had, and the person he was.

—David McSweeney

It's very strange to know, now, that there is a real person behind this journal's name, and it is unsettling to know that what we presumed to be a stranger's prankish eccentricity had not such a cavalier source. We respectfully dedicate this and all issues to the real Timothy, and nod our heads in restless kinship with him, and wish him comfort and joy. He is fortunate to have supporting him a family of such strength and compassion.

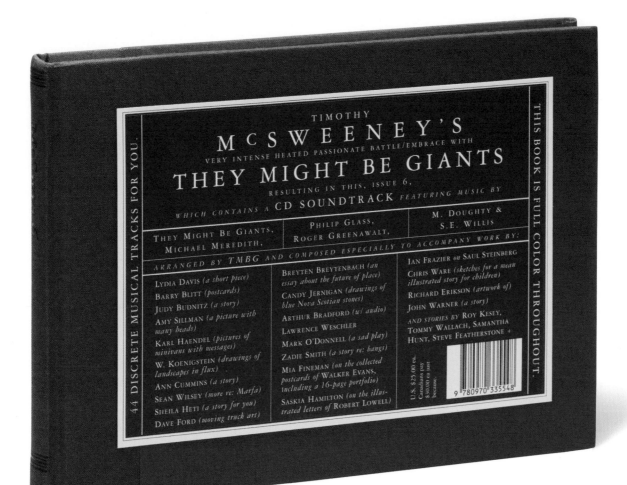

TIMOTHY
MCSWEENEY'S
VERY INTENSE HEATED PASSIONATE BATTLE/EMBRACE WITH
THEY MIGHT BE GIANTS
RESULTING IN THIS, ISSUE 6,
WHICH CONTAINS A **CD SOUNDTRACK** FEATURING MUSIC BY

44 DISCRETE MUSICAL TRACKS FOR YOU.

THIS BOOK IS FULL COLOR THROUGHOUT.

THEY MIGHT BE GIANTS,
MICHAEL MEREDITH,

PHILIP GLASS,
ROGER GREENAWALT,

M. DOUGHTY &
S.E. WILLIS

ARRANGED BY *TMBG* AND COMPOSED ESPECIALLY TO ACCOMPANY WORK BY:

LYDIA DAVIS *(a short piece)*
BARRY BLITT *(postcards)*
JUDY BUDNITZ *(a story)*
AMY SILLMAN *(a picture with many heads)*
KARL HAENDEL *(pictures of minivans with messages)*
W. KOENIGSTEIN *(drawings of landscapes in flux)*
ANN CUMMINS *(a story)*
SEAN WILSEY *(more re: Marfa)*
SHEILA HETI *(a story for you)*
DAVE FORD *(moving truck art)*

BREYTEN BREYTENBACH *(an essay about the future of place)*
CANDY JERNIGAN *(drawings of blue Nova Scotian stones)*
ARTHUR BRADFORD *(w/ audio)*
LAWRENCE WESCHLER
MARK O'DONNELL *(a sad play)*
ZADIE SMITH *(a story re: bangs)*
MIA FINEMAN *(on the collected postcards of WALKER EVANS, including a 16-page portfolio)*
SASKIA HAMILTON *(on the illus-trated letters of ROBERT LOWELL)*

IAN FRAZIER *on* SAUL STEINBERG
CHRIS WARE *(sketches for a mean illustrated story for children)*
RICHARD ERIKSON *(artwork of)*
JOHN WARNER *(a story)*
AND STORIES BY ROY KESEY, TOMMY WALLACH, SAMANTHA HUNT, STEVE FEATHERSTONE +

U.S. $25.00 ea.
Canadians pay
$30.00 ca just
because:

9 780970 335548

"The Ballad of Timothy McSweeney"
by They Might Be Giants

Walking alone on the streets of Boston,
A man with a name that everybody knows,
Please recognize our notable namesake,
Timothy McSweeney's is a journal of prose, and music, and art....

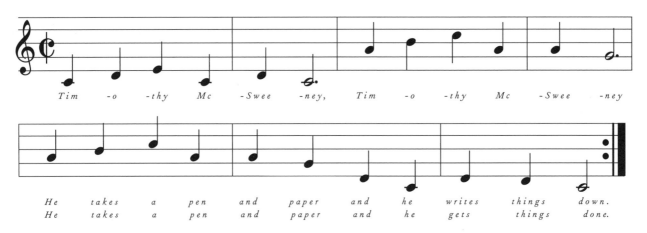

Tim -o -thy Mc -Swee -ney, Tim -o -thy Mc -Swee -ney

He takes a pen and paper and he writes things down.
He takes a pen and paper and he gets things done.

McSweeney's 6

(2 0 0 1)

LAWRENCE WESCHLER: The way I remember it, by the time of the sixth issue I had been pestering Sean and Dave with so many ideas for visually themed pieces that they just decided to devote the better part of an entire issue to such material. I ended up editing it, and looking back at it just now, it sure was a great packet of stuff. Ian Frazier's achingly poignant elegy to his frend Saul Steinberg, along with previously unpublished Steinberg drawings! Saskia Hamilton's survey of letters by Robert Lowell featuring his doodles! Mia Fineman's sampling of Walker Evans's marvelously loopy postcard collection!

MIA FINEMAN: I had just spent the better part of two years shuffling through papers and ephemera in the Metropolitan Museum's Walker Evans Archive, which includes Evans's collection of some nine thousand penny picture postcards from the early twentieth century. *McSweeney's* was clearly the perfect place to publish a selection.

LAWRENCE WESCHLER: In retrospect it's fun to scope out the landscape theme that seems to have pervaded the entire issue, starting with the pages from Austrian émigré Walter Koenigstein's colossal fantasy travelogue (over 150 blackbound notebooks documenting his imaginary meanderings through an American Southwest entirely of his own invention, his only rule being he never tore out a page); followed by Dave Ford's oddly parallel though entirely different sort of automatic travel documentation (in his case, the result of hanging leaking ink-filled bottles over empty pages in the back of his flatbed truck as he journeyed across many of the selfsame vistas Koenigstein had only imagined); and then as well, the late Candy Jernigan's micro-landscapes of individual blue pebbles from a summer she had spent with Philip Glass along the Nova Scotia shore. Dave had the inspired idea of supplementing all this with an audio soundtrack, a CD, the first time McSweeney's had attempted such a thing and one of the first times I'd seen (or rather heard of) such a thing anywhere—compounding the inspiration by inviting They Might Be Giants to invent separate tracks for every single piece in the issue.

ARTHUR BRADFORD: Dave mentioned to me that they were putting together an issue which would have a corresponding CD, and I was pretty excited about that, so I said please count me in. The funny thing was I didn't understand that this issue was mostly about the excellent band They Might Be Giants doing a soundtrack to the written work. They were all nicely tolerant of my interruption on this theme.

ROY KESEY: I had a weird short thing titled "The Workshop," so I emailed it in. A few months later I heard back: Dave liked it but wanted to talk about it. And over the phone (me in Peru and him in Brooklyn) Dave said, "It's good, but it has that open ending, and so do a lot of other stories in the issue, and I was thinking maybe we could close yours." And I thought, "My ending, it isn't really so open." But I didn't say that. Instead I said, "Oh?" And he said, "Yeah." Then he talked his way through the story, but he stopped before getting to the end. And he said, "You see what I mean? It feels like there's something missing." Which was true. The last three paragraphs were missing. They'd somehow gotten chopped off the end. So I sent him those last three paragraphs, and we all lived happily, give or take, ever after.

JOHN WARNER: I'd read Roy Kesey's piece just after he wrote it and suggested that he send it to

McSweeney's. When they took it, Roy emailed to thank me, mentioning how there was also going to be a soundtrack to each story in the issue done by They Might Be Giants. I was instantly envious and set out to find something that could earn the same honor. My story ("Tough Day for the Army") was really just the first five hundred or so words of what I thought was going to be an experimental novel that I'd written about fifteen thousand words of. (Only the story version has ever seen the light of day.) By coincidence, Issue 6 was coming out when Dave was visiting Chicago (my home at the time) for a reading. I bought a copy at one of his appearances and listened to the track accompanying my story on the way home in the car. I think my initial thought was simply, "Wow, that's cool."

DAVE EGGERS: At that Chicago reading, we invited audience members to compose and recite Condoleezza Rice haikus. At the time, Rice had only been National Security Advisor for a couple months, and so we were still getting acquainted with her politics and her five-syllable name. The Condoleezza Rice haikus that earned the most audience applause were rewarded with copies of Issue 6, which had just arrived from Iceland.

LAWRENCE WESCHLER: As I think back on that issue, perhaps the most sublimely whacked-out thing in it was Chris Ware's contribution. Art Spiegelman had told us about an entry Chris had submitted to the *Little Lit* compilation that Art and his wife Françoise Mouly had been putting together: a book of pieces aimed at children by top-notch graphic talents. But Chris's contribution, Art told me, had proved just too grim to be included (and that's saying something coming from the creator of *Maus*!). We asked Chris if we could take a look, and it was grim all right— perhaps not the best thing for little kids but right near perfect for us. And indeed, that initial approach led directly, several months later, to our collaboration with Chris Ware in Issue 13.

Two of Candy Jernigan's portraits of blue rocks and the inside back cover, where the CD was mounted.

...t in the past; OPRAH: Oprah, Oprah; THE
shovel and the buckskin gloves roll me out a
g for an oil can eating butter pecans honey get
an old new car all this by hand my hands and
why don't you come outside with me? West
deep inside and inside the other one there is
got yourself to keep you warm West Virginia
party who will be partial to you sugar maples
another deep inside and inside the other one
he state across the way West Virginia you con-
will be partial to you sugar maples [undeci-
r deep inside and inside the other one there is
ah yeah right yeah right, etc.; IT'S GETTING
h ah yi boya rah la ea ea ea ya; (SHE THINKS
ve both grew up but I heard she changed from
the accent in her speech she didn't have grow-
don't a lot about it's been years since I moved
s talking to herself not too simple and not too
d but you might know she's not the accent in
he accent in her speech she didn't have grow-
d she thinks She's Edith Head, now one more
e's Edith Head, now; MR & MRS NUCLEAR:
yes your hair hangs although my mind [unde-
es as you incline you head and although I like
bangs are that on which the world hangs I'm
as that while fully intentional and in case you
r hat bangs are that on which the world hangs
ngs although my mind [undecipherable] I dig
ur head can you murder with your style believe
world hangs I'm only holding your hands so I
now I want it faster better now I want it faster

better now; BE PATIENT: Be patient be patient patience has its own rewards repeat be patient be patient patience has its own rewards be patient be patient the [undecipherable] is rockin' forget [undecipherable] the voices are singling now the voice is in your head your sleepy your sleepy now it's time to go your sleepy; GRASSROOTS [INTERNET] REVOLUTION: Grassroots internet revolution; SWIMMING HOLE: La la la la la la la la la la la la la la la la la oh la la la la la la la la la la la la la la la la la oh wew wew wew wew la la la la la la la la la la la la la la la la la la la la la la la la la la la la la la I'm saying yeah that's, that's what I'm saying yeah that's, that's what I'm saying yeah that's, that's what I'm saying yeah that's, that's what I'm saying even my t-shirt even my t-shirt even my t-shirt even my t-shir... ARMY IS TIRED NOW: The army is tired now tired of swinging so sad all its defenders have moved along and it's so sad the army things like a child drowning in a vat of molasses how would a ch... ne will answer [undecipherable] ing I'm sure it's in the laun... like a photograph of your grand- sad like a zero on the LED father at the age of 27 but g sadder than a frog plucking a banjo frog that's about as njo-playing frog let us examine the sadness it's extremely s... banjo is the frog aware that he sad? I believe that he is awa... a frog that plays a banjo is quite so self-aware I believe is th... [undecipherable] American flags [undeci- pherable] is yellow it's really d a year in Robert Lowell's electric chair jailbirds entanglement a... ble] reappraisals in the air I am 40 given a year in Robert Lowell's tranquilize a [undecipherable] sub... LINCOLN WASHINGTON & THAT JEF- FERSON GUY: Lincoln Washington down, down, down, down, down, down, down, down to the bottom of the sea by and I'm a sailor man down, down, down, down, down, down, down, down, do... IN YOUR WORDS: Erstwhile [undecipherable] I know I'm one in a long chain I came to get my nes I know they're one in a long line I came to get my [undecipherable] and I know there's truth in your words buried inside of your words yeah, I've leaned a thing or two from hard times spent with you and I know there's truth in your words buried inside of your words yeah, I've leaned a thing or two from hard times spent with you; R U TOGETHER: R U together? Together together together together together

This CD was going to
be left blank, because it is a
pretty thing when blank, but
then we remembered how likely
you were to leave it atop your
stereo, uncased, and thus how likely it was that you would then forget what this CD was, exactly
whose music was on it (in it?), and
then you would maybe even go
and record over it—songs by other
bands even—using some terrible
new software, and in doing so
make us all sad. So we put some
words on it. This. Hi.

They Might
Be Giants
vs.
McSweeney's

McSweeney's 7

(2002)

ELIZABETH KAIRYS: Dave and I wanted to package this as a stack of old-school books, individually bound and held together by an old-fashioned book strap. We liked the look of the raw bookboard shell wrapped around the collection of vibrant-covered stories. Oddi helped us choose the bookboard and rubber band. We decided that each booklet would feature artwork by a different artist, and I worked with the writers to choose those artists.

KATHERINE STREETER: Elizabeth called me to do the cover art for Courtney Eldridge's story, "The Former World Record Holder Settles Down." Visual metaphor was assumed to be the way to go, as opposed to literal interpretation—that's how I usually prefer to work anyway—and I had total freedom to come up with my own concept. As I look back at my sketches, I remember that I spent quite a bit of time thinking about various sporting events. After the issue was published, I received Courtney's copy in the mail by accident. Her contact info was in the package, and it turns out she and I lived on the same block. So for a day or two, whenever I passed strangers in the neighborhood, I wondered if they were her.

MELINDA BECK: I probably sent Elizabeth one sketch just to let her know what I was planning to draw for the cover of A. M. Homes's story. But that sketch, like all of my sketches, is in a landfill somewhere. I chose to focus on the married couple. The figures' external features reflect how they act. She is sharp and pointy with an exposed interior. The husband sits like a child on her lap, as the pages of the story escape from his mouth. At the time I did this piece I was a bit frustrated with my own ovaries and I think that anger worked itself out here.

ERIC WHITE: In revisiting the drawing I did for "The Ceiling," I realize it was done under the influence of 9/11, and everything that event had to offer. I can't believe it was only six weeks afterward. My connection to *McSweeney's* at that point was through Elizabeth Kairys, a great designer and one of my favorite people. In a way this piece plays off of Rubin's face/vase optical illusion from the early 1900s, and also brings in this multiple-exposure idea I've been using in my work for about ten years now. I don't remember anything about the story, but I do remember really liking it, and based on the drawing I assume it was about dysfunctional relationships—my favorite.

JOHN WARNER: The cover for Allan Seager's "This Town and Salamanca" is a scan of the back flap of one of my copies of Seager's memoir, *A Frieze of Girls*, that I'd purchased at a used bookstore a couple of years before. It's the first thing that popped into my mind when I was told that the package would be its own booklet and we needed a cover. The stains and discoloration are all naturally occurring and existed prior to my ownership and seemed symbolically appropriate. (Maybe too obviously so.) For several years I'd wanted to try to publish something that would remind the world of Seager's existence. My motives were personal, since he was my great-uncle, but I'd been long fascinated by his biography: NCAA champion swimmer, Rhodes Scholar, championed as the next big thing in the short story by the guy (E. J. O'Brien) who had declared Ernest Hemingway as the previous next big thing, wrote the book (*Amos Berry*) that inspired James Dickey to take up poetry. Plus, he wrote some pretty damn good novels and stories. If not for some bad luck and an uncompromising nature when it came to the aesthetics of his own work, he could've been or even should've been a writer

69

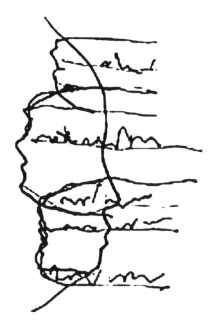

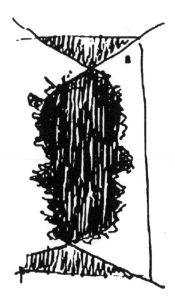

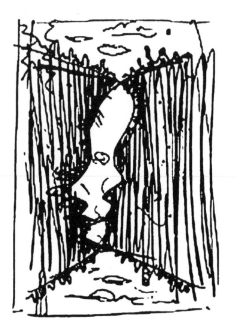

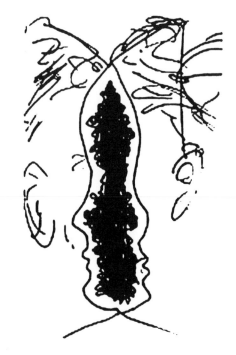

*Sketches and finished cover art by
Eric White for "The Ceiling," a short
story by Kevin Brockmeier.*

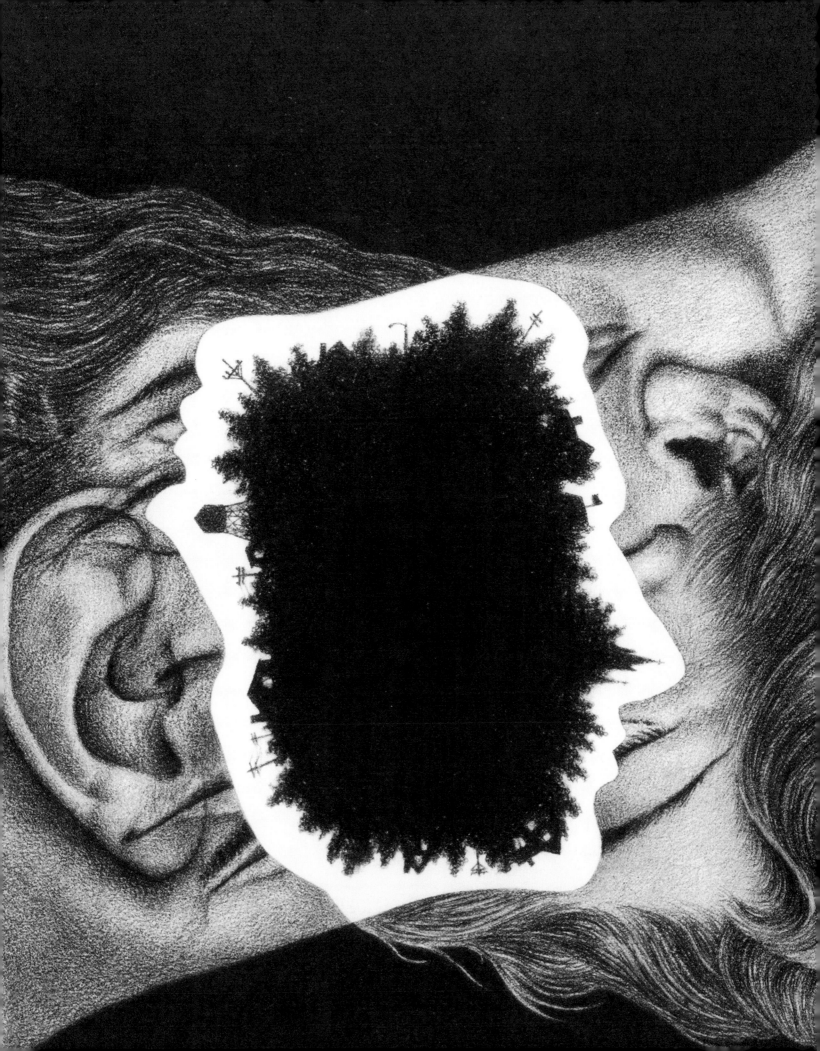

to: Elizabeth
From: Katherine

She sits on other mans
Lap = husbands hands
come in From Border w/ Ball ①

She + husband Hold bowling
ball - other persons legs are her
chair - Pin are in Background ②

She's in chair in Boxing
ring - husband looks
in ③

Husband hands her the ball -
reference to many Balls (many trys)
and Pins have numbers on them =
represent number of men ?... ④

My Favorite ←

*Sketches and finished cover art by
Katherine Streeter for "The Former
World Record Holder Settles Down,"
a short story by Courtney Eldridge.*

still widely known today. Previous to *McSweeney's*, though, there wasn't a place I could imagine publishing what I wanted to do, an appreciation or even a celebration, as opposed to a rather dry piece of history or worse (in my mind), literary scholarship. It really was as easy as telling Dave what I had in mind and him saying it sounded interesting. There's a lot of freedom in only being bound by what sounds interesting.

TIM BOWER: Painting the cover for Ann Cummins's "Red Ant House" is a blur. I remember at the time I was doing a lot of stuff for Elizabeth and *Salon*, and I suppose that was the conduit to the assignment.

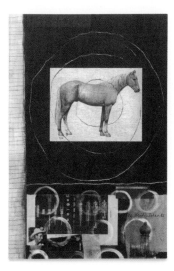

Cover art by Elizabeth Kairys for "Little Little Big Man," a story by Heidi Julavits. Kairys was guest art director for Issue 7.

Cover for "This Town and Salamanca," a forgotten story written by Allan Seager in the 1930s. The cover art largely consists of the back cover of a water-stained copy of Seager's 1964 novel, A Frieze of Girls.

Art-free cover for William T. Vollmann's "The Old Man," an excerpt from Rising Up and Rising Down, *the author's 3,000-page essay on the history of violence.*

Cover art by Tim Bower for "Red Ant House," a story by Ann Cummins.

Cover art by Chris Ware for "The Return of the Amazing Cavalieri," a story by Michael Chabon.

Cover art by Melinda Beck for "Do Not Disturb," a story by A. M. Homes.

The deadline was quick, and the pay sucked, but I recall that in exchange for those impositions, the art direction was light. These are very typical conditions, a trade-off I agree to frequently, but the exception here was that the text was a little gem. The image came to me immediately, and was approved as fast. The girl in the piece was quirky, almost possessed or damaged. I hope that's accurate, because that is what I'm left with. And everything took place on the moon, or near the moon, didn't it? A whole strange world of remoteness, so I took the color out of it, not to make it dark, but to skew the sense of place. *Lord of the Flies* on the moon, with a little girl, who looked like an old lady, or a vegetable.

McSWEENEY'S

8

McSweeney's 8

(2 0 0 2)

ELIZABETH KAIRYS:
When I lived on Valencia Street, I'd wake up every morning to see a huge flock of birds swooping past my window. "The Birdshow," I called it. My fascination with the Birdshow led to this cover. Dave and I talked a lot about how to make it feel dynamic and tactile, and we eventually came up with the emboss.

JONATHAN AMES: "The Nista Affair" was my first piece for *McSweeney's*.

"Birdshow" artwork by Elizabeth Kairys.

I think the original premise of the magazine—to publish stories rejected by other magazines—had changed, but one day I was looking through my computer and I came across this piece that I had written about six years before which had been rejected by *Harper's*. It's a true story about how someone played a rather cruel hoax on me, assuming different false identities through the mail and so forth, and all of it having to do with something I had written.

ELI HOROWITZ: Around this time, I was slowly emerging from a stretch of dead ends and basement grouchiness. I had just moved to Berkeley and was trying to keep busy: selling bowls made of old records at a flea market, riding my bike to the campus arcade to play a game called Beastorizer, painting pictures of babies. One night I went to a McSweeney's event in the city—I think it was David Byrne, Michael Chabon, and Dave. Dave talked about this 826 thing that was getting underway—the details were fuzzy, but he mentioned they needed help building the place, and my previous job was construction work, though I'm pretty terrible at it, so I volunteered. My first day there I built a little sandpit for plank-display. The next day it was mysteriously gone. Anyway, I helped set it up for a month or two—among other things, I bought Karl, the first puffer fish—and then when the pirate store was ready to open they needed someone to sit at the cash register. No one was coming in the store, so I'd sit there and read books. Dave saw this, I guess, and meanwhile he was deep in his own novel, *Velocity*, and he must have been desperate for feedback, because he asked me to read it. I'm not sure I had ever edited anything—certainly not a novel. But I read the thing in a few nights and then we met in the pirate store after closing—I think this was shortly after we had discovered a dead starfish rotting in the vat, perhaps the most disgusting smell I have ever encountered. Anyway, we talked, he seemed pleased, and over the next few months more and more projects started falling my way. I was still manning the cash register—having long conversations with William T. Vollmann while ringing up lard purchases. After a while Dave asked if I wanted to come onboard for real, and I said okay. I was managing editor right from the get-go. I had no idea what I was doing.

IF "NO"

IF "YES"

76

Reviewing Unsolicited Material

A good number of the stories we publish come to us unsolicited, by mail or by email. Ideally, a writer won't have to wait more than three months before hearing back from us. We're always trying to be as fast and respectful as we're able.

May 1st

May 1st

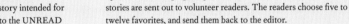

DON'T-OPEN DRAWERS *May 2nd*

The top two drawers on our baker's rack are for unsorted incoming mail, which is screened by an editor before being passed on to readers. The editor who does this these days is paranoid, and feels obligated to give everything a first glance to ensure that the next great author will not be lost in the shuffle. Every envelope that contains a short story intended for us (we get some missent submissions) is sent to the UNREAD drawer for further evaluation.

E-SUBMISSIONS *June 1st*

Electronic submissions are handled a little differently. There are a lot more of them, but as with the physical submissions a reader will look at each and every one. This is grueling, cold-blooded work. Once it's done, and the unusable stuff (guides to pooping in public places; op-eds about being a grandpa) has been removed, sets of one hundred stories are sent out to volunteer readers. The readers choose five to twelve favorites, and send them back to the editor.

UNREAD DRAWER *May 9th*

Once a story arrives in the UNREAD drawer, it's ready to be read by an intern or junior staffer. The interns and staff are specifically urged to find new voices, and pay particular attention to authors who are sending their submission specifically to us (as opposed to a mass-mailing with xeroxed cover letter). If the reader doesn't think the story appropriate for us, he or she will put a "no" on the envelope. At that point, it will go to the 2ND/3RD LOOK drawer, because every submission must be read three times before we pass on it. On the other hand, if the story stabs you dead with every damn sentence, it might be ready for the YES drawer. Any single "yes" vote promotes a piece to that drawer right away.

2ND/3RD LOOK DRAWER *May 23rd*

The 2ND/3RD LOOK drawer contains everything that's been read one or two times already; stories stay here until three readers agree that they can be turned down. The 2ND/3RD LOOK drawer is often more backed up than the UNREAD drawer, because interns dream of being pioneers and wish to read only untrammeled literature. Every effort is made to stamp this attitude out of them.

YES DRAWER *June 15th*

If a reader likes a story, it goes straight to the YES drawer. In fact, even if it's already gotten as many as two "no" votes, a single "yes" always outweighs the opposition. A story doesn't have to be perfect to earn a "yes," but it should be good enough to seem like a real contender for publication—it should, at least, make the intern-reader consider tattooing its sharpest phrases onto his or her body, reciting its author's name during intimate moments, etc.

DON'T-OPEN DRAWER

This drawer is not used very much, but sometimes there is a need for it.

NO (OR, THE REJECTION PROCESS)

If a story isn't right for us, it will end up here. Stories that didn't make the editor's initial sweep go down here, as do those that have earned themselves three "no" votes. When this drawer fills up, interns send apologetic and appreciative notes back to the writers, and these stories are recycled by the Sunset Scavenger Company and made into post-consumer products. Stories that made it a little farther might get a more encouraging response from an editor, inviting the writer to submit again, and then be recycled into higher-end products: artisanal greeting cards, maybe.

EDITOR EVALUATIONS *July 15th*

Once a story has been tapped for further consideration by an intern, it returns to the editors. At this point, it's in a pool along with stories that were promoted during the first DON'T-OPEN drawer sweep, stories by writers that we might already know and like, stories that have been specifically recommended to us by mayoral proclamation—anything that for one reason or another has become a contender. When it's time to put together an issue, this pool will be winnowed down to its burning center—maybe a dozen pieces, or fifteen, or the five or six that fit best with a certain project. A few might be held onto for additional consideration down the line, but most things that have made it this far will either be accepted or rejected in one round, with a single issue in mind. Tears are shed, hearts are broken, harsh emails are exchanged, but after much fury and indignation, we'll have found our component parts. Everything else is delivered sorrowfully back to its maker, with much thanks for sending it in.

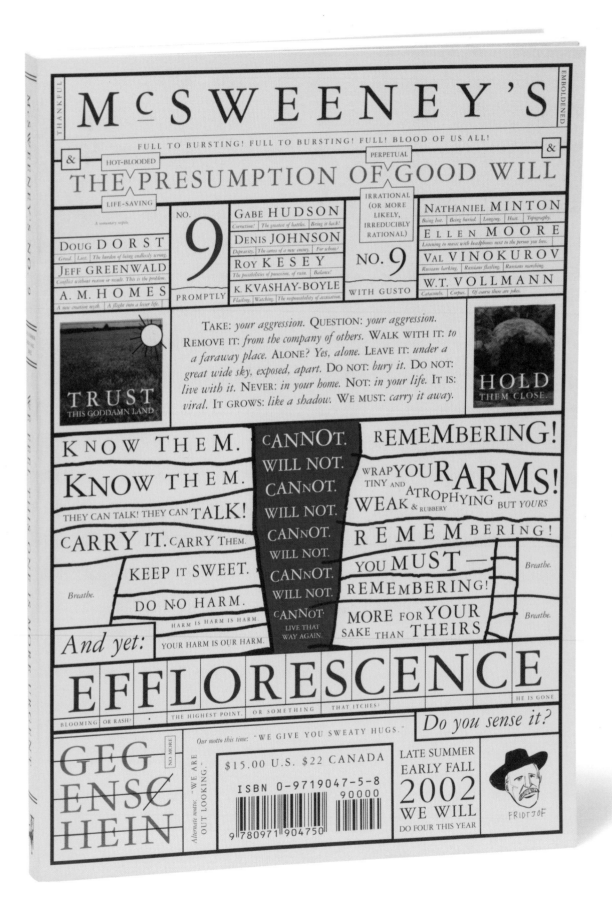

THANKFUL — EMBOLDENED

McSWEENEY'S

FULL TO BURSTING! FULL TO BURSTING! FULL! BLOOD OF US ALL!

& HOT-BLOODED — PERPETUAL &

THE PRESUMPTION OF GOOD WILL

LIFE-SAVING

A summary report.

NO. 9 — PROMPTLY

Doug DORST
Greed. Lust. The burden of being endlessly wrong.

Jeff GREENWALD
Conflict without reason or result. This is the problem.

A. M. HOMES
A new creation myth. A flight into a lesser life.

Gabe HUDSON
Correction! The greatest of battles. Bring it back!

Denis JOHNSON
Depravity. The caress of a new enemy. For whom?

Roy KESEY
The possibilities of possession, of ruin. Balance!

K. KVASHAY-BOYLE
Flailing. Watching. The responsibility of accusation.

IRRATIONAL (OR MORE LIKELY, IRREDUCIBLY RATIONAL)

NO. 9 — WITH GUSTO

Nathaniel MINTON
Being lost. Being buried. Longing. Hurt. Topography.

Ellen MOORE
Listening to music with headphones next to the person you love.

Val VINOKUROV
Russians barking. Russians flailing. Russians searching.

W.T. VOLLMANN
Catacombs. Corpses. Of course there are jokes.

TAKE: *your aggression.* QUESTION: *your aggression.* REMOVE IT: *from the company of others.* WALK WITH IT: *to a faraway place.* ALONE? *Yes, alone.* LEAVE IT: *under a great wide sky, exposed, apart.* DO NOT: *bury it.* DO NOT: *live with it.* NEVER: *in your home.* NOT: *in your life.* IT IS: *viral.* IT GROWS: *like a shadow.* WE MUST: *carry it away.*

TRUST THIS GODDAMN LAND

HOLD THEM CLOSE.

KNOW THEM.

KNOW THEM.

CANNOT. WILL NOT. CANNOT. WILL NOT. CANNOT. WILL NOT. CANNOT. WILL NOT. CANNOT. LIVE THAT WAY AGAIN.

REMEMBERING!

WRAP YOUR ARMS! TINY AND ATROPHYING BUT YOURS WEAK & RUBBERY

THEY CAN TALK! THEY CAN TALK!

CARRY IT. CARRY THEM.

REMEMBERING!

Breathe.

KEEP IT SWEET.

YOU MUST— REMEMBERING!

Breathe.

DO NO HARM.

MORE FOR YOUR SAKE THAN THEIRS

Breathe.

HARM IS HARM IS HARM.

And yet: YOUR HARM IS OUR HARM.

EFFLORESCENCE

BLOOMING OR RASH? — THE HIGHEST POINT. — OR SOMETHING — THAT ITCHES? — HE IS GONE

Do you sense it?

Our motto this time: "WE GIVE YOU SWEATY HUGS."

GEG ENSC HEIN

NO MORE

Alternate motto: "WE ARE OUT LOOKING."

$15.00 U.S. $22 CANADA

ISBN 0-9719047-5-8

9780971904750 90000

LATE SUMMER EARLY FALL **2002** WE WILL DO FOUR THIS YEAR

FRIDTJOF

McSweeney's 9

(2 0 0 2)

ELI HOROWITZ: This issue emerged in the midst of McSweeney's moving to San Francisco from New York and the 826 Valencia tutoring center getting going. Everything's hazy. The McSweeney's office was basically in the 826 tutoring center, so when the kids came in, we'd either find somewhere else to work or just teach instead. I read a lot of possible stories, thinking "I have no idea whether that's a good story," and then I read "Saint Chola" by K. Kvashay Boyle and thought "That's a good story!"

VAL VINOKUROV: In June 2001 I was at a writers' conference in St. Petersburg, Russia, and Dave was there, too. I decided to talk to Dave because nobody else would, and he seemed so starkly out-of-place: Russians tend to look down at their feet, while Dave tilts his head up like a surfer dude. I spent much of my time trying to persuade him not to do foolish American things like renting a car and driving solo to Moscow without being able to read Cyrillic or knowing how to bribe cops with proper decorum. There's a perfectly good train, I said. I failed to convince him. Apparently Dave survived. After he heard my lecture on *skaz*, he said, send it to McSweeney's, we'll print it in a memorable font. I convinced Nathalie Babel's agent to let me retranslate Isaac Babel's "Salt" to go along with the essay.

ELI HOROWITZ: This issue was printed in Baltimore. I have no idea how we picked the printer we picked.

BARB BERSCHE: The dollar was getting weaker by the second—it just wasn't affordable to print in Iceland anymore—particularly for paperbacks. This was the only book we printed in Baltimore, but I still get email updates from the printer with special pineapple recipes. Their logo is a pineapple.

DAVE EGGERS: At this point, it had been a while since I'd done one of the old all-text covers, and so it was time to experiment in that direction again. And because Issues 1 through 3 had all been based on standard computer-aided geometry, I thought I'd start with some hand-drawn lines, to break the grid up a bit. And I wanted to try incorporating photography, too—those are pictures I took in Nebraska (left) and Iceland (right). I look at this cover now and it's a tough one—the words are so raw and the look so loose that I don't love it so much. I can't believe how pained the words are. I think I was getting at something from that particular moment in time, and that time has passed of course.

ELI HOROWITZ: The inside covers were a bit too shiny and too purple.

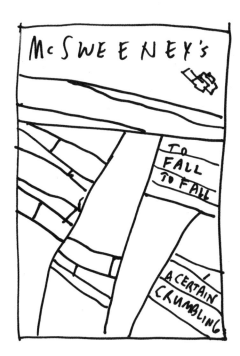

An early cover sketch for Issue 9.

*On the back cover of Issue 9, this painting—*Garden Variety *by Scott Greene—was accidentally printed in reverse.*
Here it is again, but unmirrored. At last.

DAVE EGGERS: Typically I do the design first and add the text in after. I did it that way this time—I drew randomly and then assembled it in Quark, and then decided what text to put in all the windows and holes. There are a bunch of themes running through, and references to the Beatles (No. 9, No. 9), Jonathan Richman ("with gusto"), so many things. The back cover painting was something I saw at a gallery in Mill Valley, California. I just walked into this place and saw it, and found it really startling and profound. So I asked the gallery and later the painter, Scott Greene, if we could use it on the back cover. That was that, really.

ELI HOROWITZ: I think Scott Greene's painting on the back cover—*Garden Variety*—was accidentally

reversed. The satellite dishes are pointing right when they should be pointing left. Sorry, Scott.

NATHANIEL MINTON: We did a group reading for Issue 9 in San Francisco with five or six authors. It was the first reading I'd done. The next day Eli spent an hour trying to talk me out of my lifetime subscription.

GABE HUDSON: Eli's basically a peaceful guy, but I once saw him take a tire iron to the head of some writer who was popping off at the mouth. Eli's also the only West Coast editor I know with a black belt in Brazillian Jujitsu. When I was working with him on my story for Issue 9, I asked him why he did jujitsu instead of karate or kung fu. He said something about how much he enjoyed choking motherfuckers into submission.

I.

by STEPHEN DIXON (2002)

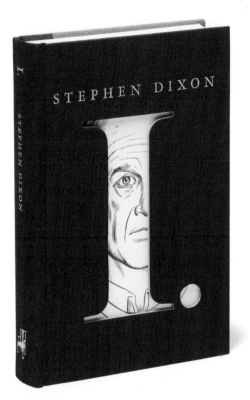

The die-cut cover for Stephen Dixon's I. *(2002),
with a portrait of the author by Daniel Clowes on the frontispiece.*

DAVE EGGERS: Stephen Dixon's *I.* must have been the first jacketless book we did. We don't have any big problem with jackets, but this started a period of about six years when I don't think we used a dust jacket. We just started having fun experimenting with the materials, with different ways of wrapping the cardboard, binding the books, using foil stamps and tip-ons and die-cuts. Elizabeth Kairys, I think, came up with the idea of cutting the entire letter "I" into the board.

DANIEL CLOWES: Dave asked me if I wanted to do a portrait of Stephen Dixon, whom I had never heard of. I was hesitant, but I wound up really liking the manuscript, and sought out some of his other work. The main thing that appealed to me was that he wanted nothing more than a straight portrait, so I didn't have to worry about imbuing the image with "content," as is usually the case with illustrations—i.e., using the portrait to sell a thesis. Also, I liked his face and thought it would be fun to draw. Still, it was for no money as I recall, and I had sworn off all non-paying work.

But, along with the manuscript Dave sent along Dixon's handwritten notes for what he thought the cover should be. They were, as expected from the author of these self-focused stories, obsessively precise and (over) explicated in lengthy detail, with many drawings and diagrams. It wasn't until I read the whole stack of notes a second time that I noticed the date at the top of the first hand-scrawled page was September 11, 2001. At that moment, I knew I had to do the cover. If he couldn't be bothered to give a moment's thought to the end of Western civilization, how could I be so petty as to worry about a few dollars?

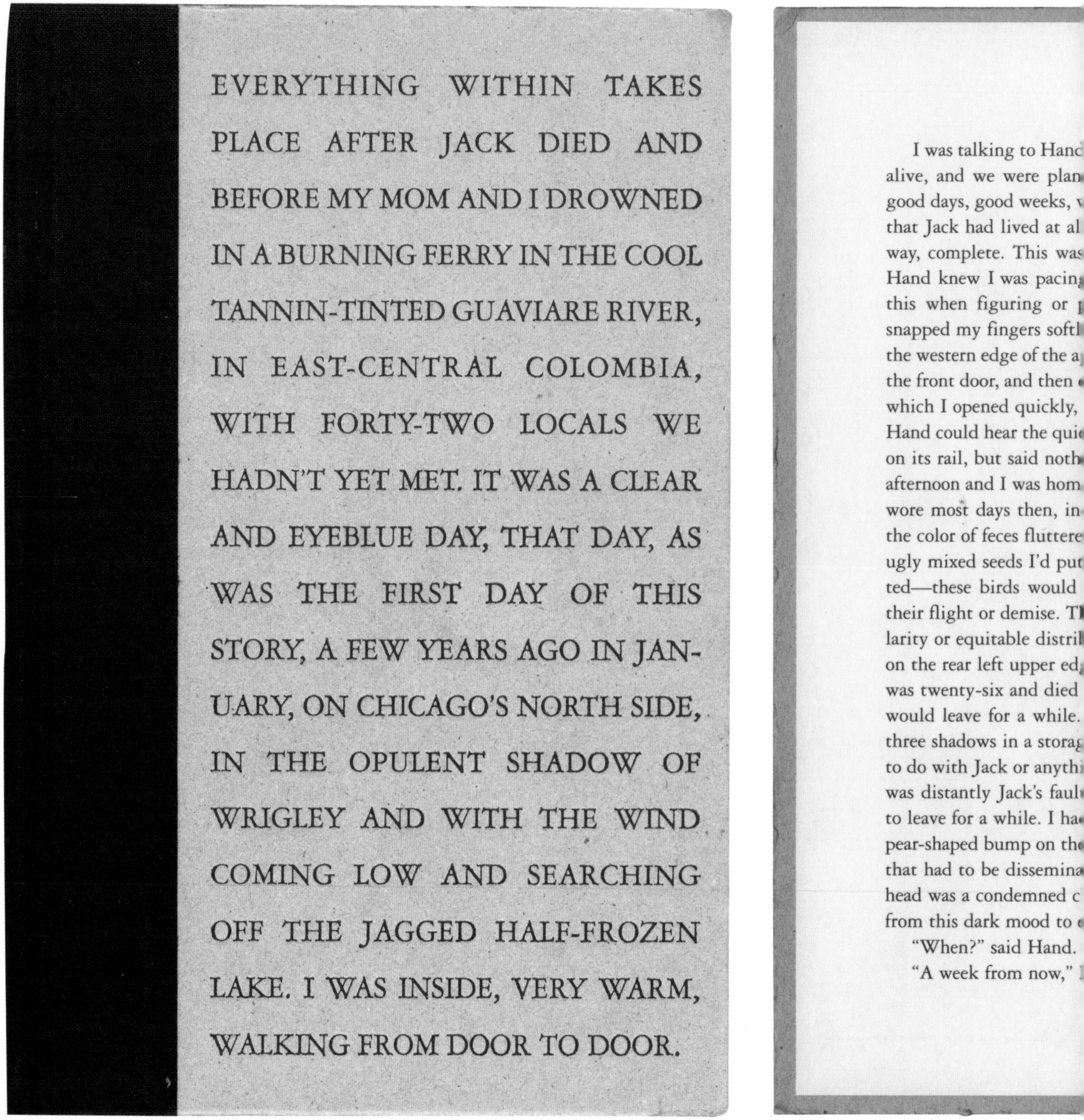

EVERYTHING WITHIN TAKES PLACE AFTER JACK DIED AND BEFORE MY MOM AND I DROWNED IN A BURNING FERRY IN THE COOL TANNIN-TINTED GUAVIARE RIVER, IN EAST-CENTRAL COLOMBIA, WITH FORTY-TWO LOCALS WE HADN'T YET MET. IT WAS A CLEAR AND EYEBLUE DAY, THAT DAY, AS WAS THE FIRST DAY OF THIS STORY, A FEW YEARS AGO IN JANUARY, ON CHICAGO'S NORTH SIDE, IN THE OPULENT SHADOW OF WRIGLEY AND WITH THE WIND COMING LOW AND SEARCHING OFF THE JAGGED HALF-FROZEN LAKE. I WAS INSIDE, VERY WARM, WALKING FROM DOOR TO DOOR.

I was talking to Hand
alive, and we were plan
good days, good weeks,
that Jack had lived at al
way, complete. This was
Hand knew I was pacing
this when figuring or
snapped my fingers softl
the western edge of the a
the front door, and then
which I opened quickly,
Hand could hear the qui
on its rail, but said noth
afternoon and I was hom
wore most days then, in
the color of feces fluttere
ugly mixed seeds I'd put
ted—these birds would
their flight or demise. T
larity or equitable distri
on the rear left upper ed
was twenty-six and died
would leave for a while.
three shadows in a storag
to do with Jack or anythi
was distantly Jack's faul
to leave for a while. I ha
pear-shaped bump on the
that had to be dissemina
head was a condemned c
from this dark mood to
"When?" said Hand.
"A week from now,"

The text of Dave Eggers's 2002 novel You Shall Know Our Velocity! *begins on the book's cover and continues immediately on the inside front cover. The unusual design confused some booksellers, who returned the book as defective.*

of my two best friends, the one still
to leave. At this point there were
we pretended that it was acceptable
his life had been, in its truncated
ne of those days. I was pacing and
knew what it meant. I paced like
ing, and rolled my knuckles, and
without rhythm, and walked from
ent, where I would lock and unlock
o the back deck's glass sliding door,
my head through and shut again.
of the door moving back and forth
The air was arctic and it was Friday
the new blue flannel pajama pants I
or out. A stupid and nervous bird
the feeder over the deck and ate the
here for no reason and lately regret-
days and I didn't want to watch
ilding warmed itself without regu-
to its corners, and my apartment,
t its heat rarely and in bursts. Jack
months before and now Hand and I
d my ass beaten two weeks ago by
t in Oconomowoc—it had nothing
se, really, or maybe it did, maybe it
immediately Hand's—and we had
s on my face and back and a rough
wn of my head and I had this money
nd so Hand and I would leave. My
a with a ceiling of bats but I swung
ria when I thought about leaving.

---

then, and now he was a dabbler, with some experience as a recording engineer, some in car alarms, some in weather futures (true, long story), some as a carpenter—we'd actually worked on one summer gig together, a porch on an enormous place gingerbread-looking place on Lake Geneva—but he left any job where he wasn't learning or when his dignity was anywhere compromised. Or so he claimed.

BAKER & TAYLOR RETURN AUTHORIZATION FORM

RTA # S323797

USE THIS FORM FOR MAKING RETURNS OTHER THAN OVERSTOCK.
ALL CLAIMS MUST BE MADE WITHIN 45 DAYS FROM RECEIPT OF GOODS.

ACCOUNT #	CUSTOMER PO #
L313114-00000	6746

PACK DATE	ATS #
1/20/03	SOM9580712BT

QTY	REASON CODE	TITLE CUSTOMER REFERENCE ID. #	ISBN	UNIT PRICE AFTER DISC.
		CALCIUM FACTOR THE S 0000000006	0963370324	11.13
		CHARMING THE HIGHLAN 0000000009	0743453069	4.40
		FOUND DEAD IN TEXAS 0000000021	0786248416	25.95
		ON TOP OF THE WORLD 0000000038	0060510293	14.53
		SMALL TOWN 0000000046	0060011904	13.97
		YOU SHALL KNOW OUR V 0000000057	0970335555	19.80

2 copies — defective 2nd page glued to inside front cover

CUSTOMER NAME:
BANGOR PUB LIBY
B/O ACCOUNT
145 HARLOW ST
BANGOR ME 04401

2

3

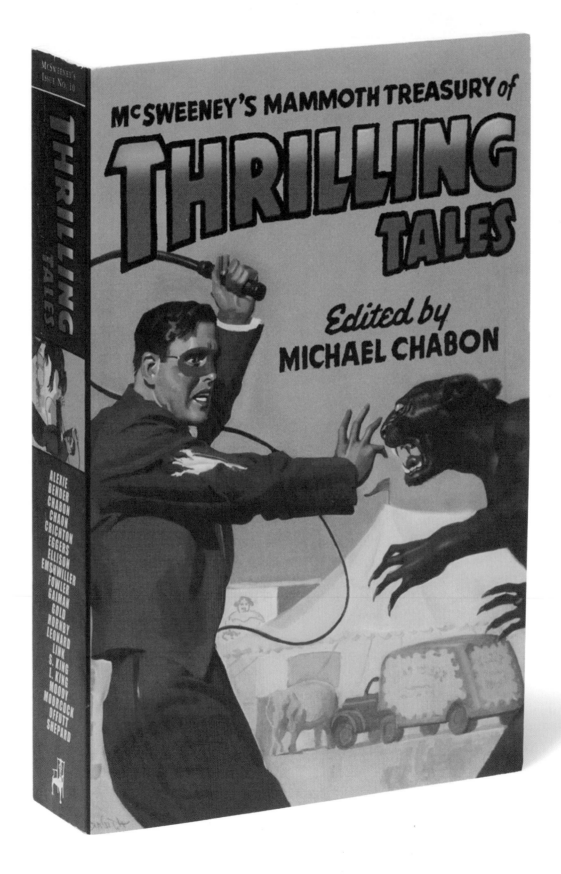

McSweeney's 10

MICHAEL CHABON: The way I remember it is that my wife and I were eating dinner with Dave and his wife, Vendela—this was in, I think, the spring of 2002—and I was kind of blathering on and on about how if I had a magazine of my own, I would solicit short fiction from our best "genre" writers and genre fiction from our best "mainstream" writers, and try to smash them together in the hope that some kind of matter-antimatter explosion would occur, leading to a renewal of the short story's neglected tradition as an intensely literary home to science fiction, horror, mystery, etc., and there would be illustrations, and painted covers, and so on, and so on. Dave at some point—having listened very politely and attentively for half an hour or so—just finally had to put a stop to it. He called me on my bullshit. Not that my intentions or my feelings about the short story were bullshit; simply that it was easy for me to sit there and spout, but what good was there in it? "Why don't you do it, then?" he said. "We can let you guest-edit an issue. We need something for Issue 10, anyway."

GLEN DAVID GOLD: When Chabon asked what genre I'd picked, I said "ghost story," because I wanted to write a ghost story. He said, more or less, "Great!

Because Stephen King, Neil Gaiman—" (he went on to list everyone who's good—you know, Chaucer, Milton, Basho, J. D. Salinger, Metallica, whoever else was in the anthology before all the people they cut) "—they're all writing ghost stories, too." Which may or may not have been true. But it appealed to my cowardly side. So I said, "Is anyone else writing an elephant serial-killer story? No?" So I switched. Then it turned out five or six guys were writing elephant serial-killer stories. I got competitive: this is going to be the best damned elephant serial-killer story of all time. And mine was the only one they printed. I only had to cry a little bit to make that happen.

DAVE EGGERS: This was also the first fundraising book we did through McSweeney's. Nick Hornby had done *Speaking with the Angel* a couple years before, a great collection of original fiction that benefited Tree House, a school for autistic youth in London. So we knew the model could work; when Michael proposed "Thrilling Tales" we thought that we could do a McSweeney's edition for subscribers and a separate edition that would be co-published with Vintage. That way, Vintage paid an advance for the book, which went directly to 826 Valencia. Michael didn't take a dime, and we

The original source of the cover art, by H.J Ward, a top pulp artist of the 1930s. Every issue of Red Star Mystery *featured this masked daredevil in a different delicate situation.*

Above: A 1930s pulp magazine from Michael Chabon's collection (left) and the Table of Contents for Issue 10.
Chabon's pulp collection was extensively pored over and mined during the design of Issue 10.

Below: The opening spread for Elmore Leonard's story, with an illustration by Howard Chaykin.

How Carlos Webster Changed his Name to Carl and Became a Famous Oklahoma Lawman

By ELMORE LEONARD

The fate of a bank robbing murderer resided in two scoops of peach ice cream on top of a sugar cone.

Carlos Webster was fifteen years old the time he witnessed the robbery and murder at Deering's drugstore. It was in the summer of 1921. He told Bud Maddox, the Okmulgee chief of police, he had driven a load of cows up to the yard at Tulsa and by the time he got back it was dark. He said he left the stock trailer across the street

105

raised a really healthy amount of money for our programs.

BARB BERSCHE: This issue was a big learning experience, business-wise. We were so focused on getting funds to 826 that we came close to forgetting about our own expenses. The journal was the way we made our ends meet, so it was hard to find a balance between giving away the proceeds and paying the rent.

ELI HOROWITZ: We put some old-timey ads inside, to give it that pulp-paper-back feel. They all came from Chabon's collection. It was my dream to sell an ad on the back cover to a novelty company—not for the money, just to have it. Like most dreams in this world, it died without ever really being explored.

DAVE EGGERS: A lot of the related paperbacks of that era—the 1930s and '40s—used a two-column format, so we thought that would be appropriate. It created huge typesetting headaches, though. It was very hard to get it to look right. But we wanted the ads to be there occasionally on the outer columns, and so we went with it. The Vintage and foreign editions all scrapped the two columns.

ELI HOROWITZ: Chabon found the cover image, too, in an old issue of *Red Star Mystery*. Howard Chaykin did the interior illustrations.

MICHAEL CHABON: I had been working with Howard—one of my all-time favorite comics artists, creator of *American Flagg!* and of course

Monark Starstalker—on the *Escapist* comic book. I was thrilled just to be able to say the name "Howard Chaykin" a couple of times a week, let alone work with the man. I liked working with him. Howard is funny and smart and encyclopedic. He knew pulps and pulp art as well as anyone alive. I just had a feeling he would do a good job.

ELI HOROWITZ: Vintage organized the cover lettering. David Coulson did it. We were up against various deadlines on this one, and I didn't know what I was doing and meanwhile Dave was finishing his novel—it was pretty hectic. He and I were constantly making speedy late-late-afternoon drives to the last-to-close FedEx drop-off spot.

DAVE EGGERS: The issue is really heavy, and I can't figure out why. The Vintage edition is a lot lighter. I guess we used heavy paper. It has the weight and feel of a brick.

ELI HOROWITZ: Issue 10 was also the first appearance of our fifty-six-issue declaration—that line about the quarterly stopping after fifty-six issues. I remember typing that for no reason at all—I guess I just liked how it sounded. Originally the heading said, "This has been Issue 10 of *McSweeney's*. There have been nine before. There are forty-nine to come." I wrote that for no reason, and expected it to be cut. But then Dave took a look and his only comment was to make it forty-six instead of forty-nine. I guess he knows our limits.

Above: The back cover of the Issue 10 subscriber edition, featuring an inexpensive health-insurance plan offered only to the McSweeney's faithful, with promotional text by Jorge Luis Borges.

Next pages: Artwork from Marcel Dzama's book The Berlin Years (2003).

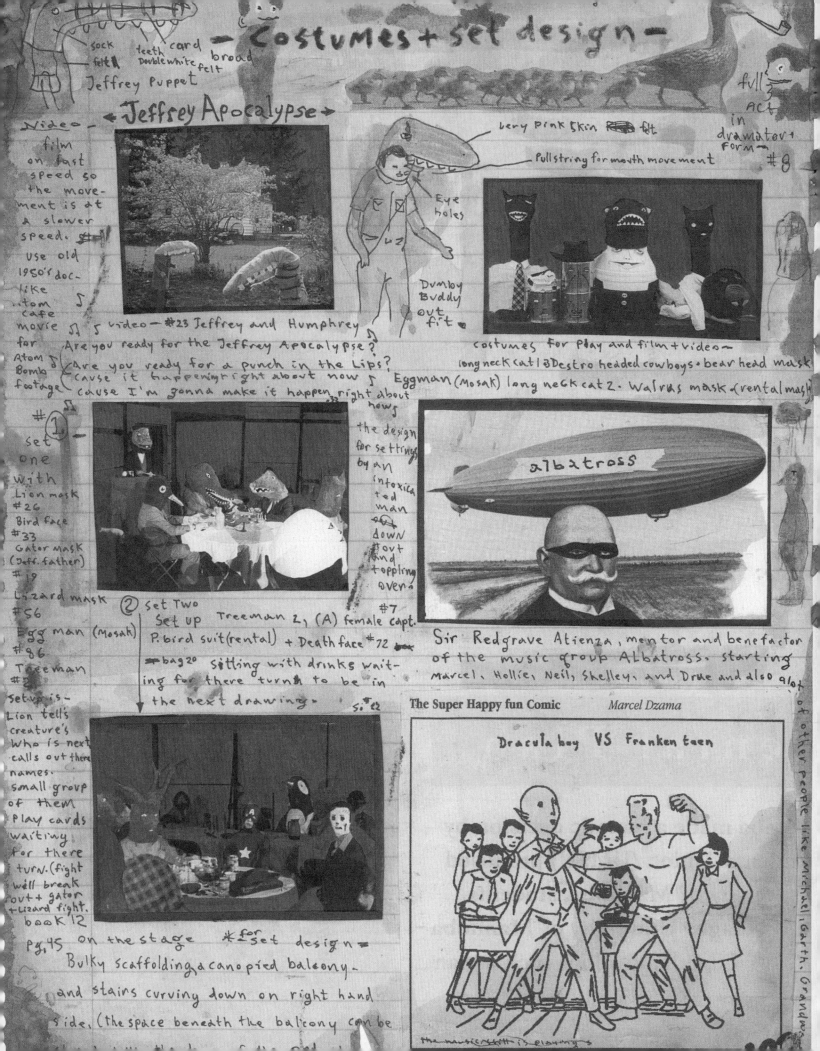

— Costumes + set design —

sock teeth card broad
felt Double white felt
Jeffrey Puppet

full
3
Act
in
dramatory
Form →
#8

← Jeffrey Apocalypse →

Video — film on fast speed so the movement is at a slower speed. #1
Use old 1950's doc-like atom cafe movie for Atom Bomb footage

very pink skin felt
Pullstring for mouth movement
Eye holes
Dumby Buddy out fit

video — #23 Jeffrey and Humphrey
Are you ready for the Jeffrey Apocalypse?
Are you ready for a punch in the Lips?
Cause it happening right about now
Cause I'm gonna make it happen right about now

costumes for play and film + video —
long neck cat 1 3 Destro headed cowboys + bear head mask
Eggman (Mosak) long neck cat 2. Walrus mask (rental mask)

#1 →
set one with
Lion mask #26
Bird face #33
Gator mask (Jeff. father) #19
Lizard mask #56
Egg man (Mosak) #86
Treeman #3

the design for settings by an intoxicated man down + out and toppling over.
#7

② Set Two
Set up Treeman 2, (A) female capt.
P. bird suit (rental) + Death face #72
bag 20 sitting with drinks waiting for there turn to be in the next drawing.
so #?2

set up is —
Lion tell's creature's who is next calls out there names. small group of them play cards waiting for there turn. (fight will break out + gator + Lizard fight. book 12
pg. 45

albatross

Sir Redgrave Atienza, mentor and benefactor of the music group Albatross. starting Marcel, Hollies, Neil, Shelley, and Drue and also a lot of other people like Michael, Garth, Grandpa

The Super Happy fun Comic   *Marcel Dzama*

Dracula boy VS Franken teen

on the stage #for set design —
Bulky scaffolding a canopied balcony.
and stairs curving down on right hand side. (the space beneath the balcony can be

the music keith is playing

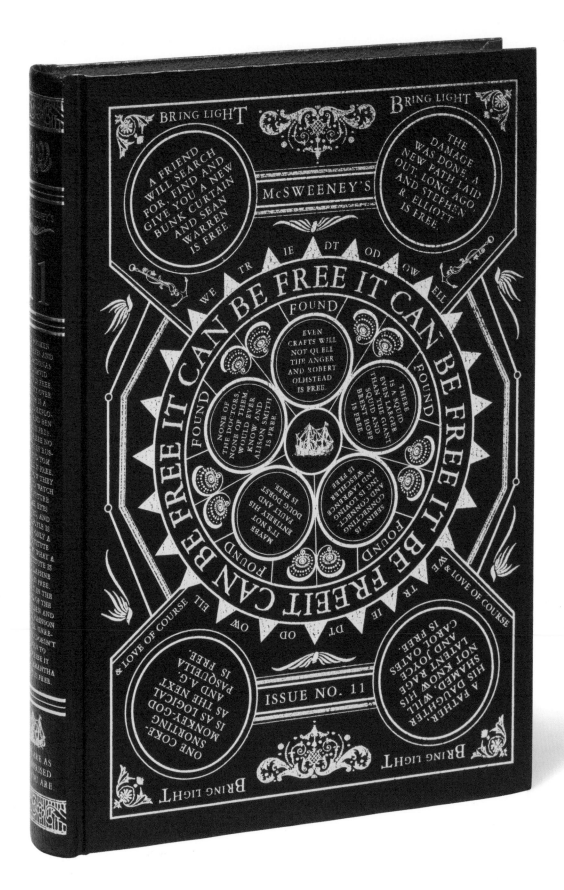

McSweeney's 11

(2 0 0 3)

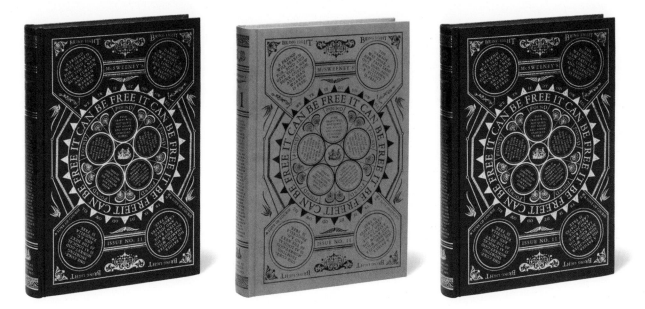

The four covers of Issue 11, finished with different colors of foil stamping and leatherette casewrap.
McSweeney's is indecisive.

BARB BERSCHE: The situation with the different covers for Issue 11 was a happy accident. Dave wanted to use a rich leatherette, but Oddi, our printer in Iceland, had only a limited quantity of four different leatherette colors on hand at the plant. There wasn't enough of one leatherette to cover all the issues, and I guess it took too long to custom-order more. So we just decided to go with it and use all the leatherettes that they had. When they ran out of one color, they started production with the next. In the end, we ended up with 9,000 black; 8,300 brown; 1,800 orange; and 900 blue covers.

STEPHEN ELLIOTT: My three stories in *McSweeney's* 11 grew into eleven stories (oddly enough), and those linked stories became my novel *Happy Baby*, which was co-published by McSweeney's. Issue 11 also included a DVD about the making of *McSweeney's* 11.

DAVE KNEEBONE: By the time Issue 11 rolled around, I'd been hired to handle business stuff at McSweeney's—managing distribution and subscriptions. Every so often I'd bother Eli, saying "We should stick a DVD in there." And he was like, "Yeah, but there's a lot of extra crap you've gotta go through," and I'd remind him that my friend Matt and I had just graduated from film school, so we could shoot, edit, and produce the thing ourselves. Dave had been thinking about doing something like this before I arrived, but I think my pestering probably helped it to happen when it did.

DAVE EGGERS: I think it was inevitable that we would do a DVD. We'd done the CD for Issue 6, and we thought that there could be nothing more absurd than watching a DVD about the making of an issue of a quarterly literary journal. The task was to make it boring enough but not too boring.

91

The inside back cover of Issue 11, with DVD and directions for use.

DAVE KNEEBONE: We had some huge ideas at first—we talked about doing an original, choose-your-own-adventure-style film, with a single story going off in multiple directions—but those ideas fell away when we realized we only had a couple months. We decided to just focus on the writers in the issue, something that would add to the pieces that were already there. The obvious first idea was to film the writers reading.

STEPHEN ELLIOTT: On the DVD I talk about what it's like being a celebrity author hanging out with Eminem, who refers to me sometimes as "the white Slim Shady." That DVD was probably the highlight of my literary career. It's been downhill since then.

DAVE KNEEBONE: We shot all the writers in a week and a half or so, traveling to New York for the East Coast writers like Tom Bissell and David Means and down to Santa Barbara for T. C. Boyle. Joe Pacheco was a major help in New York, taking us all over Manhattan. And he shot the Jonathan Ames "Cribs" piece, where Ames shows off his apartment in Brooklyn. Thomas Burns—a film-school friend, a great shooter who was then in New York—pitched in, too. In Tom Bissell's apartment, after he and David did their readings, we got some great footage of the two of them playing some hockey thing—I think it was for Sega Genesis. After that, we thought it would be funny to shoot as many writers as possible playing video games. As we were heading out to Joyce Carol Oates, Tom gave me the video game controller and said, "Just take this—just see if she'll do it." When we asked Joyce, at the end of her shoot, if she'd be up for holding the video-game controller and pretending to play, she was like, "Sure! I'll do anything." So we gave her the controller, and we basically had to explain what it was for. She'd never played a video game in her entire life. A few moments later we filmed her pushing the buttons and pretending to stare at a television. I think she sold it pretty well.

DAVE EGGERS: Kneebone did a great job with the making-of video, and then we figured we needed a director's commentary track. But we wanted the director of all directors to do it. I can't quite guess why he said yes, but he did. Francis Ford Coppola actually did the director's commentary for the video.

DAVE KNEEBONE: That day with Francis Ford Coppola was easily one of the greatest days of my life. Dave and I were both pretty nervous, driving up to Coppola's amazing spread in Napa. We pull up to this little bungalow—a little writing studio and office he has up there—get out of my truck, and knock on the door. The door opens and standing barefoot in bermuda shorts is Francis Ford Coppola, saying "Come on in! Come on in!"

DAVE EGGERS: Francis Ford Coppola is an incredibly friendly and warm man. Every so often you can see him outside his café in North Beach, sitting with some food and wine and friends, graciously saying hello to anyone who might walk by and recognize him. For such a legend, he's very accessible and open. After he gave us a tour of the winery, we showed him the DVD. The funniest thing about the whole project was that he did the whole commentary without having seen it before.

DAVE KNEEBONE: When we brought out the DVD, we asked him, "Would you like some background on the project before you start the commentary?" And he said, "Nah, just turn it on and I'll start talking."

DAVE EGGERS: He just watched it and commented on it. But without sound! He couldn't have the sound on

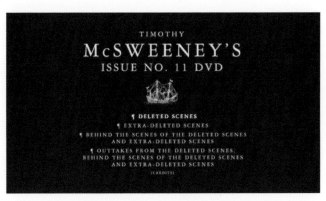

The soundtrack to Pollock (starring Ed Harris) tinkles in the background of the Issue 11 DVD menu screen.

Outtake: Samantha Hunt objects to donning an expressive shawl for the reading of her story, "Blue."

Deleted scene: Doug Dorst, impervious to sandwich-eating distractions, reads from his story, "The Candidate in Bloom."

Alternate angle: Intern Andrew Leland, impervious to Dorstian distractions, eats a sandwich as Doug Dorst reads.

at the same time, so we just pressed play, without the sound, and he commented on what he saw.

DAVE KNEEBONE: He just starts riffing, telling stories about his grandfather—who was a bit of a lothario, it seems—and making comments about the ladies in the video, and the camerawork.

ELI HOROWITZ: When my face appeared, he said something about me looking like his brother—I think his name was Augusto. I'm very proud of that.

DAVE EGGERS: The thing most people don't know about Coppola is that he's very funny. Very dry. Listening to him comment on this documentary he's never seen, Kneebone and I were dying. We were off-camera, but we couldn't hold it together. I had to leave the room many times while he talked. I still think it's the best thing about the DVD.

DAVE KNEEBONE: When it was over, he said, "That was fun. You guys want a glass of wine?" And we were like, "Yeah!" So he led us to the tasting room of his winery, and we all sat down at a table overlooking his vineyard and drank a glass of wine. It was one of the greatest moments of my life.

DAVE EGGERS: After the making-of documentary, and the commentary track, we figured we should make a documentary about the editing of the making-of documentary. The idea was just to point the camera at the film editor for twenty minutes.

DAVE KNEEBONE: That editor was my roommate and partner, Matt.

DAVE EGGERS: We just asked him to sit there and actually edit. We wanted it to be excruciatingly long. I think it was his idea to be in his underwear.

MATT BLACK: No, they insisted I be in my underwear.

DAVE EGGERS: Okay, maybe the underwear was our idea. We let him wear boxers, though. Even though briefs would have been funnier. And then the audio commentary for the editing-of occurred to us. You have to have an audio commentary for something like that. Sarah Vowell and John Hodgman seemed the natural fit when you need two people to comment on a guy in his underwear. I think they spent months rehearsing and rewriting their parts. They took some classes, I think. Did some research. And from what I hear, Sarah and John were in their underwear while commenting on Matt in his. Not in a lewd way. It was summer in Manhattan, and it's very warm.

SARAH VOWELL: Actually, we were wearing long underwear. Under our clothes. Also, we had on spats. Hodgman and I are all about sartorial decorum, unlike the rest of you West Coast slobs. Basically, I feel like commenting on the making of the making of this DVD is the most important thing I have done in my career. Up until this moment, of course. Clearly this here commenting on my commentary for the making of the making of video wins out as an even more important contribution to American letters. I still get the chills remembering the moment

Opposite: Joyce Carol Oates enraptured by Sega NHL '98. Above: Author-pugilist Jonathan Ames models his boxing robe during the filming of "Lit Cribs," a guided tour of Ames's Brooklyn apartment. Photos by Joe Pacheco.

DVD editor Matt Black takes a drink of water during the "Editing of the Making of" segment of the Issue 11 DVD.

that underwear-wearing editor got up out of his chair and left the room and just the whole mystery and tension and suspense of the aftermath and all the questions that his exit asked. For a minute there, we wondered: Where did he go? And by extension, where are we, as a literary community, going? And whither America, if not humanity itself? Turns out, if I remember correctly, the guy just went to get a cup of tea or something, but the whole time he was gone was a moment of profound existential inquiry. And in that moment Hodgman and I were like Huck and Jim, adrift on a raft of possibility.

JOHN HODGMAN: You have to understand, I didn't know Sarah very well at this time. We had only met a few times, during which I didn't speak much, due to fear. She was already so smart and talented and accomplished (only more so now), whereas I was just starting out as a writer after a long detour into professional literary-agenting. And now, in what would become a traditional part of the McSweeney's experience, I was being suddenly asked to collaborate with someone I was a fan of. As if we were peers. As if we were the same. As if I and people like Sarah Vowell and David Byrne and They Might Be Giants all naturally hung out together anyway, or shared a summer house. So I felt like a fraud, and I didn't know what I was doing. I can't say the DVD helped. It was just some guy sitting in his underwear. I remember making a lot of comments about the Tazo tea Sarah had been gracious enough to serve me. And at the time, I wasn't even being *paid* by Tazo tea. So that tells you how hard it was for me to come up with something to say. But then, after hour 89 or so of watching Matt in his underwear, I confess it started to make sense. Maybe it's something hypnotic they put in the subliminal track, but what McSweeney's has constantly taught me is that we are all the same. Creative people, when they are not asses, understand that in fact we do all live in the same rambling house, no matter where your "career" stands; and the smart and gracious ones will always be game to play along, so long as the game is not stupid and greedy. They might even be nice enough to serve you tea.

HEIDI MEREDITH: I love seeing our little one-room office on the DVD. That space was so tiny and crowded, and we were so many.

DAVE EGGERS: There were honestly between eleven and fourteen of us there on any given day, in a one-bedroom apartment meant for, well, one person.

ANDREW LELAND: The DVD making was amazingly fun. Francis Ford Coppola says mean things about me in his commentary, I think. Sean Wilsey saying that when Daphne Beal picks up the laundry, the laundry is "always very well picked up" is one of my favorite moments on the DVD, if not on the planet. It was very difficult to keep a straight face and eat a sandwich while Doug Dorst read his story.

DOUG DORST: The DVD shoot was a baffling experience. Andrew Leland was doing a strange, wiggly burlesque with a sandwich while I was reading my story. Steve Elliott showed up on the set with a woman I'd never seen before, insisting that she was my wife, and kept asking me how it felt to "wear the cuckold's horns." Eli Horowitz promised me that I'd get a trophy for Coolest-Author-of-the-Issue, for which I'm still waiting. Oh, and I got a parking ticket.

Above: The entrance to McSweeney's circa 2003. A ladder inside 826 Valencia leads up to a tiny room with a small wooden deck.

Above: This shack, on the roof of 826 Valencia, is where the majority of McSweeney's staffers worked 2001–2005.

Below (left to right): Thriving office workers Eli Horowitz, Heidi Meredith, Dave Kneebone, and intern Gideon Lewis-Kraus.

Rising Up and Rising Down

by WILLIAM T. VOLLMANN (2003)

WILLIAM T. VOLLMANN: I just worked and worked until it was done. Then I worked some more. That was about it.

SUSAN GOLOMB, VOLLMANN'S AGENT: When Bill approached me about representing him after several years of his going it alone, he told me a condition of my being able to handle his backlist and future works was to sell his 4,000-page manuscript on the motivations and ethical complexities of violence. A manuscript that must be published in its entirety, with additional pages of annotation and footnotes, oh, and plentiful illustrations! Bill referred to this project as "my ball and chain." I found several editors at mainstream houses who very much wanted to publish this book and labored mightily to convince the powers that be to do it, but alas, no major house could see how to handle the logistics of printing, pricing, shipping, and distributing such a lengthy and serious (read: unprofitable) work.

AMIRA PIERCE, MS. GOLOMB'S ASSISTANT: On the bottom shelf of one of our filing cabinets in the office sits a copy of the manuscript from when Susan was first sending it out. In a box that was originally used for 5,000 fresh white sheets of copy paper, there are almost 4,000 xeroxed pages of maps, diagrams, photographs, essays, expositions, and stories, with page numbers that Bill wrote in by hand. Sometimes, I pull it out and whip the top off for a new intern or a friend coming by the office for the first time.

CHRIS SWEET, FAN-WEBSITE ADMINISTRATOR: I first became aware of *Rising Up and Rising Down* about fifteen years ago. Some kind soul emailed me a list of Bill's works-in-progress and *RURD* was one of several titles on that list. At the time, I didn't know anything about the book. All I had was a title. As the months and years passed, the legend surrounding the

book grew. The delight in reading the occasional excerpt, published in various literary journals, was often accompanied by a profound sense of disappointment, because I never thought the entire project would see the light of day. The likelihood that a publisher would ever be found seemed mighty slim.

DAVE EGGERS: I saw an excerpt of *RURD* in *Grand Street* in 1998, and I tried to find out when it would be published as a whole. I wrote to Vollmann, offering to publish any other excerpts from it, and that led eventually to his giving us "The Old Man," which we published in our seventh issue of *McSweeney's*. Meanwhile, I'd heard—I think from Vollmann— that he had a publisher for the entirety of *RURD*, and so I was waiting for that to appear. A while later, I saw him read one night at Black Oak Books in Berkeley, and during the Q&A he mentioned that *RURD*'s publisher had backed out, and the book was orphaned. So I went home, did some rudimentary math, and wrote him a letter to the effect that McSweeney's might be able to figure out a way to get the book out. This was in the winter of 2001, and after a few months, Bill and Susan and [McSweeney's president] Barb Bersche and I figured out a way to do it. And we did all this before we even saw the book.

ELI HOROWITZ: Bill came down to San Francisco in June of 2002. A group of us met him at the office, and we all sat in a circle. Bill had prepared three memos: "For Designer," "For Fact-Checker," and "For Editor." Somehow "For Editor" ended up in my hands. Then we all went out to dinner. I sat next to Bill, and during the dinner he kept making comments to me beginning with "Since you're my editor..." At the time, I wasn't even a full-time employee.

DAVE EGGERS: Eli Horowitz had been a volunteer carpenter when we were building 826 Valencia. He and I would talk about books, and he seemed very astute and hardworking, so eventually he became the logical candidate if McSweeney's ever hired a managing editor. Until that point, the place had always been a two- or three-person operation, without any other full-time editors. But when we committed to Vollmann's book, that forced the issue—we had to have some full-time editing help. Eli was hired, in large part, to bring Vollmann's book into the world. It was not easy; it aged him mightily. Eli was twenty-four when we hired him, and he's now seventy-three, and looks older than that.

DEVORAH LAUTER, INTERN AND RESEARCHER: When we first went to see the manuscript at Vollmann's house, he took us to lunch at the original Tower Records, one of Sacramento's favorite landmarks, which is now a restaurant covered in tropical decor, with a lot of fluffy flowerless plants and zebra stripes. Vollmann said we could come over any time, and he'd even give us a key if we needed one. And I'll never forget how Eli looked up and smiled: he was so proud that we were all here in this tropical Sacramento restaurant, working with someone as friendly as Bill. There aren't many people as friendly as William T. Vollmann. That was all before any of us knew what we were getting into.

ELI HOROWITZ: Each of those early conversations left me exhausted; I was trying so hard to keep up, but there was just so much to keep up with. I was like the blind man feeling different parts of the elephant, trying to guess what kind of animal it is—or is it a bunch of different blind men, each feeling one part? Anyway, I was in over my head, but I didn't want Bill to worry. I took a lot of notes and asked a lot of questions.

CHRIS SWEET: When I finally heard that McSweeney's would be publishing the book, it made perfect sense. It made my year.

ELI HOROWITZ: Fact-checking took a long time. He didn't make many errors, but there were just a lot of facts to check. Production was also pretty complicated.

Dave and I designed the book's template and set it up in Quark. Then for each chapter, Owen [Otto], or I, or whoever, flowed the text; Devorah and Ben [Bush] inserted all the images they found; Gabe [Roth] did the copyediting; someone else entered his changes; I went back through and cleaned things up; Dave made his marks; fact-checkers made their fixes; design changed a bit; Vollmann made his comments; I smoothed things out again; and so on. And there are about seventy chapters, and each was its own document.

SUZANNE KLEID, FACT-CHECKER: The actual work of fact-checking was incredibly tedious. Eli would hand out one-hundred-page chunks of the manuscript to each of us and we would head out to the Doe library at UC Berkeley, highlighters in hand. The vast majority of the facts were quotations—from as many as five or six different sources on each page. I found myself having dreams about Trotsky.

GABRIEL ROTH, COPY EDITOR: Copyediting this book was difficult. Vollmann writes in the voice of a man who's going to examine every assumption and pursue every thought; he uses ornate grammatical constructions and really intricate punctuation. The syntax feels almost seventeenth-century in its crazy rigor; it's like Burton's *Anatomy of Melancholy* or something.

ELI HOROWITZ: I finally read the whole book in November and December [of 2002]. In terms of line editing, I was in charge of the theoretical chapters, and Dave did the journalistic chapters. I tried to focus on structure and clarity. I broke down his arguments into basic steps and then made a complex grid to analyze and compare each chapter. It was a different sort of editing. But the writing itself was always so strong, and unlike anything I had ever encountered.

KARA PLATONI, RESEARCHER: I learned many small useful facts in the course of working on *RURD*. One of them is how to correctly spell Kalashnikov.

DEVORAH LAUTER: We needed hundreds of books from the UC Berkeley library, and since Ben Bush was the only one with a UC library card, he was the only one who could check out the books—and even then a limited number of them. We had to find a place to hide the stash inside the library between Ben's pick-ups, a place we could leave them for weeks. What we really needed was a library connection, or some kind of secret vault/trapdoor/hidden bookshelf.

ANDREW LELAND, FACT-CHECKER: I remember checking citations and quotations, and noticing that many of the pages I was looking for were already marked with scraps of paper. Then we found out that Vollmann had done a lot of his research in the same library. It was a thrilling feeling—the bibliographical equivalent of pressing my hand into those Hollywood handprint-in-concrete things, or maybe like tracking Vollmann through the analytical snow.

DEVORAH LAUTER: Finally, we developed a workable solution to the library-book problem. We ended up with a compliant graduate student and some false papers. It turns out that if a book has a green CHECKED OUT slip sticking out of it and it's sitting in a "study carrel," which only grad students are allowed to have, no one will mess with them, i.e., try to reshelve, check out, touch, or even come near your books. The problem was getting hundreds of these fake checked-out slips. After a little sweet-talking I managed to get ahold of enough to last several months. It was a close call, I was almost found out.

GABRIEL ROTH: The difficulty of this book went beyond tracing the shape of the sentences, one after another. *Rising Up and Rising Down* is about the subjects that provoke the strongest feelings in people: violence, obviously, but also love and hate, race and class and gender, hunger and pleasure and tyranny and freedom. It was hard to scrutinize it with a detached, clerical eye for very long. I took a lot of breaks. To read it is to argue with it. I tried not to, because it slowed me down and lowered my page count, but there were plenty of times when I wanted to throw Vollmann across the room.

SUZANNE KLEID: Ninety-nine percent of the time Vollmann hadn't made a single mistake. In those few instances when he'd actually misspelled a name, or put a phrase out of place, we got kind of excited.

BRIAN NEFF, FACT-CHECKER: I would have a stack of twenty or so books, which more often than not would contain something on the Nazis, something by Julius Caesar, *The Art of War*, *House of Pain*, Goebbels's diaries, *Women in Prison*, *Studies in Homicide*, and maybe de Sade's *Juliette*. I would sit down next to a group of Cal students, diligently plugging away at their calculus homework, and just wait for the looks to start. Invariably they would come. Eventually it seemed like everyone at the table was looking at me over the top of their books. I always wondered what those people thought I was doing with all those books on violence and sex and war.

SUZANNE KLEID: Dave would sometimes cheerfully exclaim that he thought the fact-checking could get done by the end of the summer [of 2002]. Among ourselves, we whispered that this thing was so huge it was never going to be finished. When that summer ended, I handed my highlighters off to a new group of interns who then toiled for another full year.

KARA PLATONI: I was doing some research for the "Defense of Animals" chapter. Since radical activism seemed to be a good place to start, I went in search of the Animal Liberation Front, a clandestine international organization that endorses the damage or destruction of property for the sake of animal welfare. I was lucky enough to find someone's email address, and even luckier that they wrote back. So Vollmann drafted a deeply philosophical and intricate list of questions for the ALF, I sent the questions to my anonymous contact, she submitted them to the group for a response, the answers were sent back to me, I sent them to Vollmann. Fine. Months elapsed. I forgot all about the list. I went out on a first date with a guy who, in the course of the evening, was revealed to be a dedicated vegan. He seemed dreadfully put out and surprised when it was revealed that I am not.

Unaccountably surprised. Then it turned out that pre-date, he'd done a Google search on my email address, which had turned up only one result: Vollmann's questions, posted on the ALF Web site. These were questions like: If you could push a button that would vaporize the entire human race while leaving the rest of terrestrial life intact, would you do it?

BRIAN NEFF: The downtown Oakland library is a strange place. They have a surprisingly good collection of books, but on any given day, no matter what time of day you go, there is an equal chance that you will find it full of either psychopaths or school-children, and I have to say that on some days I couldn't tell the difference.

ELI HOROWITZ: I became weary, and sometimes went crazy. By the end I was fairly miserable. June of 2003 was probably the worst. I went to sleep thinking about this book, and woke up thinking about it. In the morning I'd have my laptop out and be working before I got out from under the blankets. But even then, there were always moments when I stepped back and realized what we were working on, and I would get real excited about the whole thing.

KAREN LEIBOWITZ, HOUSEMATE OF ELI HOROWITZ: Over that year, Eli simply didn't have the time to fulfill even the minimal requirements of a properly socialized American man. I mean, I remember a time before the book when he would trim his hair every four or five days. While he was doing the book, we were lucky if he cut it every two weeks, you know what I mean? And the homemade sauerkraut he used to make—that fell by the wayside. Falling up falling down indeed.

DAVE EGGERS: I didn't know that Eli was so worn out. He always seemed so chipper, and he appeared to have everything in hand. He'd grown a very long beard, I remember, and began burying his food, but otherwise there were no obvious indications of the book's effect on his life. We talked a lot about the book while editing it, and I remember that we would

both periodically have moments where we'd say, "Oh sweet Jesus, this is great, this is so fucking great!" We'd read over a particular section and feel that we were a part of something truly magnificent. That kept everyone going.

ELI HOROWITZ: Whenever I forgot what I was working on, something would jump out and grab me by the throat—an episode in Yemen, or the photo portfolio in the "Remember the Victim" chapter. I got chills, actual chills.

MATT FRASSICA, INTERN: In the last few days before the book had to go to press [in July 2003], Eli sat the summer interns down at the tables in the writing lab. "Guys," he said, "I've called you here today because you have all done an excellent job, and I am proud of you. You have worked hard, and deserve praise. But a couple of days ago, as I was thinking about this book and what is best for it, I consulted this reference." He picked up a thick user's guide to Quark XPress 4. He flipped to a page he had marked. "This is how David Blatner, the author of *The QuarkXPress 4 Book*, begins Chapter 8.11, 'Indexes: It was Mr. Duncan, my elementary-school librarian, who first impressed the importance of an index into my malleable young brain. A nonfiction book without an index, he said, wasn't even worth putting on the library shelf.' Now, if David Blatner's elementary-school librarian says it's so, then I say it's time we give Vollmann an index. What do you think?" No one contradicts an oracular computer manual—or Eli—so we divided the book up and scanned it for its major moral actors.

ROSE LICHTER-MARCK, INTERN: I won't soon forget that "Team Index Pizza Party" day. The interns combed every page of *RURD* while Eli stood over us and yelled obscenities at Matt Frassica, who was slacking. We were compiling a list of the "major moral actors" of the book. People were writing up the names on the dry-erase board so that we would all be documenting the same people. When we were done, that board read like a who's who of atrocity.

MATT FRASSICA: Vollmann discusses Julius Caesar, Napoleon, Hitler, Cortez, Eichmann, Pol Pot, King Egil, and so on in establishing his moral calculi. He also occasionally mentions Eli, and discusses the process of editing that the book had undergone. So we decided to index Eli: Horowitz, Eli; I.416, III.587, V.363-4. The next day, Eli removed himself from the index, which I suppose was his prerogative as editor.

RICHARD PARKS, INTERN: In a way, the index is an insidious thing, because the innocent act of looking up a single name might make you crazy. The connections are everywhere, so it's never as simple as culling a single date or place name. Even the smallest association Vollmann makes threatens to explode into a matrix of history.

MATT FRASSICA: About a week before we had to send the thing off to the printers, I went to dinner and then came back to do some late-night fact-checking. But once inside, Eli handed me a walkie-talkie. "Tell me what's missing, and I'll print it," he said. He was printing a full copy of *RURD* from his computer, which was up a ladder in the old 826 Valencia office. The printer was down the ladder and on the opposite end of the writing lab from his computer. That night, Eli printed and I sorted all seven volumes of *RURD*, checking to make sure the titles of the chapters matched their entries in the Table of Contents, that the drop caps were spaced right, that no pages went missing. After an hour, the walkie-talkie batteries started to die, and they would emit warning shrieks every five minutes.

ROSE LICHTER-MARCK: For the most part, all of us worked well together; there were, however, a few crises. Toward the end of July, we were going through the final manuscript one last time. Eli wanted each page to be checked by two pairs of eyes, so we worked in pairs. I was partnered with a girl who was there for the first day of her internship, and she had no idea what she had stumbled into. She was dividing her volume by chapter into different piles, and when it was time to put it all together, there were about

100 pages missing. It was a little frantic for a while: when you're dealing with 3,000+ pages, disorganization is a code-red emergency. I think she wept.

RICHARD PARKS: About the first week of August, in the home stretch, I almost destroyed the entire project—for reasons I can't exactly go into. I imagine that if you were to ask Eli today, he'd say that it's as true as it ever was: Never trust an intern with 3,000 pages of manuscript text and the *New York Times*'s FedEx account number.

GIDEON LEWIS-KRAUS, GENERAL ASSISTANT/ ASSOCIATE: I had been around McSweeney's for much of the *RURD* project, but I had somehow avoided working on it. At the beginning of August, however, an extremely frustrated William T. Vollmann called one morning and asked for Eli. Eli was on vacation. Could he then talk to one of the interns who worked on the book? The summer interns were gone, and I was the only person available to talk to him, so I got on the phone. He had just received the final galleys from the printer, and there were myriad things he wanted changed. I sat there with him, going through seven volumes of PDFs on Eli's computer, for almost four hours. We somehow ended up spending a lot of time talking about the intricacies of transliteration.

ELI HOROWITZ: Even after I thought everything was done, there were a bunch of little problems with the printers, and each time something flared up, a tremendous weariness would pass over me. Then we finally got the actual books. They looked good. I was happy.

DAVE EGGERS: This is the most proud we've been of anything we've ever done. This kind of book is what McSweeney's was set up to do, and we just have to thank Bill for letting us bring this book into the world. He had faith in our little group, and we very much appreciate it.

WILLIAM VOLLMANN: When I finally saw it, I was so happy I almost cried.

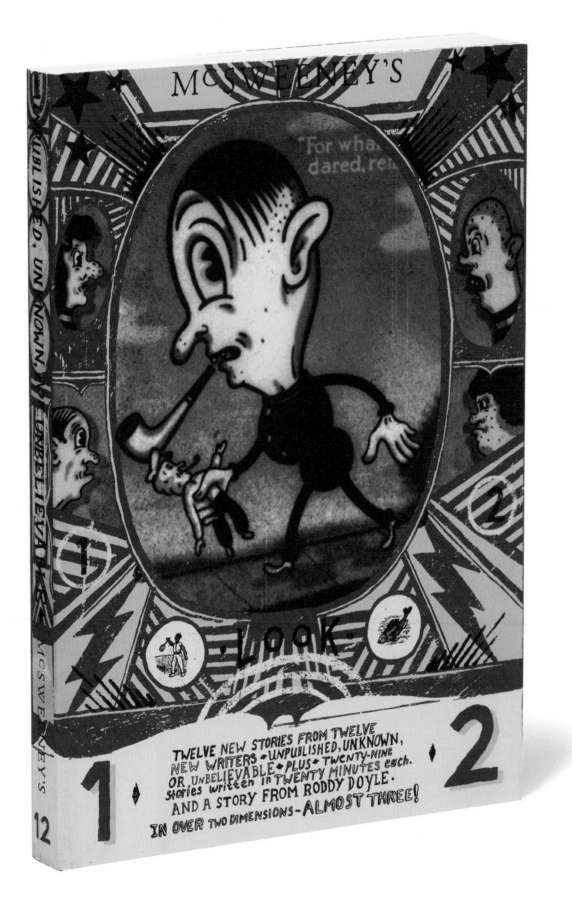

McSweeney's 12

(2003)

ELI HOROWITZ: A lot of decisions about this issue sort of just happened. The title pages feature examples of DanceWriting. DanceWriting is a way to communicate dance movements using stick figures on a standard, five-lined musical staff. Dave Kneebone had seen it somewhere.

DAVE KNEEBONE: I cannot, for the life of me, remember where I saw the DanceWriting. Likely it was from a semi-sober Googling session. That happened a lot during those halcyon days.

ELI HOROWITZ: I'm pretty sure Issue 12 was printed with Westcan, up in Winnipeg, Manitoba—our first issue with them. This is the only quarterly with French flaps, which are extensions to the cover of a paperback book that fold and function like the dustjacket flaps on a hardcover book. They're kind of expensive—not hugely, but more than seems right. Not enough bang for the buck. Printing on the inside cover is a lot cheaper. You could add twenty or fifty pages to a book for the price of French flaps. The expense has something to do with having to run the book through some trimming machine twice instead of once. Chris Young at Westcan can explain it better.

CHRIS YOUNG: French flaps come at an expense since, as Eli pointed out, they require a second pass on the perfect bind. On the first pass we would collate the text signatures, glue the spine edge, and trim the fore-edge flush. Then we would hand-feed the collated book block back through the binder, this time attaching the cover and trimming the head and the foot. If we tried to trim the head, foot, and fore-edge on the first pass, the French flaps that extend past the fore-edge by approximately one-sixteenth of an inch would be trimmed off. I hope this makes sense.

ELI HOROWITZ: There is an eyehole in each of Issue 12's French flaps. For a reader to use the eyeholes, the book needs to be standing up, like a triangular building. The original design concept was that it'd be like a carnival booth—"Step right up and see the amazing 3D hippo!" Along the way, the booth aspect got dropped but the carnival aspect remained. The stereoscopic image you see through the eyeholes—a hippo—happened because I had a plastic hippo on my desk. I put it out on the porch railing—we were in our rooftop-shack office at the time—and snapped a couple pictures. The weird thing is, I was the one pushing for the stereoscopic image, but I've never been able to see those Magic Eye posters. I once maybe got this hippo to pop in my brain, but mostly I was like a deaf composer here. It looks like we printed the interior on colored paper, but it was actually white paper printed to look that way. This was our first sectional issue, I think, and it bothered me to just stick it all together. In later issues this would lead to more bizarre formats, but here the tinting seemed like a good small solution, a way to differentiate the new writers and Roddy's long *Commitments* follow-up and the twenty-minute stories.

RODDY DOYLE: I originally wrote "The Deportees," a story in eighteen chapters, one chapter a month, for a multicultural paper in Dublin called *Metro Eireann*. ("Eireann" is one of the many Gaelic words for "Ireland." Life is never dull when your country has more than one name.) It was a fresh little terror once a month, because I'd no idea how to continue the story. Each chapter was eight hundred words, so I lost interest once I reached my quota—until I had to fill it again the next month. I kept adding characters, and forgot completely about one. It took a year and a half. In that time I also wrote half a novel, a screenplay, a stage play, a book for children, and buried a dog.

DAVE DALEY: The twenty-minute-story idea all started when Dave Eggers agreed to submit a story to the paper I was working at, the *Hartford Courant*. But a couple days before the deadline, he emailed to say the story wasn't coming together as hoped—but that he had a new idea. He'd been up late the night before and written a bunch of super-short stories under time pressure. He'd given himself an hour to write three stories. Did I want to see those? If so, he'd do a couple more that night. Could three stories written in an hour—twenty-minute fiction—

actually be any good? The newspaper guy in me was intrigued. Deadline fiction. It actually seemed like a better fit for a daily paper than a short story. Dave sent five of them the next day, and they were funny little worlds unto themselves. There was such beauty to the idea—sit down to write with a deadline and maybe it forces out something true, something personal, something that might have been self-edited given all the time in the world. I became obsessed. I harassed Dave until he agreed a collection of twenty-minute fiction would make a good *McSweeney's* project. Would it pay something so I could quit my thankless newspaper job? Dave advised against that. But I've never had so much fun with a project.

Illustrator Christian Northeast's mock-up of the stereoscopic architecture (above), with the final art, including view flaps, spread to the right.

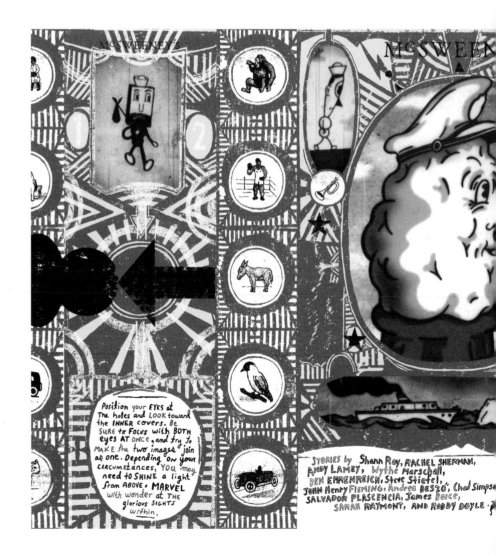

I wrote wish lists that went for pages, then emailed all the authors I could find asking for an hour of their time to write three twenty-minute stories. They were allowed to revise, if they wanted, but the story itself had to be on the page in twenty minutes—and we wanted to know when the clock started. Those who I couldn't find email addresses for got handwritten letters at their homes. The strangest thing? People did it. Every day, I'd find new stories in my email from Rick Moody, Jonathan Lethem, Myla Goldberg, Nicole Krauss, Douglas Coupland, Aimee Bender, Charles Baxter, Paula Fox, Sam Lipsyte, Aleksandar Hemon, it went on and on. My favorite writers, who had no business answering emails from me, let alone

writing stories upon my request, all said yes. Every day the mail brought even more—and sometimes, better still, amazing rejections—long, funny, personal notes from the likes of Richard Ford and Joan Didion, explaining in what must have taken much more time than twenty minutes why they couldn't possibly write a twenty-minute story. In the end, more than one hundred writers—and musicians, too, like the Old 97's Rhett Miller and Luna's Dean Wareham—turned in three twenty-minute stories. Some of them cheated. Most of them confessed it to another writer who did this, and that person always turned them into me. Oh, I know. You cannot hide.

McSweeney's 13

DAVE EGGERS: I forget how we started talking about it, but we had run some of Chris's work in Issue 6, and around then I asked Chris if he'd ever be interested in guest-editing an all-comics issue of the magazine. These ideas usually pop up in the spur of the moment, and this sometimes drives Eli crazy; I'm generally too eager to give issues, or sections of issues, away to other people. I might have asked Chris in person, actually, when we were doing a few events together after Issue 6. I don't have much of a filter for these things; if I'm standing in front of Chris Ware and an idea pops into my head that he should take over a whole issue, I just blurt it out.

CHRIS WARE: Dave asked me sometime in mid-2002, I think, and I agreed to it in December of that year.

DAVE EGGERS: At that point I just gave him the reins. I knew he could design the whole thing if he wanted to, and that's what he did.

CHRIS WARE: The understanding was that I had six months to put it together. It was printed in April of 2004, however, so it, um, took quite a while longer than I'd expected it to.

ELI HOROWITZ: Chris just killed this so hard, from start to finish. Basically all I did was say, "Sure, you can do that too" twenty times—add a cartoonist,

The earliest draft of Issue 13, the all-comics issue.

include the minicomics, stamp on the jacket. But from conception to execution to every detail, that's Chris.

CHRIS WARE: Dave and I met at least once in the midst of my putting it together. Though he hadn't seen any of what I had done already, he was very encouraging and annoyingly didn't appear to be concerned about it at all.

DAVE EGGERS: We honestly didn't see the issue until we got the color proofs from the printer. Ware did every last inch of the issue. We're really hands-off when we're working with people who know what they're doing. I think Chris was originally kind of surprised we didn't need to see much along the way, but honestly, when we know something's going to be done well, we have a habit of just putting it out of our minds.

CHRIS WARE: Regarding the size of the book, I thought the native *McSweeney's* scale was already comfortable to hold and would emphasize the literary end of the comics spectrum, so I stuck with that. The foldout dust jacket (which grew out of Gary Panter's visual history of comics and inspired my own "metaphysical defense" of comics on its reverse) was intended to point towards comics' popular origins in America as daily and large-size Sunday newspaper pages. I was regretful that I couldn't accommodate

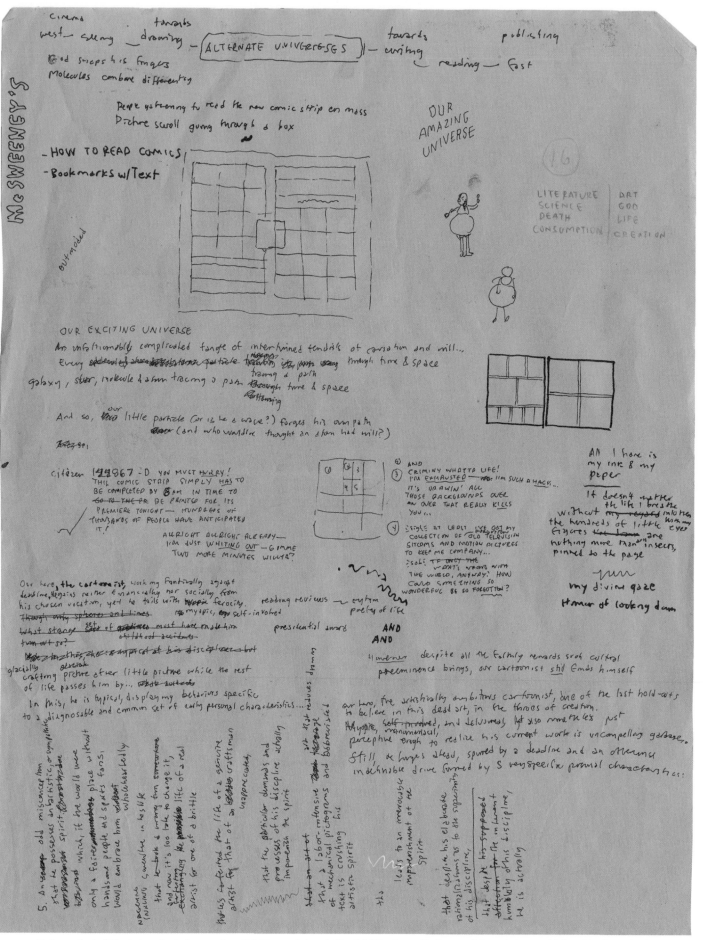

Early notes for the foldout jacket, wherein the guest editor, Chris Ware, worked out the idea of dividing the two sides between religion and science, and daily and Sunday comic strips.

larger, more eye-popping work elsewhere, but that would have made for a completely different comics anthology. My aims were to create a dignified volume that somehow covered the entire history of American cartooning (even if some points were only glossed over or hinted at) and to make the book into something of a living organism, where the design not only contained, but also defined the ideas within it. My model was Art Spiegelman and Françoise Mouly's *RAW* magazine, which I think Dave also has mentioned as an inspiration.

ELI HOROWITZ: By the way, this was our first book with TWP, the printer in Singapore that we now use frequently. Françoise Mouly recommended them.

CHRIS WARE: I knew that the book would reach the mailboxes of a thoughtful, literate readership and so it was my chance to stealthily make a good case for thoughtful, literate comics. So I made a list of my favorite artists and invited them to contribute either reprinted or new work.

RON REGÉ, JR.: When Chris Ware contacted me to be in the anthology, he told me that there was no need for me to do something new. Reprinting something I had already done would be fine. But I was anxious to get to work on something new. I realized that this *McSweeney's* anthology was going to reach a lot more people than anything I had done before, and I wanted it to be good! (At the time, very few cartoon short stories made it into the kinds of bookstores that carry *McSweeney's*.)

BEN KATCHOR: Contributing was absolutely painless and therefore I don't remember much: where I

The mock-up from page 114, but folded into its three dimensional form as it would appear wrapped around the book itself.

was, or what I was doing at the moment. I associate Chris Ware's physical voice with the request and so I assume he telephoned me. In a very polite manner, he asked me to select a few pages from my "Hotel & Farm" series. I chose about ten episodes that were my favorites for reasons of story and drawing. Chris also asked me to hand-letter the title page for the section. I was happy to contribute to this anthology because I felt it would be seen by many people who might otherwise not see my strips. I have only a pleasant, although vague, memory of the entire process.

JOHN PORCELLINO: It was in Chicago. Somebody had some old issue of *McSweeney's* or another—I had never seen one before. I remember thinking, "This exists in its own world." A few years later, Chris asked to reprint some of my comics in a special issue he was editing. Of course I said yes.

CHRIS WARE: My approach to the organization of the issue tilted on such concerns as color compatibility, composition, and whether or not the cartoonists loathed each other. I endured many panicked nights worrying about my odd conjunctions and visual rhymes (such as Philip Guston bumping up against Mark Beyer and Charles Schulz's discarded legal pad sketches versus Lynda Barry's notebook page comics). As it turned out, I only had to edit out a couple of things or find the appropriate tuckpoints between subjects for it all to work, ruining just two friendships in the process.

MARK NEWGARDEN: Chris Ware was a thoughtful editor. In the issue, we decided to reprint some of my black & white *Little Nun* strips in color. Chris asked me to spec my colors in the manner of an early-20th century Sunday page cartoonist. That method is to indicate the chosen color only in the first instance of a space or an object in a strip and then let the engravers follow suit in all its succeeding reappearances. This request was perhaps a tad absurd in the age of the digital paintbucket but it did make my job microscopically easier, and I appreciated it.

CHRIS WARE: To break up the rhythm of the colored pages, I solicited short essays or stories in some way related to comics from a few real writers I knew, and I also asked John Updike if I could reprint his essay about his early aspirations as a cartoonist, because it so beautifully describes what it feels like to put ink to paper. I hand-lettered such things as the title above Charles Burns's title page comic cover and all of the dust jacket lettering, but I stuck with *McSweeney's* tried and true "Garamond 3" font for the body copy to keep a consistent feel from the publication's earlier issues.

ANDREW LELAND: Every issue of the quarterly is an "anthology" of sorts, but this one really felt different to me in that regard. I found myself saying, at Book Expo America in particular, "This is arguably the best anthology of the contemporary graphic novel in print. It's also an issue of the quarterly."

RON REGÉ, JR.: I had just read an interview transcript in *Harper's* and knew that I wanted to turn it into a comic. I was pretty nervous about putting a story on such a sensitive subject into wide circulation. I was very much aware throughout the process that I

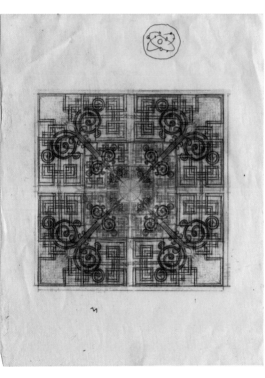

An early design by Chris Ware for the ornament on the newspaper foldout jacket which links Gary Panter's obverse strip outlining the history of comics to the metaphysical argument of the issue's cover. Later, Ware developed the more "atomic particle collision" design which finally appeared.

was representing the story of someone real. I still wonder if one day I'll get a message from Arin Ahmed. I'm still not sure what I would say. I decided right away that I didn't want to draw anything in a literal way in this comic (best to leave that to guys like Joe Sacco), and had been developing a set of archetypal "characters" in other work at the time. I feel bad that I made the Israeli defense minister look like an evil devil, but I've decided to draw all militarists this way. Arin's story is told by a set of characters I've developed to portray young adults in today's world, dressed in pajama-like, cartoon prison uniforms. When I figured out that the story would be over 20 pages, Chris asked if we could double them up by turning them sideways on the page. I understood, but wasn't that excited about it. Chris called to apologetically suggest a compromise—that the story be printed as its own little booklet. I thought it was a great, great idea—and it's been fun to hear stories about the booklet getting separated from the anthology, or discovered later—it has a bit of a life of its own. I especially like the way that it doesn't include any info at all about who made it, or when!

CHRIS WARE: I guess one would think the backstory of assembling a comics anthology would be embroidered with lots of wacky anecdotes, but I only remember the enterprise being extremely privately painful and emotionally stressful. I would be remiss in not remarking on how Eli Horowitz's easygoing attitude regularly relieved my intellectual and artistic constipation.

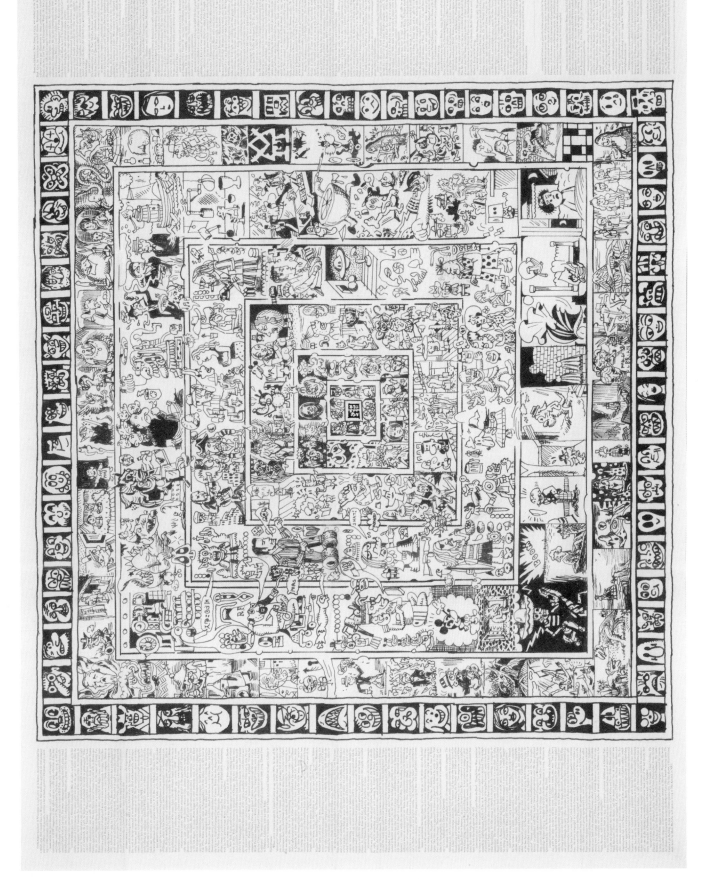

The jacket interior: Gary Panter's history of comics.

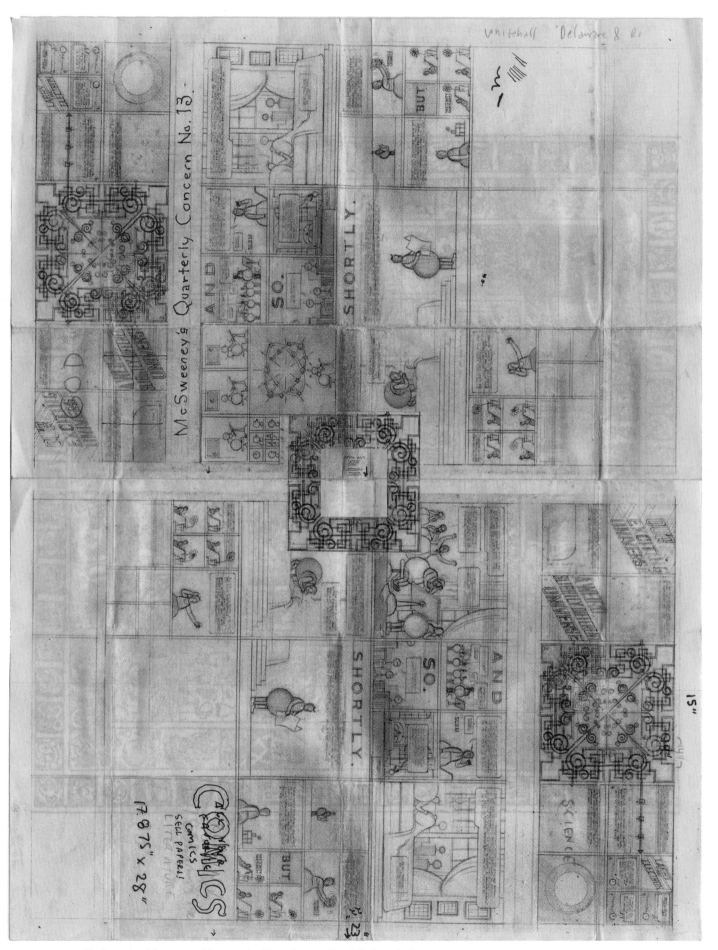

The first version of the newspaper foldout cover in miniature form, soon discarded in favor of a character design more abstract and in tune with particle physics.

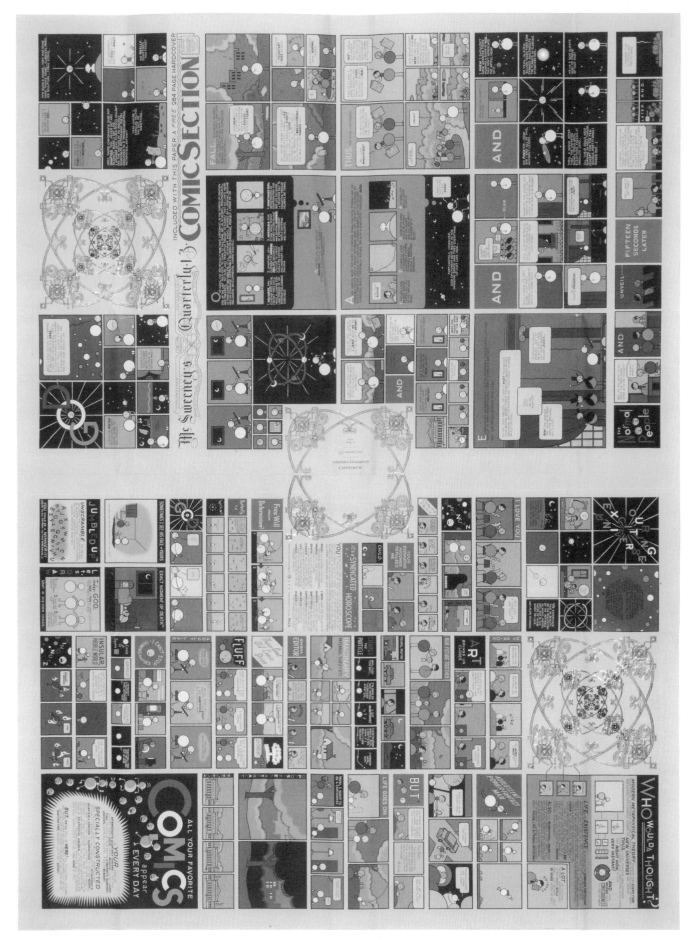

The finished newspaper foldout cover by Chris Ware.

The copy of the first printing that Eli Horowitz sent to Chris Ware, with Post-its indicating corrections for the second edition. Ultimately, three editions were printed—the quarterly's biggest print run ever.

Pages 2 and 3 of the third edition, showing a copyright-page typo that Eli Horowitz missed ("may not reproduced") and title-page artwork by Charles Burns and lettering by Chris Ware.

Pages 16 and 17—half of Dan Clowes's four-page strip. It's one of the only full-bleed pieces, which makes it run into the gutter a little bit.

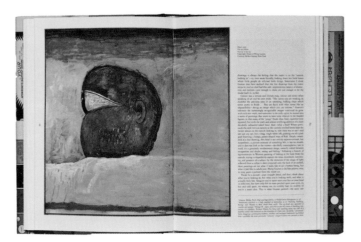

Pages 88 and 89—part of Chris Ware's appreciation of Philip Guston (Guston's Head appears on this spread). No typos.

Pages 136 and 137—the beginning of Kim Deitch's six-page strip describing a visit to a death-row inmate.

Pages 14 and 15: Robert Crumb's two-page strip, which features a couch with the color and texture of a tongue.

*Pages 132 and 133, part of Art Spiegelman's contribution,
which was excerpted from his book* In the Shadow of No Towers.

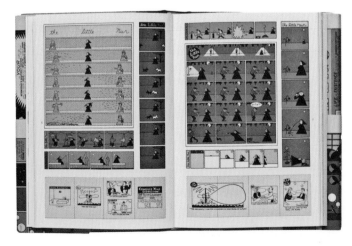

*Pages 54 and 55: comic strips by Mark Newgarden,
some of them signed by "Matisse," "Mondrian," and "Ponne Tomplinksi."*

*The two minicomics carried in the jacket's pockets, by Ron Regé, Jr. (in color)
and John Porcellino (in black and white).*

THE BELIEVER	FIFTY-SIXTH ISSUE: INSTANT SON	SEPTEMBER 08
THE BELIEVER	FIFTY-FIFTH ISSUE: BRIOSO	JULY/AUGUST 08
THE BELIEVER	FIFTY-FOURTH ISSUE: TMESIS	JUNE 08
THE BELIEVER	FIFTY-THIRD ISSUE: WORD SMILES	MAY 08
THE BELIEVER	FIFTY-SECOND ISSUE: THE FILM ISSUE	MARCH/APRIL 08
THE BELIEVER	FIFTY-FIRST ISSUE: LAGNIAPPE	FEBRUARY 08
THE BELIEVER	FIFTIETH ISSUE: ERGODIC	JANUARY 08
THE BELIEVER	FORTY-NINTH ISSUE: THE ART ISSUE	NOVEMBER/DECEMBER 07
THE BELIEVER	FORTY-EIGHTH ISSUE: NONCE	OCTOBER 07
THE BELIEVER	FORTY-SEVENTH ISSUE: BOEUFCAKE	SEPTEMBER 07
THE BELIEVER	FORTY-SIXTH ISSUE: SYREETA	AUGUST 07
THE BELIEVER	FORTY-FIFTH ISSUE: OUBLIETTE	JUNE / JULY 07
THE BELIEVER	FORTY-FOURTH ISSUE: AZABACHE	MAY 07
THE BELIEVER	FORTY-THIRD ISSUE: LITOTES	APRIL 07
THE BELIEVER	FORTY-SECOND ISSUE: GRAVID	MARCH 07
THE BELIEVER	FORTY-FIRST ISSUE: BLANDISHMENTS	FEBRUARY 07
THE BELIEVER	FORTIETH ISSUE: MAJUSCULE	DEC 06/JAN 07
THE BELIEVER	THIRTY-NINTH ISSUE: EXIGENCIES	NOVEMBER 06
THE BELIEVER	THIRTY-EIGHTH ISSUE: BROOMCORN	OCTOBER 06
THE BELIEVER	THIRTY-SEVENTH ISSUE: CRAMBO	SEPTEMBER 06
THE BELIEVER	THIRTY-SIXTH ISSUE: LAMBKINETTE	AUGUST 06
THE BELIEVER	THIRTY-FIFTH ISSUE: GLOAMING	JUNE/JULY 06
THE BELIEVER	THIRTY-FOURTH ISSUE: JUNK OF PORK	MAY 06
THE BELIEVER	THIRTY-THIRD ISSUE: HOLUS-BOLUS	APRIL 06
THE BELIEVER	THIRTY-SECOND ISSUE: PLANGENT CORN	MARCH 06
THE BELIEVER	THIRTY-FIRST ISSUE: TEETHSOME	FEBRUARY 06
THE BELIEVER	THIRTIETH ISSUE: PENTIMENTO	DEC 05/JAN 06
THE BELIEVER	TWENTY-NINTH ISSUE: SPOONBREAD	NOVEMBER 05
THE BELIEVER	TWENTY-EIGHTH ISSUE: BITUMEN	OCTOBER 05
THE BELIEVER	TWENTY-SEVENTH ISSUE: BOOMTOWN	SEPTEMBER 05
THE BELIEVER	TWENTY-SIXTH ISSUE: PRESSURE FACE	AUGUST 05
THE BELIEVER	TWENTY-FIFTH ISSUE: GNASH	JUNE / JULY
THE BELIEVER	TWENTY-FOURTH ISSUE: HOAX FED	MAY 05
THE BELIEVER	TWENTY-THIRD ISSUE: FUTURE SALAD	APRIL 05
THE BELIEVER	TWENTY-SECOND ISSUE: COUCHFIRE!	MARCH 05
THE BELIEVER	TWENTY-FIRST ISSUE: ARABLE	FEBRUARY 05
THE BELIEVER	TWENTIETH ISSUE: RHATHYMIA	DEC 04/JAN 05
THE BELIEVER	NINETEENTH ISSUE: HARTSHORN	NOVEMBER 04
THE BELIEVER	EIGHTEENTH ISSUE: CARRY	OCTOBER 04
THE BELIEVER	SEVENTEENTH ISSUE: SEPTEMBER 04 BUNSHOFT!	
THE BELIEVER	SIXTEENTH ISSUE: CARAFE	AUGUST 04
THE BELIEVER	FIFTEENTH ISSUE: BLOWSY	JULY 04
THE BELIEVER	FOURTEENTH ISSUE: CASSINGLE	JUNE 04
THE BELIEVER	THIRTEENTH ISSUE: WODGE	MAY 04
THE BELIEVER	TWELFTH ISSUE: PORCHCRAWLIN'	APRIL 04
THE BELIEVER	ELEVENTH ISSUE: FLYERETTE	MARCH 04
THE BELIEVER	TENTH ISSUE: LODESTAR	FEBRUARY 04
THE BELIEVER	NINTH ISSUE: CÚSPIDE	DEC 03/JAN 04
THE BELIEVER	EIGHTH ISSUE: NECKFIRE!	NOVEMBER 2003
THE BELIEVER	SEVENTH ISSUE: ROTUNDA	OCTOBER 2003
THE BELIEVER	SIXTH ISSUE: MAKE IT SO	SEPTEMBER 2003
THE BELIEVER	FIFTH ISSUE: ON TIME, ALL THE TIME	AUGUST 2003
THE BELIEVER	FOURTH ISSUE: STEADY!	JULY 2003
THE BELIEVER	THIRD ISSUE: ALL IS WELL	JUNE 2003
THE BELIEVER	SECOND ISSUE	MAY 2003
THE BELIEVER	FIRST ISSUE	MARCH 2003

The Believer

(2003)

HEIDI JULAVITS: My involvement with *The Believer* came about because I was irritated. In the summer of 2002, I found I'd been irritated pretty regularly, and my irritation could be directly attributed to the reading of book reviews. The review that inspired me to email Dave Eggers—to vent this irritation—was a review, or rather a series of reviews, about Rick Moody's book *The Black Veil*. Many of these reviews were powered by an unmistakably anti-intellectual undercurrent that echoed the

Opposite: The spines of the first 56 issues of The Believer.
Above: The cover of the May 2006 issue, featuring Charles Burns's portraits of (clockwise from top left) Orhan Pamuk, Nicole Holofcener, Jim White, and a kangaroo.

that Dave embodies, he knows how to intuit that a person might be decently good at something they've never in their life attempted to do. I believe this was some time in October. The year was definitely 2002. At this same time, Vendela Vida, whom I'd known since 1993 when we were grad students at Columbia, was in the process of creating her own magazine of long-format interviews.

VENDELA VIDA: My interest in the long-format interview began in January of 1993

anti-ambition, anti-style, anti-language, anti-writer, anti-fiction undercurrents I'd been sensing in those many other reviews that spurred my initial grouchiness. I expressed my email dismay to Dave, and he wrote back, "We should start a book review."

By "we" I thought he meant "the people currently employed at McSweeney's"; I responded, "Absolutely." A few days or maybe it was a few weeks later, he wrote me an email that, to my memory, contained a message to the effect of, "You're on." Meaning, he would back a book review–type thing and I was responsible for putting it together. At this point, I had absolutely no experience with magazines or magazine editing. Of the many varieties of genius and foresight

when I started interning at the *Paris Review*. Every night I would borrow a back issue of the *Paris Review* from the shelves of the office on East 72nd Street and read an old "Writers At Work" interview, and every morning I would return the issue to the office's shelves and borrow another. Each interview sent me on a different jag. I would read a conversation with Grace Paley and seek out everything I could find of hers, and then I would get obsessed with a Philip Larkin interview and check out anything the library had of his that I hadn't yet devoured. I was young and had a broken foot and lots of time. Plus: I had made it until January without buying a winter coat, and I was determined to make it to spring without

119

buying one, which meant spending a lot of time inside.

That cold winter of reading "Writers at Work" interviews informed not only the books I sought out, but also my small disappointment with interviews published in other magazines. Why were other interviews with non-writers so brief? Why so zippy? Was the zippiness a function of the editing process or a true representation of a ping-pong-paced exchange? Why, if in a given week, I read an interview with a musician in one magazine would I be guaranteed to find him or her profiled and interviewed in at least four other publications with the same date on their front cover?

I had an idea for a magazine that would feature four untimely interviews per issue, all with different types of people—artists, scientists, puppeteers, anyone doing something interesting or thinking in a new way. Each issue would contain one question, the same question, that was asked of each interviewee and this question would be published in red. Why red? I don't know. In any event, *The Believer* now publishes three or four in-depth interviews an issue, the bulk of which are not related to the release of a film, book, or album. The red question thing, though—that's something, five years in, we still haven't done. Maybe we'll start doing it in blue.

HEIDI JULAVITS: Quickly we realized that this "book review" and this "long-format interview magazine" could combine to become one entity that would cover pretty much everything from books to politics. We also realized we needed some help, and contacted Ed, also at Columbia with us in the early '90s, who kindly agreed to join us in this folly of an enterprise—in short, putting out a 140-page monthly magazine with three editors and no office.

ED PARK: I started working full time at the *Village Voice* at the end of 1995, and I spent several years as a copy editor. On some days the work was light and I would read novels at my desk, along with the rest of the department, and fantasize about grand unified theories of literature. By 2002 I was writing pretty regularly for the paper, mostly film reviews,

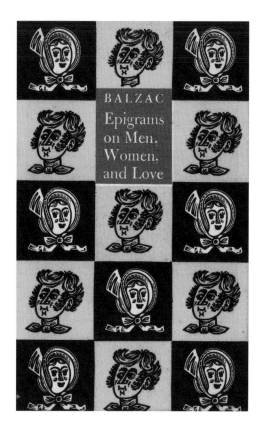

One of several old cover designs that inspired
the design of The Believer.

and occasionally filling in for other editors, which is how a piece of mine came to be included in the *Voice Literary Supplement*. It was an essay on W. G. Sebald and William Gaddis, both of whom had posthumous works out that year, and both of whom had cited Thomas Bernhard as an influence. Inspired by the "rolling prose" of all three, I wrote the piece as a single unbroken paragraph—a tactic another editor probably would not have greenlighted.

It had to be done that way, I thought. It was form married to function: the authors' obsessive styles merging with (or directing) the reviewer's. A friend later told me that a higher-up had grumbled about the essay's slablike visual density—this was around the time the editorial side had been lectured by the art department about the value of multiple "entry points" on a page.

Shortly after the piece appeared, I received an email from Heidi, who is the kind of person likely to have "Thomas Bernhard" in her Google News

Some early sketches, by Dave Eggers, for the cover of The Believer.

alerts. She complimented me on the piece, which was nice, and asked if I might be interested in helping edit a new magazine about books, to be published by McSweeney's, which was unspeakably amazing. The magazine would run long essays and interviews. It would favor ink over pixels. It would not emphasize timeliness or traffic in potshots, or (at least for starters) run any ads. Just one interesting thing after another. It would basically go against every bit of received wisdom, and I couldn't believe how great it sounded. I thought I should play it cool and wait a day before writing Heidi back to say yes. I broke down at five minutes.

HEIDI JULAVITS: Fortunately, we were able to utilize the McSweeney's infrastructure (for copyediting, printing, and distribution), thus sparing us one of the biggest headaches suffered by most new magazines. We hired a managing editor who lasted one issue before being replaced by Andrew Leland, then a college student at Oberlin. He dropped out of Oberlin to join our staff. I don't know how his family feels about this, but we give thanks, on a daily basis, to an unspecified higher power for Andrew's committed delinquency on our behalf. We managed to get our first issue on the stands in March 2003, and for those first six months every issue was a cross-continental fire drill, lots of last-minute article replacements and

humorous typos we failed to catch. It took more than a year before we weren't stressing every month that we wouldn't have enough text to fill the next magazine. Part of me misses those fire-drill days; part of me really does not.

ELI HOROWITZ: Originally I wasn't involved, and then, I was. I remember we were way behind schedule on the first issue, and one day we just decided *Today is the day we get it done*. So I drove up to Dave and Vendela's and I made a list and just started plowing through. Headlines, charts, all title-page and TOC nonsense. Did I write a "Child" piece for that issue? I think "Child" was my idea in the first place, and I regretted it as soon as I suggested it. I also interviewed Kumar Pallana. That was a highlight. Several months before, a friend had told me that he lived in Oakland. I did a bit of searching and found his phone number. Then I just sat on it—what do you do with something like that? I didn't feel like I could call just to chat. Then when I thought of the interview, that alone seemed to justify *The Believer*'s existence—now I had an excuse to talk to the man, rather than just mentally stalking him.

DAVE EGGERS: On the design side, I knew that monthly magazines always lost money for years and years, and even starting one on any normal scale

would cost hundreds of thousands of dollars. So the task at first was to come up with a format that would be cheap to maintain. Actually, cheap on the staff side, but careful enough on the production side that people would buy it.

ANDREW LELAND: So Dave designed the first issue of *The Believer* as a template that could be updated by one or two people every month.

DAVE EGGERS: The conditions or constraints on the design were like this: We knew it had to look and feel different than normal magazines. Nothing glossy, nothing standard-sized. We knew we didn't want to depend on advertising. We didn't take ads for the first four years. We knew the design staff had to be minimal, or basically nonexistent.

So the general task was to design a template that was clear and memorable, and simple and unchanging enough that one person could maintain it. Up till this point I'd done most of the design and production on *McSweeney's*, and so I knew a vast design staff wasn't necessary to put out a text-heavy magazine. But could we make a monthly that was interesting enough to look at but simple enough for one 22-year-old to maintain?

That's where Andrew came in. He had been an intern the summer before, and when he left, he told

Opposite: Twenty Believer *drawings by Tony Millionaire, 2003–2009.*
Above: An incidental illustration by Ryan Dodgson
from the November/December 2008 issue.

us, "Don't let my being in college disqualify me from any jobs that might open up." So when this job opened up—the single guy who would have to do all the basic design and production, headline writing, and managing-editing of a monthly—we thought of Andrew. I called him one day and offered him the job. He would have to skip his senior year, though. And he did.

ANDREW LELAND: Eli called me and told me they might be able to offer me the job, but they were queasy about making me drop out of college, and Dave wanted to wait until he got back to San Francisco to make the final decision. There was about a week between that first phone call and the call from Dave where I was actually offered the job. I promptly stopped attending all of my classes, and spent each day pacing insanely around my house in a bathrobe, chain-smoking, pounding espresso, and driving my housemates crazy. It's a good thing I ended up getting the job, because if I hadn't, I probably would have failed all my classes that semester. Dave Kneebone picked me up from the airport with the advanced copies of the first issue of *The Believer*, which had only been described to me over the phone, in the abstract. My feeling was that I would have dropped out of college for pretty much any job McSweeney's offered me, but when I actually beheld issue one, the way it looked, the list of contributors, and, once I began to go through it, the writing—the true extent of my good fortune began to dawn on me.

Vendela once said she thought the first issue looked more "workmanlike" than the others. I don't know what she meant, but I like the sound of it and I wish I could make workmanlike issues for her. I have very soft hands.

VENDELA VIDA: By "workmanlike" I meant that when you stare at that first issue, it looks sort of like an apartment that someone has just moved into and set up just so—the unstained (and still uncomfortable) couch is centered against one wall, the books are lined up straight on the shelves, and the desk looks like no work has ever been done on it. It takes a while for the place to look like a home—for the pictures and invitations to be magneted to (and fall to the floor from) the refrigerator, for the tassels of the rugs to get knotted, for the blank spaces on the walls to be filled in. That's what I meant by workmanlike—the first issue still looks unlived in to me—which, I suppose is accurate; we were still settling into its pages.

DAVE EGGERS: With the *Believer* cover, I was looking for something bold and simple, something that you'd see across the room and know what magazine it was. I'd loved what Chip Kidd did for *The Paris Review*, that iconic but malleable format, and wanted *The Believer* to have that same sturdiness.

Around that time I'd just been given an old book that had a sort of grid on the cover, and I'm inclined toward grids and lines and boxes in design anyway, so I started sketching with grids.

ED PARK: On the *Believer* Web site it says that the magazine's working title was *The Optimist*. Another working title was *The Balloonist*—one reason why my

An incidental illustration by Esther Pearl Watson
from the February 2007 issue.

article on Charles Portis, in the debut issue, has a balloon/gas theme running through it. One of Portis's characters (in *Masters of Atlantis*) was a veteran of the army's "Balloon Section" in WWI, and the piece ends with a nod to Marx's formulation "all that is solid melts into air," which hooks back up to the lede (about how Portis had the newspaper job once held by Karl Marx). We didn't end up using the name, but it turned out to be a great way to organize the article. I haven't written a similarly long piece for *The Believer* since. Maybe the trick is to come up with another working title, write around it, and abandon it?

ANDREW LELAND: Ever since Issue 2 [May 2003], I've done most of the interior layout and Alvaro Villanueva has picked the cover colors and tweaked the look of the headlines.

Dave wrote and designed the two-page "Schema" spread—"A History of Magic Realism"—in the first issue, with the help of an intern named Tommy Wallach. Every issue to date has included a Schema, which we also call "the chart." These are usually designed by Alvaro or by Brian McMullen, who often writes his. Most of the magazine's original design elements remain: The cover still features four portraits by Charles Burns, situated in the corners of a nine-square checkerboard grid. Headlines occupy the rest of the squares. The first page of the magazine is still a place for notes. One-pagers—like "Tool" or "Light"—still have their original format and are interspersed among the essays and interviews which still have the original layout. The table of contents is still on the back cover. The last page of *The Believer* has always been the "In the Next Issue" page, where projected articles and essays for the next issue are advertised.

The bottom third of this page is one of the magazine's regularly miscellaneous spaces: We used to print a list of books mentioned in the magazine; sometimes it was book recommendations; for a time we did something called "Blurb Libs"; once we ran Karan Mahajan's three-column list of Bollywood movies adapted from American movies which were adapted from British novels; nowadays I usually put unwieldy, awesome spot illustrations there.

VENDELA VIDA: And we all live in different places—mainly New York and San Francisco—and so we've never had an official editorial meeting with all of us in the same room.

HEIDI JULAVITS: One of our first staff meetings happened, I think, almost a year and a half after our first issue was released. Vendela, Ed, and I were working an outdoor book fair in New York. Andrew wasn't there, but for some reason we were calling it our first staff meeting. We joked that the initial order of business should be to lay somebody off, but the only person we could lay off was Andrew, since he wasn't there to defend himself, but we all agreed that if we laid Andrew off there would be no magazine. So we tabled the layoff discussion, and instead used our staff meeting to troubleshoot ways to keep our tablecloth from blowing off (we bought a six-pack of Goya Malta cans). This spring, Ed and I and our interviews editor, Ross Simonini, met for vegan food at an ayurvedic restaurant, and then we went and played with Ed's baby. That is a recent example of a staff meeting.

Tony Millionaire's illustration
for Chris Bachelder's essay
"Doctorow's Brain," February 2007.

ROSS SIMONINI: Most of the interviews are born when a writer sends me or Vendela an email asking to have a conversation with a person they know or admire or find fascinating. I'll read a little about the interviewee and try to track down any published interviews to see how articulate or verbose or tight-lipped or overexposed they might be. If I like the idea, I'll pass it along to Andrew and Vendela and any other editors who might have an opinion on it. If the idea sounds good to everyone, I usually ask the writer to send me more ideas on possible lines of questioning. I pretty much always ask the writer to avoid questions that have been asked in previous interviews and to find some sort of unexpected digression or topic to discuss. (Some of the best *Believer* interviews have been cases where a musician talks about cooking or an actor talks about literature.)

MEEHAN CRIST: I joined the *Believer* staff in early 2005, when Heidi was swamped with work and needed help. At first I was reading and managing submissions, but that soon morphed into editing the one-page reviews of new books. My editorial "training" was a half-hour of coffee with Heidi at Max's, a café in Morningside Heights, Manhattan. She handed me copies of a few reviews that worked well—Gary Lutz on *The Pornographer's Poem*, a poetry review by Stephen Burt, a few others—and basically said, "See what's going on here? This works. We want more of this." I tried not to burn my tongue and mumbled something like, "Sure. Okay. I can do that."

ANDREW LELAND: Heidi, Ed, Vendela, Ross, and Meehan Crist send me edited pieces in Word format. I spell-check them and flow them into the design template and read them usually for the first time in Adobe InDesign—the layout software—tweaking for style as I go. After it's flowed I'll send it to the copy editor, give it to an intern to fact-check, contact a gallery or photographer if necessary to get art, or give Charles Burns or Tony Millionaire his assignment.

TONY MILLIONAIRE: Many, many years ago I was asked to do some very small illustrations for *The Believer*. The idea was that I'd do them for a few months and then another illustrator would take over the job, then another, etc. As it turns out, I am extremely qualified for the job, and there was not another illustrator who could fill my shoes. Some of the assignments turned out to be quite simple—a cat with weird eyes, a kid at a lemonade stand selling novels for five hundred thousand dollars, etc. The portraits are always fun, especially if it's someone nobody recognizes. I drew Patton Oswalt six times, couldn't get the likeness right away, it ain't easy. But the most difficult are the illustrations about writing. I'm no writer, as you can tell by my use of the word "ain't," and I'm not much of a reader, especially now that I live in a city where I don't ride subways or trains. These articles that go on and on about the craft of writing drive me out of my mind. I can't draw a picture of an anthropomorphized book chasing after a whatever anymore; I've done it about six times, so I have to do all this thinking and so forth and it's really hard. So anyways that's my beef.

ANDREW LELAND: Once I have all the pieces for a particular issue, I'll start assessing the pagination, seeing if I need to compress (with jump pages) or stretch (with spot illustrations) the pages. Then I'll start entering copyedits and factchecks and sending PDFs to the authors. Once the authors are signed off, art starts coming in, and I can tighten the issue, addressing typography concerns and color-signature distribution. I show the pages to Dave and Vendela, write the cover- and table-of-contents headlines, and send to Alvaro for him to tighten. Once Dave and Vendela are signed off, I'll upload the high-res RIP-ready PDF to Westcan. At this point, the magazine is "closed."

NICK HORNBY: I visited 826 Valencia for the first time in April 2003. The first issue of *The Believer* had just been printed, and it looked beautiful. I picked one up. "This looks fantastic," I said to one of the editors who happened to be there.

"Thanks," she said.

"No, really. Gorgeous. Wonderful."

"I'm glad you like it," she said.

"I really do." I still wouldn't put the magazine down. I wanted to be asked to write for *The Believer*. I thought that if I said nice things about it for a long, long time, thus preventing the kind editor from getting on with his or her busy life, he or she would cave in and offer me work of some kind, but s/he didn't. And I was too proud to beg. The Temptations probably wouldn't have understood that particular dynamic, the older visiting writer from another country sniffing round a fashionable magazine for younger people. Pride is essential at a moment like that. I loved my visit to 826, but I came away slightly despondent.

A couple of months later, I got an email asking me if I wanted to write about music for *The Believer*. I had only recently given up the job of music critic for the *New Yorker*, so I made an alternative suggestion,

something I'd been thinking about for a while: a column about books that tried to describe our struggles with reading, the way we bought books and left them lying around unopened, the way we gave books up, the path that leads us from one book to the next. They agreed, with no apparent reluctance. I don't know

Unpublished incidental illustration from Jason Polan's series of people interacting with animals, from the July/August 2008 issue.

what had happened in the months between my visit and the email they sent. Probably they received millions of letters complaining of the absence of older, wiser, balder heads from their pages. But I stuck at the column for the next five years, on and off, the longest I've ever stuck at any regular gig for a newspaper or magazine. They never once gave me a reason to resign was the trouble, so in the end I had to invent my own. I'll regret it, possibly very soon.

VENDELA VIDA: One of my favorite things about the magazine is something we didn't plan: the smell. To me, the magazine smells like sawdust the morning after it's rained. First thing I do when an issue comes back from press is look to see how the cover came out, the second thing I do is hold it up to my nose.

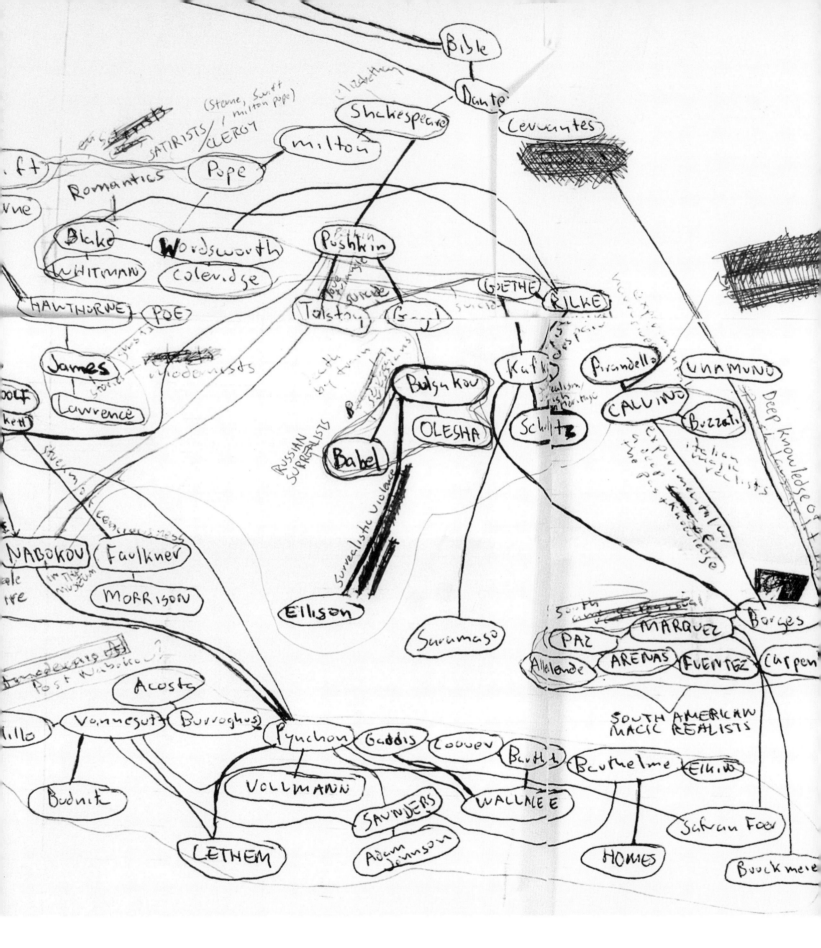

Tommy Wallach's research for "A Brief History of Magic Realism," the first Believer Schema, *from Issue 1, March 2003. The finished piece is on the next page, with a handful of other Schemas.*

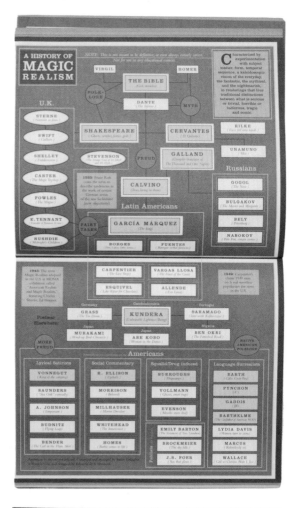

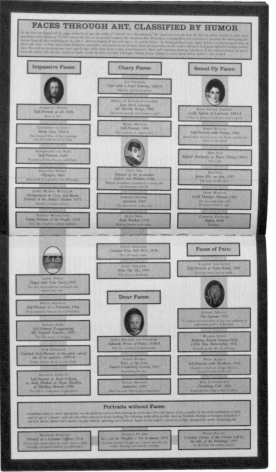

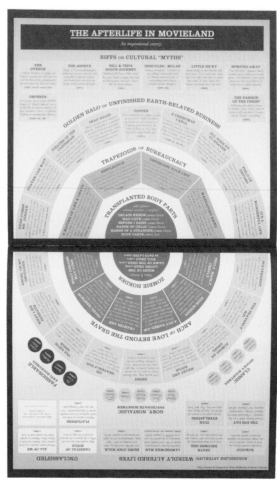

March 2003
*"A History of
Magic Realism" by
Dave Eggers, Tommy
Wallach, et al.*

October 2003
*Ben Greenman's
"1920: A Historical
Map of a Typical Year"*

November 2003
*Alex Kitnick's
"Faces Through Art,
Classified by Humor"*

August 2004
*Brian McMullen and
Steven Villereal's "The
Afterlife in Movieland"*

November 2004
*Kevin Moffet's
"The Heaven and
Hell of Specialty
Magazines"*

February 2005
*Brian McMullen's
"Non-Essential Stock
Photographs, Vol. 1"*

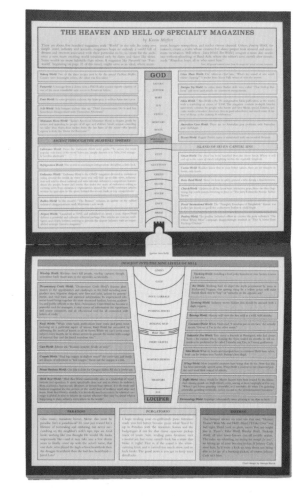

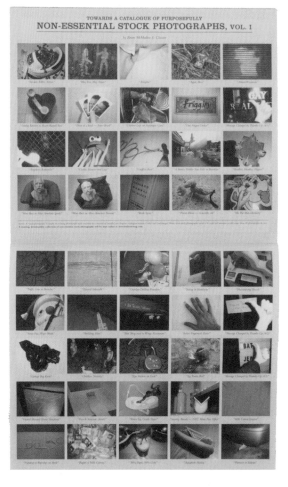

May/June 2005
*Utrillo Kushner's
"The Kingdom of
Singing Drummers"*

October 2005
*Jennie Gruber and
Brian McMullen's
"Golems at Large!"*

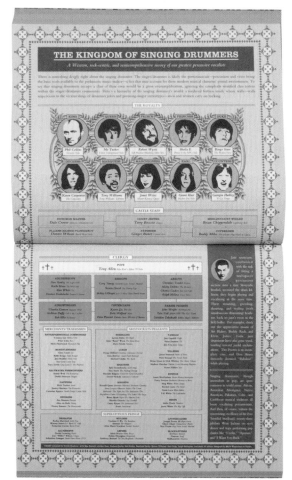

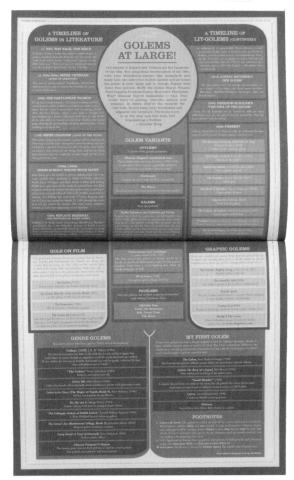

CHARLES BURNS DRAWS THE FORTY-FIFTH BELIEVER MAGAZINE COVER

by Charles Burns

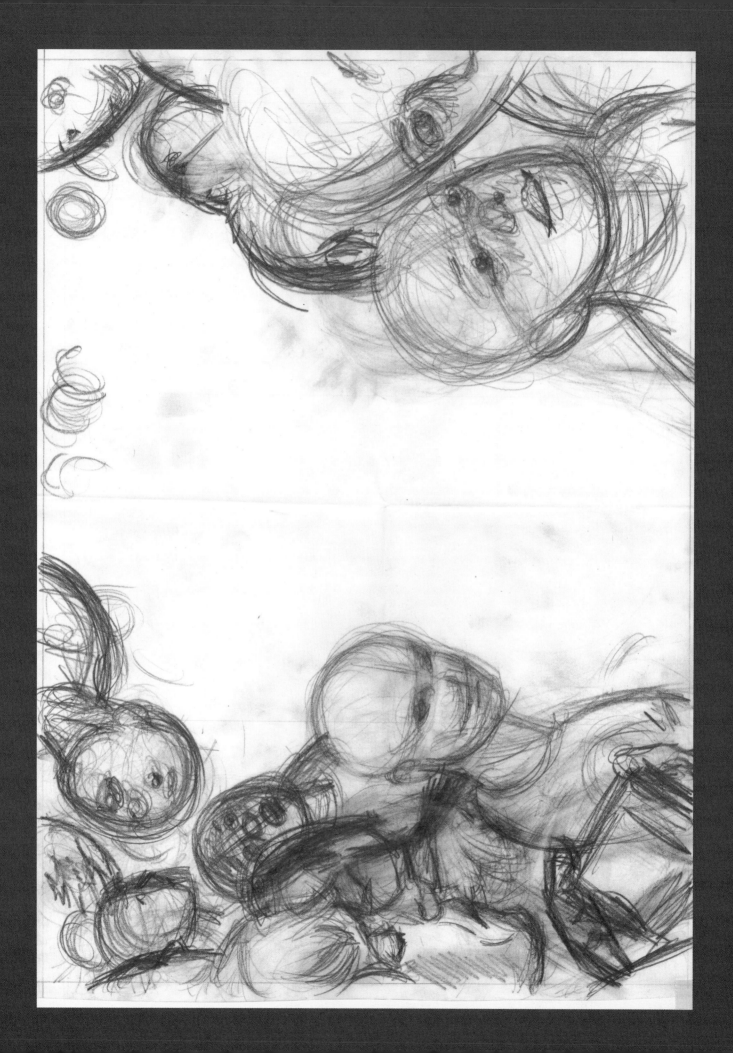

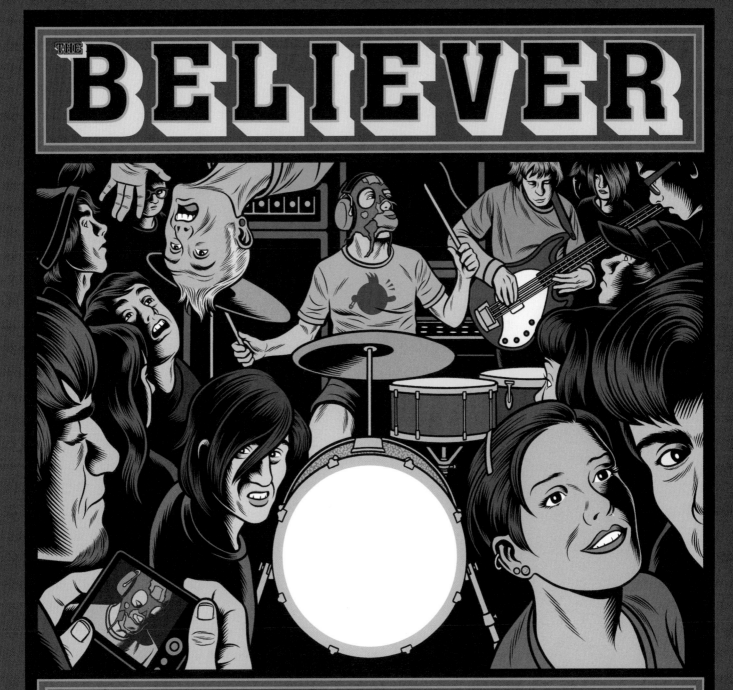

THE BELIEVER

THE 2007 MUSIC ISSUE

JUNE/JULY 2007 ★ $10

Including a CD of twenty songs by Sufjan Stevens, **Aesop Rock**, Grizzly Bear, **Lightning Bolt** (pictured above), and many others. **ALSO**: The search for Bill Fox (Cleveland's lost genius); **Paul Collins** finds rock's rarest instrument; Miranda July talks to the Blow. PLUS: Of Montreal, wax manifestos, **David Gates**, Trent Reznor and Hegel, synthetic larynges, & lots more!

0 97377 57012 0

4 5

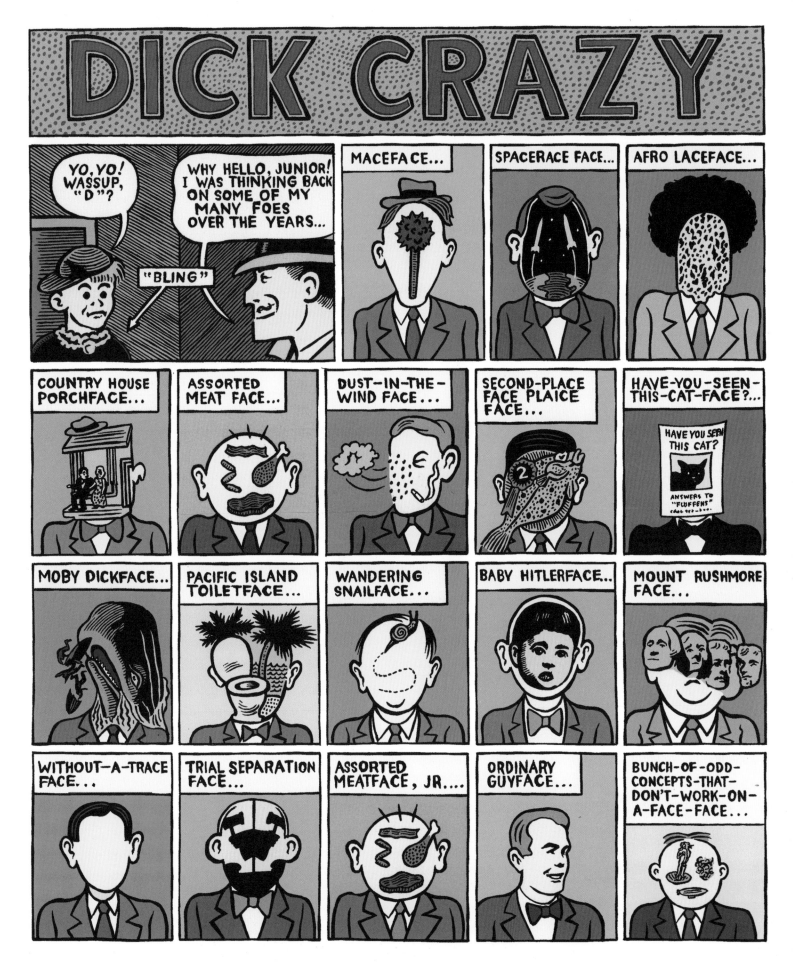

Opposite: Detail of Michael Kupperman's cover illustration for Stepmother, *a fairy tale by Robert Coover (2004).*
Above: A page of comics by Michael Kupperman from The Believer.

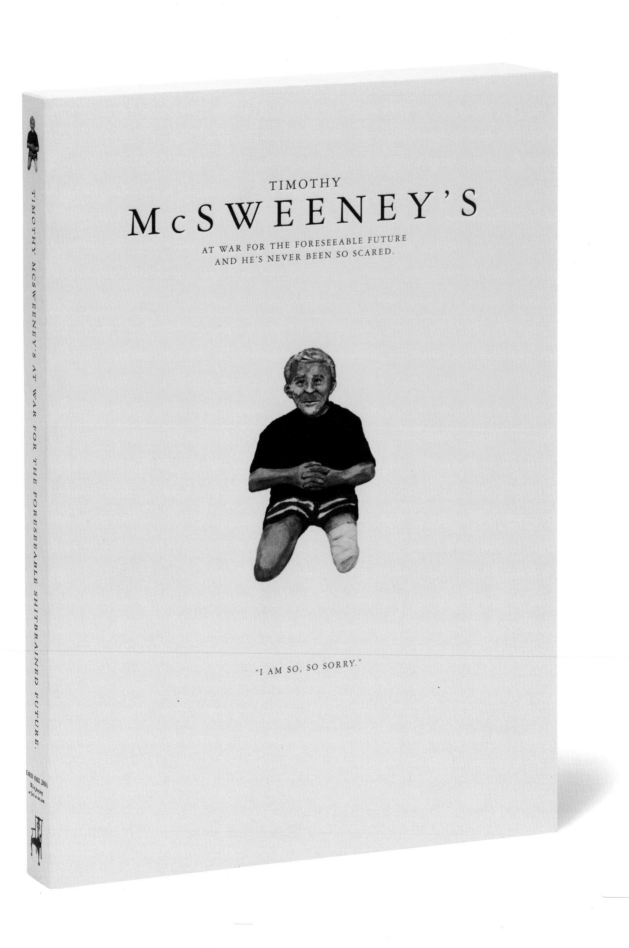

McSweeney's 14

(2 0 0 4)

DAVE EGGERS: I'd just read a piece in the *New York Times Magazine* about soldiers who had lost limbs in Iraq, and it was a revelation. I don't think Bush or Cheney had any idea of all of the secondary consequences of starting a war. Because they never served in the military and are generally incurious people, it's very easy to see how thousands and thousands of amputees would come as a surprise to them. I was so angry about it all that I painted a picture of Bush as a double-amputee. You can be absolutely sure that the President wouldn't lose two limbs for whatever goals he had in Iraq. Maybe it's a simplistic way of looking at it, but that's how I saw it at the time: Anyone sending the young people to have their limbs blown off in Iraq should be willing to make the same sacrifice. So I did this painting.

"It was worth it!"

Sketch by Dave Eggers of George W. Bush as an amputee.

ELI HOROWITZ: For the title-page art, Dave had the idea of dirigibles. I didn't know much about them at this point. Because I was living in Berkeley, I was able to get a day-pass to the university library. There, I found a few old histories—mostly French—of early flying machines. I tried to pick the handsomest or nuttiest ones. All the interior illustrations are printed in blue because we liked the look of two-color printing. This was a pretty standard paperback so, honestly, we were just trying to jazz things up a bit.

JOSHUAH BEARMAN: I think my essay really benefited from the two-color printing. The piece—a twenty-four-page investigation into Xinjiang, China's growing swarm of great gerbils—underwent quite an edit, as I recall. At first, there were a lot more lines in there like: "The Charming Dipodil (*Gerbilus amoenus*) is a cute little fucker native to Northern Africa." A little of that goes a long way, it turns out.

Illustration by Peter Kim for Joshuah Bearman's article: a size comparison between a Mongolian gerbil (left) and a great gerbil.

ELI HOROWITZ: For the cover, the plan was to do all the text as a color stamp, so you could see and feel the words pressed into the paper. The printer talked us into a less expensive option: standard offset printing with a "deboss" on top, to simulate the stamped effect. I'm still not really happy with how it came out. I don't like simulating—it almost never feels satisfying. We've tried to avoid that kind of shortcut ever since.

HEIDI MEREDITH: We got a lot of feedback on this issue from our subscribers, both good and bad. Some people were offended by the cover. It probably had more to do with with the legless portrait of our sitting president than the imperfectly debossed text.

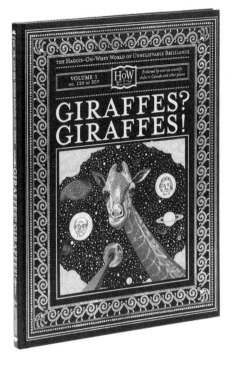

**GIRAFFES?
GIRAFFES!**

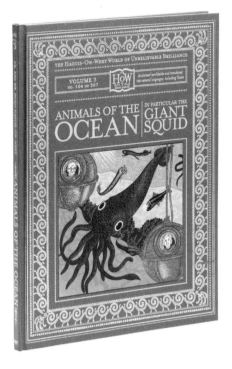

ANIMALS OF THE OCEAN | IN PARTICULAR THE **GIANT SQUID**

YOUR DISGUSTING HEAD | THE DARKEST, MOST OFFENSIVE —AND MOIST— SECRETS OF YOUR EARS, MOUTH AND NOSE

SQUID HISTORY

Unlike giraffes, squids do not have a stupid history like arriving on Earth from space on a conveyor. They instead came from a normal place: the center of the Earth. Traveling through the same tunnels the molemen once used, the squids made the slow climb to the surface once the center of the Earth became played out. Many sociologists have discussed the rationale for this migration, citing such possible factors as food and darkness. However, the real answer is identity. The squids wanted to move to where the shakers and pushers were. At the time that place was the very, very far bottom of the ocean. Unfortunately, things have changed. The bottom of the ocean is a lot more subdued now. The mastodons and sharkmen have all moved away... and yet still the squids remain. Down in the dark, murky, dark waters, spending all their days swimming aimlessly. Swimming aimlessly and killing. And occasionally one of them glows in some neon color for a while. They're better than other animals of the ocean, though. I wish I could find my shoes. The soft ones I use for walking.

AM I BEING EATEN?

People get confused when they are being eaten. Sometimes they are not being eaten, but very often they are. A general rule of thumb is if you think you are being eaten, this is probably what is happening. Some questions to ask yourself:

1. ARE ANY OF MY LIMBS MISSING?

If there is a limb missing, and blood surrounding you, chances are an animal of the ocean has used its teeth to bite off part of your body. This means that you, or at least the part that was bitten off, is being eaten.

2. IS A BEAK-LIKE MOUTH EVISCERATING MY ORGANS?

This is the work of the giant squid, when it is eating you. The squid will use its tentacles to bring you into its orifice, then its razor-sharp beak will begin shredding your organs and liquefying your bones. These are signs you are being eaten.

3. AM I LIGHTHEADED AND ALSO DRINKING MY OWN BLOOD?

These are two common symptoms of being eaten. Often, when an animal is consuming your limbs, you lose a good deal of blood. This can cause lightheadedness. Also, when you are being pulled under the surface in the jaws or tentacles of an animal of the ocean, you will gulp water. And much of this water will be mixed with your own blood.

4. AM I INSIDE AN ANIMAL'S STOMACH?

If you find yourself inside a stomach, you have likely been eaten.

WHICH OF THESE MEN HAVE BEEN BITTEN BY A SEA CREATURE?

A B
C D
E F

ANSWER: A-YES, B-YES, C-DON'T BE SILLY, D-YES, E-YES, F-YES

ORDER IN WHICH SQUIDS WILL EAT YOU	MALE, AVERAGE HEIGHT	WOMAN, AVERAGE HEIGHT	CHILDREN, ALL SIZES
	1. Legs	1. Arms	1. Left arm, left leg
	2. Arms	2. Torso	2. Lower torso
	3. Head	3. Head	3. Right arm, right leg
	4. Torso	4. Lower torso	4. Upper torso
	5. Lower torso	5. Legs	5. Head

The Haggis-On-Whey
World of Unbelievable Brilliance

by DR. DORIS AND MR. BENNY HAGGIS-ON-WHEY

(2004)

MARK WASSERMAN: One day I got a typically cryptic email, something like: "I'm working on a weird book. do you want to design it?" We instantly connected on the overall visual style of the books; I was already a big collector of '50–'60s science books.

DAVE EGGERS: This is a series that's honestly hard to explain why it exists. I can't remember why we felt the world needed such a thing. We wanted to create a series that looked, at first glance, like some kind of real series of reference books for kids. We wanted them to look like the kinds of books TIME-LIFE used to publish. But ours would be full of entirely false information.

TOPH EGGERS: There really should be a study into why it's pleasurable to fib to kids. You have to weigh the fibbing part against the joy kids, or anyone, might get while imagining this all to be true.

DAVE EGGERS: We started by creating this scientist, Dr. Doris Haggis-On-Whey, who sort of came about because we knew Florence and Irving Hochman, a lovely couple who used to come to 826 Valencia for many of the events. While Toph and I were vaguely talking about a series of fake-info books, one day I looked at Flo and Irv and thought, these are the authors of the books. So we asked them to dress up as Doris and Benny. They had a lot of fun.

TOPH EGGERS: H-O-W is really about what happens when someone really talented gets demoted to the bush leagues. Dr. Doris is obnoxiously smart but has for some reason been assigned a children's book series.

Opposite: The covers of the first three H-O-W books, and a spread from Animals of the Ocean, in Particular the Giant Squid.

DAVE EGGERS: The first one was about giraffes. I don't know why. I think it started with Toph and I laughing about how Darwin and all his theories become harder to believe when you look at the giraffe.

MICHELLE QUINT: A few months ago, someone brought to our attention that there was a band out there called Giraffes? Giraffes! We immediately ordered five CDs off their website.

JOE ANDREOLI: Ken Topham and I were driving around in his car one day, trying to come up with a name for our band. A copy of *Giraffes? Giraffes!* had been hanging out in the backseat and one of us said it out loud. It sounded good. Real good. So we started borrowing it.

MICHELLE QUINT: I found their Myspace page and sent them a note. We wanted posters too! But I think I may have been a little cryptic at first, because Joe's response expressed concern that we might be contacting them about copyright issues.

TOPH EGGERS: It's an unfortunate revelation but I think sadness is at the heart of all children's stories. Someone's either getting lost somewhere, or growing up with some shunnable abnormality in order to learn a life lesson. In writing these books there seemed to be no reason to depart from this tradition. For me the recipe in any story is always a date or two, a real place, and hopefully either a recognizable astronomer, philosopher, or lead singer of Sugar Ray. Because the more real elements you have at the outset, the more nonsense can follow. Which of course is one of Newton's laws.

McSweeney's 15

(2 0 0 4)

DAVE EGGERS: It seemed inevitable that at some point we would do an issue devoted to Icelandic writing. We'd spent a lot of time there while we printed our first issues in Reykjavik, and our friend Arni from Oddi Printing would occasionally mention Icelandic writers we should read.

MAC BARNETT: When I reported to Eli on my first day as a McSweeney's intern, I shared my unusual situation: that I had studied Icelandic literature in college, that three days earlier my dad, uncharacteristically moved after

The band logo for Big Country, the chief inspiration for Issue 15's never-repeated logo design. Below that, an early sketch by Leif Parsons, missing the delicate gray midtone.

reading my thesis on skaldic poetry, had decided to send me on a trip to Iceland, and that almost immediately after starting interning at McSweeney's I'd be taking a three-week vacation. I expected to be fired. Instead Eli told me that a planned issue highlighting Icelandic fiction was languishing and needed someone to get excited about it. I was very excited. I was also terrified to go to Iceland by myself—I knew that it could be lonely and expensive. On my first day there, Birna Anna, the newspaper reporter whom Dave and Sean had met when they went to Iceland for the printing of Issue 4, showed me around the island. Mostly

she did it because she is a generous person, but I think also partly because she thought I was much more important than I actually was. This issue gave me a sense of purpose for my whole vacation. I lied to everyone I met and told them I was on a business trip.

BIRNA ANNA BJÖRNSDOTTÍR: The work on Issue 15 involved some pretty extensive and detailed logistics. Everything had to be translated, then evaluated, then approved or not, so there was an extreme amount of back and forth. To this day I don't think I've emailed anyone whom I'd never met as often as I did Eli while we were working on Issue 15. And every now and then Dave would check in and tell me thanks and that in gratitude for my work, Eli would wash my car. And then there was Mac, the intern (whoops, he was an intern, wasn't he?), who was on the case as well. I didn't make him wash my car. Eli has yet to show up and when he does he'll get the same deal.

ELI HOROWITZ: Birna Anna was really plugged into the Icelandic literary scene, so she came up with an initial list of authors, along with samples from each,

and helped us contact the publishing houses. We read all that, asked for some more, maybe found one or two ourselves—but she was great at putting everyone in context.

DAVE EGGERS: Around that same time, Arni from Oddi Printing reminded us that they had these huge reams of yellow cloth in their warehouse, collecting dust and taking up space. About a year before I'd designed an early cover for a book that was going to be just five short stories. Later, that book was expanded and became *How We Are Hungry*. But for a while we thought we'd just put five stories together and bind them in this yellow cloth. Somewhere along the line the book grew, and we changed the cover from yellow cloth to black leatherette, and that was fine, but we had to figure out a way to use the cloth, and the yellow sky on this cover became the solution.

ELI HOROWITZ: There was enough cloth for 10,000 full books, because I think that was our original print run of Dave's five-story book. But the print run for *McSweeney's* around then was about 20,000, so we figured that the cloth that could have covered 10,000 full books would also cover 20,000 half-books. The horizontal split seemed more interesting than just doing a traditional cloth spine.

DAVE EGGERS: Once we knew it would cover half the cover, horizontally, it made sense that that swath would be the sun. I was thinking of Iceland in the summer, which has almost uninterrupted light.

MAC BARNETT: For illustrations, we decided to use some Icelandic runes I remembered from college. I'd read about vikings inscribing magic symbols on the genitals of nábrókarstafur, the "necrobreeches" made from the skin of dead men, and that's not the kind of thing you forget. Viking literature is full of belletristic descriptions of killings and corpses and projectile vomiting. At the beginning we printed an Icelandic lock-picking spell which is supposed to be spoken while your mouth is full of a man's belly fat. It's absolutely insane but fairly representative of the genre.

DAVE EGGERS: The little sunburst around the *McSweeney's* name is a nod to the band Big Country, who always used those bursts around their logo. When I think of Iceland, I think of Scotland, and that makes me think of Big Country.

MAC BARNETT: Somewhere along the way, we decided to shrink-wrap a little tabloid in with the issue—it's a sampling of Iceland's version of *People* or *US Weekly*. The country's so small that the magazine is almost

like a yearbook: every time a new issue came out, my friends would gather around tables and look for pictures of themselves. There were also lots of pictures of Harrison Ford in there. He had apparently visited Iceland three times in the three weeks I was there.

BARB BERSCHE: The miniature Icelandic tabloid had some racy pictures on its cover. So, depending on which way Issue 15 was facing on a store's shelf, you either saw this gorgeous landscape on the front, or an unexpected eyeful of an Icelandic man's naughties on the back. This bothered some bookstores.

Right and below:
An eyeful of sample spreads from the
Icelandic mini-magazine that came shrink-wrapped
with every copy of Issue 15.

How We Are Hungry

by DAVE EGGERS (2004)

DAVE EGGERS: We were about to do a reprint of the hardcover, and we didn't want to do the same thing. The belly band hadn't held up so well, and was always shifting up and down. So we scrapped the belly band, and I just wanted a more complex stamp. The catch was I didn't have time to design one from scratch—I think we had about three days between when we knew we needed to reprint and when the design had to be finalized. And honestly, I was ready just to go with the previous cover, with the words stamped on instead of on the belly band. It would have been pretty mediocre. Then the night before I was going to send the file off, my father-in-law returned from a trip to Hungary, and he'd gotten me this book about Hungarian art deco designers from the 1930s. And I flipped through it, and there was this great flourishing sort of framework on one page. And I lifted it. I scanned it right there, altered some bits, and worked it around the existing artwork. It looked good, I think, and came together at the eleventh hour.

Early cover sketches by Dave Eggers.
When a hippogriff flies over a fire at night, what color is the hippogriff?

Two cover variations that got printed early on, before the belly-band edition.
Only a few copies of these two exist, and we're not sure where they went.

Second-edition hardcover with modified art deco stamp.

McSWEENEY'S
ISSUE No. 16

Ann Beattie   Adam Levin
Robert Coover   Harry Mathews
Roddy Doyle   Miranda Mellis
Pia Ehrhardt   Nathaniel Minton
Brian Evenson   Kevin Moffett
Denis Johnson   Hannah Pittard

UNFOLDED ONCE

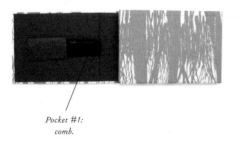

*Pocket #1:
comb.*

UNFOLDED TWICE

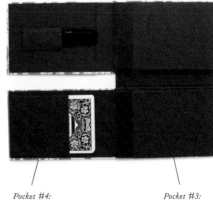

*Pocket #2:
story collection.*

UNFOLDED THREE TIMES

*Pocket #4:
deck of cards.*

*Pocket #3:
novella.*

McSweeney's 16

(2005)

*Two adventurous components of Issue 16: "Heart Suit," a story by Robert Coover
in the form of fifteen playing cards; and a comb.*

ELI HOROWITZ: I'd been wondering about a book that could be normal-size but with an enormous cover. Something that could sit on a shelf, pretend to be a normal book, but then unfurl into something else entirely. That led me to various folding contraptions, which I tested mostly by tearing napkins into various shapes.

DAVE EGGERS: The artwork on the exterior started with Joanna Davis. She's the sister of our friend Amanda Davis, a writer who died too young, in 2003. We'd always admired Joanna's art when we saw it in Amanda's house in Oakland. Joanna did these gorgeous paintings, almost monochromatic, of forests. So I kept thinking of a way we could use her stuff for a cover. But until Issue 16, we hadn't really used much in the way of illustration on the covers.

JOANNA DAVIS: I had moved to Pennsylvania and fell in love with drawing dormant winter trees. For the

first time in my life I could draw something over and over and over again without getting bored. Eli asked me to do several different drawings in a short amount of time for the cover, until we got to the perfect one. I was actively involved in all the ensuing decisions: how it was to be printed, the type of fabric, the color of the ink, etc. I yessed it all. I was so happy that my drawing was being used that they could have shredded and defecated on it before going to press and I would have been fine with it. Luckily none of the decisions involved violence.

ELI HOROWITZ: The only violence was directed at those napkins. Once we had the basic shape, I thought of the built-in pockets as a way to hold everything in on the inside. But it was important to me that the pockets be earned. I wanted the function to require the form. I didn't want to just have some stories in one pocket, some stories in another, other stories in another. So I tried to think about what kinds of things

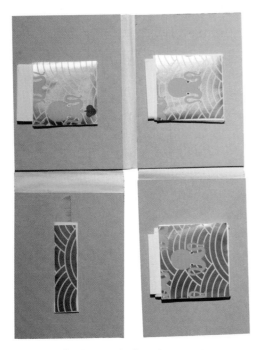

Computer sketch by George Slavik showing an unused
interior illustration concept.

would need a pocket—separate works, collections of things, objects—while meanwhile keeping my ears open for works that might fit.

ANGELA PETRELLA: When I was an intern, Eli asked me to come up with some ideas for alternative ways to present a story. His initial starting-point suggestion was "a deck of cards," and he told me to come up with two hundred ideas like that. So after many, many hours, I gave him a list of things like a waitress's pad, a reporter's notebook, a hotel guest-book, a teacher's grade book, a TV guide—every-thing ever. A few months later, I got the issue. It was a deck of cards.

ELI HOROWITZ: We figured out three items—the novella, the playing cards, and the book of stories—but we still needed a fourth. I really wanted an object in there. To fit, it had to be thin and long. And it had to be inexpensive. Beyond that, I just wanted some-thing clear, immediate, frank. I considered a ruler or a magnifying glass, but I didn't want to imply any specific purpose—I didn't want readers wondering what they were supposed to measure or examine. So I settled on the comb.

CHRIS YING: Once at a book fair, a customer looked at this issue and said, "Oh, I get it. Like, combing for good fiction." I just said, "Yeah, exactly."

ELI HOROWITZ: The comb is pretty much nonsense. I've heard the whole thing compared to a gentleman's grooming kit, which had never entered my mind.

DAVE EGGERS: This was the first issue Eli really conceived on his own, I think, so I was giving him a wide berth, but periodically checking in with him. I didn't really know what the thing would look like until he showed me the printer's mockup, which was pretty incredible. I couldn't believe they could make such a thing affordable. And then he showed me four different combs. The printer had subcontracted with a comb-maker, and they sent us four options, includ-ing an afro-pick. I don't know if I ever asked why we would have a comb in the issue.

ELI HOROWITZ: After we resolved the comb thing, there were other technical issues to sort out. For instance, the layout for Adam Levin's story, "Consid-ering the Bittersweet End of Susan Falls," took some conversation.

ADAM LEVIN: My story had a couple too many visual weirdnesses—varying typography, diagrams, and marginalia. When I realized after a couple years that the problem was impossible for me to solve, I sent it to *McSweeney's*, hoping they'd understand. After Eli accepted the story, we sussed out which weird things were essential and which weren't. I rewrote sentences and added paragraphs. Chapter 2, the weirdest-looking one—it was supposed to look like a really smart fifteen-year-old girl's marginalia in a textbook and a page of *Chumash* (a Torah in book form, with marginal commentary)—switched places with Chapter 3. It seemed best to push that weird-looking one a little further back, just like you wait 'til at least the second date before showing the girl your eleventh toe.

ELI HOROWITZ: And Nathaniel Minton, another writer we included, was really sick while we were working on his piece.

NATHANIEL MINTON: I had a fever of 104°when I got the galley back from Eli. There was this delightful drawing of a tree on my story along with a note about the comb.

ELI HOROWITZ: Issue 16 also marked the first appearance of any material from Denis Johnson's novel *Tree of Smoke*, which directly led to me attempting to build a cabin on his land in Idaho. This stemmed from the promise Sean Wilsey had made to Denis a few years earlier—that we'd build a cabin for him in exchange for being able to publish some of his work. Ann Beattie's novella "Mr. Nobody At All," the other heavy hitter in there, had been bumped from her book and was just sitting in her drawer.

A spread from Chapter 3 of Adam Levin's story, "Considering the Bittersweet End of Susan Falls."

ANN BEATTIE: "Mr. Nobody At All" came to me as a title when I pulled a book off the shelf and found the name, reading about the artist Edouard Vuillard. I guess it clicked because what we name things, as opposed to what they are, was the subject of the piece I was writing. I'd gotten tired of going to memorial services and hearing people talk about their significance in the lives of the people who were dead: their special moments; their deeply significant anecdotes. I wrote part one, then told my friend Harry Mathews that what I was working on didn't pass the *"Et alors?"* test. To explain this in-joke: a mutual friend once described a situation in which he found himself doing research for a book in France. When people listened to what he'd discovered about his subject, he'd act like he was the gossiping concierge, asking, *"Et alors?"* Anyway—I had the first part of what I was writing, but didn't think it much mattered. Harry suggested I stage a second memorial service. He was exactly right, and that gave me the idea to ask him to write his own tribute (I told him a bit—but just a bit—about the imaginary person I'd been writing about). Whew.

ELI HOROWITZ: Issue 16, along with two other books we were expecting—*The Facts of Winter* and *The People of Paper*—was frozen in customs for a couple awful weeks. It was a huge, huge pain. Apparently they were sharing a container with some other shipment from Singapore, and that shipment contained "dead animals."

Next pages: Joanna Davis's orginal artwork for the pocketed, pants-shaped Issue 16 cover.

Pages 160–161: The covers of eight books in the "McSweeney's Rectangulars" series of novels launched in 2005.

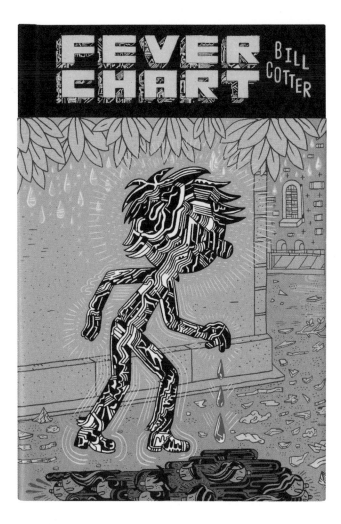

FEVER CHART BILL COTTER

A CHILD AGAIN
BY ROBERT COOVER

ARKANSAS

John Brandon

THE CONVALESCENT
by JESSICA ANTHONY

"Jessica Anthony is a writer possessed of mind-bending talents. Inconceivably, she's written a novel that's innocent and wise, grave and hilarious, bleak and hopeful. Reading it, I felt as though I'd stumbled upon a magical text that might, at any moment, disappear from my hands. *The Convalescent* is that kind of special."
—Heidi Julavits

THE PEOPLE OF PAPER
BY SALVADOR PLASCENCIA

ICELANDER
BY DUSTIN LONG

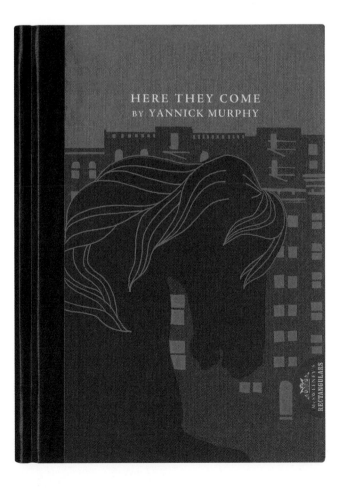

HERE THEY COME
BY YANNICK MURPHY

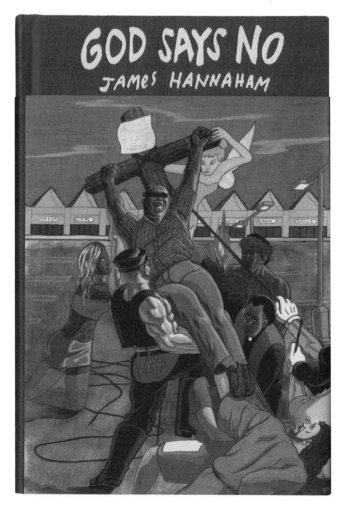

GOD SAYS NO
JAMES HANNAHAM

McSweeney's 17

(2 0 0 5)

STEPHEN ELLIOTT: I published a short story, illustrated by Laurenn McCubbin, in the *Unfamiliar* digest that was a part of this issue. The issue was bundled like a packet of mail. The whole thing was just a mess, messier even than a real bundle of mail.

A found, crumpled photograph of two drinkers in a swimming pool. Blown-up sections of this photo served as several of the illustrations in "Unfamiliar," the short-stories portion of Issue 17.

DAVE EGGERS: I guess this was the strangest issue of *McSweeney's*, and I take responsibility for its failures. I admit to liking bundles of things; I like separating the parts of an issue into as many discrete objects as possible—it gives us that much more opportunity to play with the forms and the covers. And because we had been sending our issues through the mail for so long, it seemed natural that eventually we'd experiment with the very form of mail. What if this issue looked like one big bundle of junk mail? If we had ten or so separate objects, it just seemed like a good way to play with the form of mailers, magazines, journals, catalogs. So we made a list of things we wanted to do, and started assigning them. I did hope originally to have a couple of very elaborate magazines in there, magazines that would seem like they'd been around for decades and this was just another issue. One of the magazines I'd wanted to do forever was to be called *Lesser Known Actor Weekly*. It would look like *People* or *US Weekly* or *In Touch*, with pictures of celebrities eating lunch or sunbathing, but it would be entirely about character actors whose faces you knew but whose names you didn't. I thought that would be so good. But the logistics of it were going to be very difficult, and we didn't have the money or manpower.

So we scaled down the elements a bit. I think *Yeti Researcher*, Josh's obsession, was already in the works, and we started from there.

JOSHUAH BEARMAN: I don't think I believe in Bigfoot, but I like the idea of believing in Bigfoot. Thus was born *Yeti Researcher*, the first journal devoted entirely to scholarship about the Yeti—and of course Bigfoot, Sasquatch, Orang Pendek, the Florida Skunk Ape, and other cryptic hominids worldwide. Naturally, *Yeti Researcher* was meant as nonfiction. (Like all Yeti research!) Once we decided on *Yeti Researcher* as the official organ of the Society for Cryptic Hominid Investigation, we tried to make it function that way. We assigned real articles to real people. We accepted submissions. We turned down some articles because they were not serious enough about the current state of Yeti research; we turned down others because they were too fanciful. As cryptozoological scholarship goes, we realized we had to be as rigorous as possible.

BRENT HOFF: I came across many bizarre stories while helping Josh research this thing. My favorite was a cattleman's journal entry from 1888, detailing how a Native American tribe he was wintering with brought meat to a "giant, hairy man-like creature, totally covered with thick hair, except for its palms." The tribe called him "Crazy Bear."

JOSHUAH BEARMAN: There is nothing made up in *Yeti Researcher*. Well, the ads are made up. And

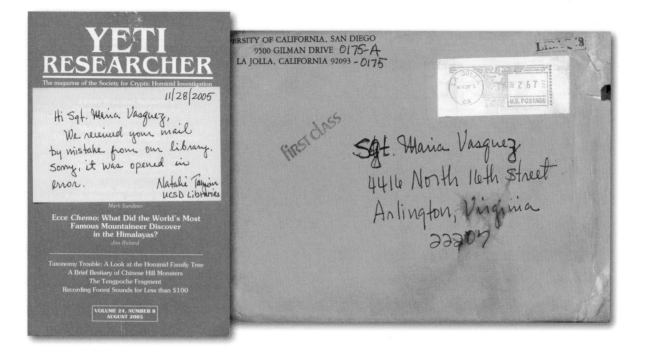

Most of the individual mailpieces in Issue 17 were preprinted with the "home address" of Sgt. Maria Vasquez. (The name is fictional, but the mailing address is real, and it belongs to the parents of McSweeney's editor Eli Horowitz.) Occasionally, well-meaning institutions would come across the issue's contents and, mistaking them for misdirected mail, forward them to the preprinted address.

maybe also the letters from readers about previous issues. But the articles, and details therein, are all real, in the sense that they cite accounts, evidence, theories, and personages of the actual Bigfoot/Yeti historical narrative. We at *Yeti Researcher* may have been guilty of some enthusiastic interpretation, but that's how theoretical breakthroughs happen, right?

BRIAN MCMULLEN: Josh wanted *Yeti Researcher* to look serious, but at least a little stylish. Like *Popular Science*, say. Dave, on the other hand, wanted it to look like a real scholarly journal, ignoring prettiness. What everyone agreed on was that it had to look real. Not like a parody or a joke. I picked fonts that were popular in the 1970s and tried to make it look like it had been around for twenty-four years and never redesigned. We scanned a bunch of old ads, and changed some text, targeting the ads to a yeti-research audience. In college I had a used geology book that smelled like old milk. I kept that smell in mind as I designed.

DAVE EGGERS: While Josh worked on *Yeti Researcher*, we started assigning all kinds of other jobs to other people. Pilar Perez started work on the art sampler, which came to be known as *Envelope*. We gathered some fiction that would otherwise have gone into *McSweeney's* for *Unfamiliar*, which was a prototype for a weekly all-fiction magazine. And then there were the weirder elements of the package. I can't remember when *Red Car and Perch* occurred to me, but I figured the issue had to have it. I emailed Brian McGinn, who had taken one of my 826 Valencia classes. By this point he was an intern at McSweeney's, and I asked him to take pictures of a few hundred red cars. That idea made me laugh—that someone would make a magazine full of just two things: pictures of red cars, and pictures of perch. I guess I knew this issue would have a somewhat limited audience.

BRIAN MCGINN: My job was to shoot snapshots of red cars wherever I saw them, noting the location of the car and describing how it made me feel. I volunteered for this job at an editorial meeting. After I'd gotten three hundred or so photos, I brought 'em to Dave, and they were combined with the occasional picture of a perch in a random location to create *Red Car and Perch*.

JORDAN BASS: The first time I heard about Issue 17 was when I came home on my Christmas break, in January of 2005. Dave sent me and an intern named Claire, who was known as "Rocket," to find a perch and take pictures of it in a variety of different locations, for *Red Car and Perch*. We looked around for a perch in the Mission but couldn't find one, so we bought a tilapia. The perch in all those pictures is actually a tilapia, which the fish-market guy assured us was related and similar-looking. We spent an afternoon walking around and putting it on different things—the

Batmobile coin ride in front of Walgreens, things in Dolores Park, etc. I think the plastic wrap interferes with the composition a little bit, but we didn't want to handle the fish too much, or put it directly on anything. There was definitely a ticking-clock feeling to carrying this fish around and putting it on people's cars, waiting for it to split open or something. I can't remember what we did with the fish afterward.

DAVE EGGERS: Meanwhile, Evany Thomas was in the middle of working on the sleeping positions book, I think, when she and I started talking about a catalog for this issue. Some kind of free mailer that would come unwanted through the mail. And the operative idea was that the catalog would offer hundreds of gift baskets, with only the most slight differences between them. That made us laugh our heads off, that we would

"Red Car and Perch," the portion of Issue 17 made to look like it was mailed to Sgt. Maria Vasquez by the law firm of Ribbon, Thacker, Talbot & Roy. It consists mainly of page after page of photographs. Each photograph prominently features either a red car or a perch, or both.

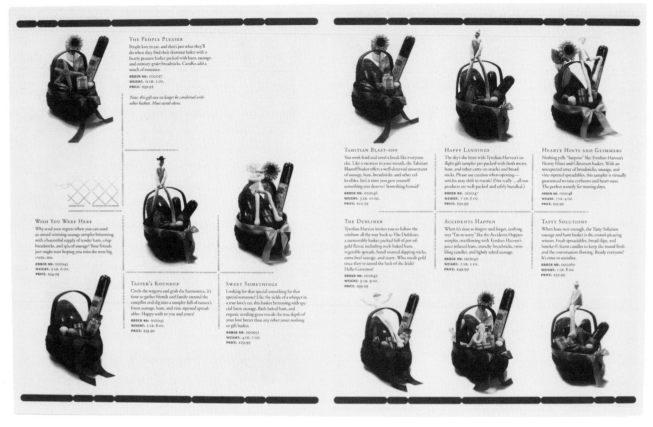

A representative spread from the "Tyrolean Harvest" sausage-basket catalog, which the printer accidentally forgot to staple in the middle. Each sausage-basket photograph contains the same elements, more or less. The difference is all in the presentation.

take about a hundred product shots with us just changing a sausage from the left side of the basket to the right. Evany took it from there.

EVANY THOMAS: The goal was to assemble the dustiest, most non-appetizing and off-looking gift basket ever, and we just went up and down the aisles grabbing anything depressing or freaky-looking. We got decorative ribbon in the most muted, non-celebratory shades possible, and picked out this horrible crumbly grass bedding in a sad, dead gray. The basket itself was divided into two spheres, and if you got the angle right, it looked like a big round ass. The meat and spreadables we got at Safeway next door, but we personalized everything by spray-mounting on Tyrolian Harvest labels that we made and printed on resume parchment. The copy for the catalog was directly inspired by one of my all-time favorite passages, found in the liner notes of a best of Julie London CD:

"If you look up 'sultry' in *Webster's Ninth Unabridged*, you might see a sketch of Julie London. Sophisticated, suggestive, caressing… her velvety song stylings whispered of cocktails, candlelight, a cigarette—and no moon at all. She didn't sing, she beckoned, and no man could doubt that Julie London yearned for him alone. Limiting an anthology to 18 great London songs is like picking bubbles out of champagne. She recorded a wealth of first-class material, and it anguishes the connoisseur to bypass so many pearls."
—Irwin Chusid, WFMU, East Orange, NJ

I tried really hard to achieve the same gleeful levels of hyperbole and strained metaphor to describe each gift basket, and I even managed to work in a direct quote ("Trying to pick just one reason why someone might hope to purchase Tyrolian Harvest's Classic Creations meat-and-breadstick sampler basket is like trying to pluck bubbles from champagne").

DAVE EGGERS: One hope for the issue was that in the bundle there would be a few prototypes for magazines that we wanted to publish somehow. *Unfamiliar* was a prototype for an all-fiction weekly magazine. We just wanted to show what such a thing might look like. *Envelope* was the same thing—a prototype for an art magazine.

CHRIS YING: As an intern, I did the lettering of artists' names for *Envelope* with some alphabet rubber stamps that Eli had. However, as could be expected, we were missing a bunch of crucial letters. I think the P's are really mutilated R's.

BRIAN MCMULLEN: In late 2004, Dave invited me to make a fantasy mailpiece for the issue. It had to be something I could produce on the cheap, in about two months of free time. Those were the only rules. My first idea was to include a pair of custom-designed tube socks in the mail bundle, as if the socks were the latest release in a garment-of-the-month club. Tube socks for April, a pair of shorts for May, sweatpants for June, and so on. Each garment would come sealed in a bag along with a mini-catalog, promoting the service. After we figured out that custom socks were too expensive, I came up with Pantalaine—a brand of affordable "plural clothing" intended to be worn by two or more people at the same time. I spent the next few weeks brainstorming ideas for clothes and then making them with Katie—my understanding and supportive wife—and a dozen talented, generous friends. For the writing and design of the mailpiece, I went for the look and feel of a Sunday-newspaper advertising circular—the kind of thing T. J. Maxx or Sears might print a hundred

An early draft of "Corrugated Miniaturist," an Issue 17 outtake. This periodical—a monthly sheet of cardboard to cut up and assemble into a miniature model of a cardboard shipping container—was created to take advantage of the corrugated cardboard sheet that got added to the mail bundle just before the issue went to press.

million of and then stuff into every mailbox in the USA. The message I wanted to communicate is very simple: Pantalaine is a family-oriented company, and proud to offer America the most dependable and affordable line of multi-person clothing available anywhere.

ELI HOROWITZ: We debuted the Pantalaine spring line, or maybe fall line, I don't know—the pan-seasonal line—at the second "The World, Explained" night, at the REDCAT Theater in L.A. Models included the writers Salvador Plascencia and Trinie Dalton and the artist Matt Greene. It was a cast of thousands, and I added some narration—mostly weak puns and what I imagined to sound like fashiony nonsense.

JORDAN BASS: When I came back again in June '05, the issue had gone to press, but *Corrugated Miniaturist* had been nixed. I loved *Corrugated Miniaturist*.

BRIAN MCMULLEN: I came up with *Corrugated Miniaturist*—a periodical aimed at hobbyists who like to make models of cardboard boxes—at the last second, after Dave and Eli decided to add a sheet of cardboard to the mail bundle.

ELI HOROWITZ: We needed cardboard in there for sturdiness, and for the barcode and pricing information. We didn't want to just leave the cardboard blank, so we gave Brian the weekend to come up with something, and he did. But *Corrugated Miniaturist* was ahead of its time.

BRIAN MCMULLEN: I think it went to the printer and Eli had a proof in hand before Dave politely intervened. He kindly praised the concept and even offered to do it later, but this particular sheet of cardboard had to be more topical—more in touch with current events than a DIY miniature packing box.

JORDAN BASS: We had a meeting out on the back deck, behind the old office, and everyone threw out ideas—I think there might've been some guidelines laid down as to usefulness, topicality, and non-wackiness. Looking at my email, this actually happened on July 28th, as on that date I have a passive-aggressive message from an intern with a different vision for it ("I mentioned the idea to Dave and he liked it. If you want me to do anything else let me know. I'm working on a factcheck but I'll probably have some extra time"). The "Citizen's Insertable Swiftness Manifest" was written that day, after the meeting, and I sent it to Dave that night. The next day he laid it out himself—he wanted it to look "as ugly as possible," I remember.

ELI HOROWITZ: When press time came, we decided to give this print broker a try. The price was right, and at that point it didn't feel like a dramatic switch. I think everything was printed at one place, but I don't really know anything for sure. That was my experience with print brokers: never really knowing anything for sure. Too many degrees of separation between you and the actual physical object. So so unfun, the printing of this issue was.

DAVE EGGERS: Because everything was mail-oriented, we had to come up with an addressee and an address. That's where Sgt. Maria Vasquez, Jr. came from. The "Jr." part still makes me laugh.

ELI HOROWITZ: All the mail was addressed to Maria Vasquez, who is an imaginary person, but the address was real—it was my parents' house in Virginia. I don't think I mentioned this to them in advance—I don't think I particularly

thought about it myself. But then shortly after the issue shipped, the mailman began delivering individual elements of the issue to my parents along with each day's mail. I guess the bundle would split apart along the way, and then all those letters and catalogs and magazines would join the mailstream and get delivered like actual mail. Despite the fact that none of it had actual postage. Sometimes the envelopes would be accompanied by little notes from post offices wherever, apologizing for the damage or delay. My parents received literally hundreds of pieces. The mailman was very confused—was Maria Vasquez living in the basement, and why was she so popular?

AMITY HOROWITZ (ELI'S MOM): Sgt. Maria Vasquez? Someone must have gotten the address wrong. I checked the phone book for someone in Arlington with that name and actually found one, but when I called I learned that her phone number had been disconnected. Then, a day or two later, a second envelope and then a third. Finally I opened the manila envelopes to try to get a clue about who she was so I could send things on. And the pictures inside looked very McSweeneyish.

HEIDI MEREDITH: I think it was hard for people to see what the issue had inside of it. It had a lot of cool stuff, but you couldn't really tell. Bookstores just didn't know what to do! Eli and I actually wrote an email (that our distributor passed to all the bookstores that ordered the issue) with ideas about how to display the issue. Some stores opened up the issue and displayed it, but that can be messy and get everywhere, so a lot of stores tried to avoid it. We got a lot of returns and had to work hard to reassure stores that Issue 18 would be a "normal" package.

The front and back of the accordion-folded Pantalaine circular, an advertisement for good deals on clothing made to be worn by two or more people at the same time.

Dear New Girl or Whatever Your Name Is

edited by TRINIE DALTON & LISA WAGNER

(2005)

TRINIE DALTON: Teaching high school wasn't my calling, but I loved the kids' creativity and humor and wanted to document it in a way that wouldn't land me in jail. I detested the teacher-police persona, *except* when I saw kids making illegal notes—because I am nosy and that's where juicy action happens. Teen soap operas. I confiscated ruthlessly while subbing. And, I let the students draw if and when they finished assignments, because the arts budgets were zero. Bring drawing and painting classes back! Teens are so friggin' talented, it blows my mind. Sometimes they drew me special pieces: unicorns and Pokemon. My faves are a rose rendered in the ballpoint-pen prison style a girl's gangster dad taught her and some crazy dangerous ninja stars and weaponry a Vietnamese boy cranked out day after day. I made three binders of masterpieces and told students I had the collection, which made them proud. I called it the notes gallery. Students were into it. Then, Lisa cooked up the book idea and we separated and selected notes based on some tweaky categories—like "Lost Love & Breakups," "Weapons & Violence," "Sex," "Rock 'n' Roll," something like that. And then we passed piles of notes to favorite artists as inspiration. My notes-confiscating dwindled as I secured my own classes. I was getting better at teaching. But I miss those chaotic days when notes were flying. Spitballs NO, notes YES! Once you get some teaching skills, you can't tolerate the notes, it's a total waste of class time. So it represents for me a special window of time, an oblivion, a camaraderie with the kids. Like, hey, I'm cool too, I like notes. I'd rather write notes than sit up here and boss you around.

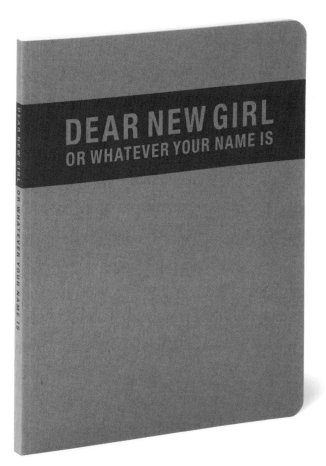

Opposite: Artwork by Kevin Christy.
Below: Artwork by Jason Holley.

ELI HOROWITZ: I had lots of *principles* on this project. Concepts. It wasn't an art book—it was an artifact. It didn't tell you what it was—it just *was*. This meant no borders, no captions, no title page, no introduction. Also, we didn't present it as a specific challenge for the artists, like "Here's the note, and here's what they did in response"—it was all mixed together, all on an even footing. I wanted people opening the book in a store to be not quite sure what they were looking at.

Some of the artists we worked with in this book became frequent collaborators later: Rachell Sumpter, Jacob Magraw-Mickelson, Leah Hayes, and Jason Holley among them. The Art Center in Pasadena, where Lisa teaches, has been a great pipeline for our illustrators—strong artists who also read, have a design sense, and are real hard workers.

LISA WAGNER: I remember the night I thought of doing this book—sending Dave some PDF fake-layouts with a sliver of an idea about doing a book on notes that would inspire drawings. He responded back so quickly and I remember thinking perhaps this was the right idea at the right time. McSweeney's is good for that kind of seizing.

I was itching to use the archive of notes that Trinie had collected/confiscated when she was a substitute teacher in L.A. I remember when she dropped off the whole collection to me, in colorful presentation binders. I was having lunch in Pasadena with a friend. She stayed and sat with us and drank some water while the notes leaned against my leg in a shopping bag. I remember that I almost forgot them.

I also talked with Jason Bitman at *Found* magazine; Jason Holley and I met with him in Silverlake for coffee to talk about dipping into their archive of notes. We ultimately landed back with the Trinie archive and felt really good about keeping the notes centric to one general place and feeling and working with Trinie again (we have done a few projects together) seemed so perfect. The idea of flying to Chicago and picking through bags and bags of *Found* notes was daunting. But Jason was very formidable and willing and spewing with creative thoughts. I kept imagining a big warehouse of mailbags filled with notes, dimly lit, white gloves, flashlights.

When Jason and I were driving up from L.A. to meet McSweeney's for our first meeting he was working on that third spread (Parima) in the book in the car. We stopped in Santa Cruz to see our friend Kim and to do some more xeroxes at Kinko's and to use their whiteout and make a fakebook of ideas with French folds, and to call Eli. I was harpying Jason to make more work while we drove up to San Francisco, and that Parima spread was entirely done in the car.

One night Eli, Trinie, Jason, and I drank beer and ate pizza and did a first edit. That seemed easy after all of our slavish ideas about how to edit this. Eli is a good editor. Deft for such a young 'un. Eli slept in our guesthouse and in the morning I saw him walking around our yard like a Moor poet. He is such a wunderkind, curious animal, snappy spitfire brain. Fun to work with him.

I remember climbing many stairs to top-floor studios in New York and Brooklyn to meet with artists. Jonathon Rosen's studio was on the Gowanus Canal and it was a hike I remember and maybe it smelled, it was August. I was pregnant and out of breath and had to find a cab. Leanne Shapton was in a Sixth Avenue walkup studio in New York. She told me about a suit she had made for herself while she was in Ireland and I remember thinking that was cool. And in L.A., driving around for studio visits and to drop off packets of notes to people. The Claytons cleaned their bathroom for me. Jacob and Joel dropped their artwork off at my studio in a little wooden box with latches. Mark Miller had a crisper full of candy in his fridge.

The cover was influenced by an old engineering book I found at the Rose Bowl swap meet in Pasadena. The print broker still has it. I like the rounded corners. I like how cryptic it is, like a secret you have to decode and the only way to do that is to study the notes and read and look back and forth through the book matching art with text and make connections.

Opposite and following pages: An assortment of spreads from Dear New Girl *by various artists. First row: Paper Rad, Christian & Rob Clayton, Paper Rad, and Joel Michael Smith. Second row: Leah Hayes, Jason Holley, and an anonymous student. Third row: Leanne Shapton, Jason Holley, Jason Holley, and an anonymous student. Fourth row: Alex Morano (student), Jason Holley, Martha Rich, and Marcel Dʒama. Page 174: Mark Allen Miller. Page 175: Paper Rad.*

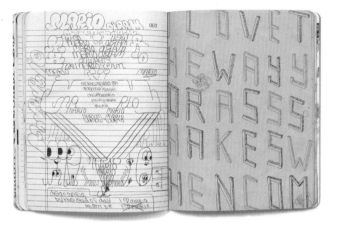

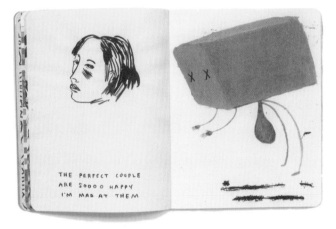

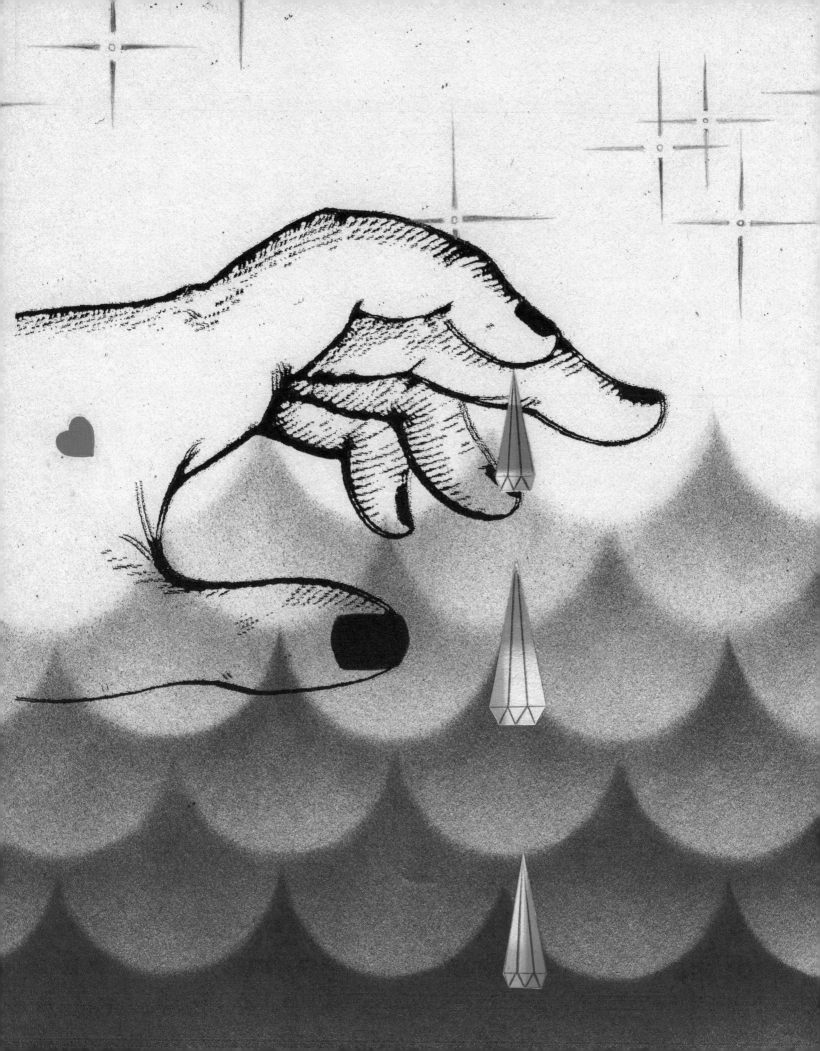

Baby Be of Use

by LISA BROWN (2005)

Above: The covers of the first four books in Lisa Brown's Baby Be of Use series.
Opposite: Preparatory sketches for Baby Fix My Car, *plus the two-page spread as it was published in the book.*

LISA BROWN: I got the idea for these books when the hard drive on my computer crashed and I was waiting for it to get fixed. I was bored, with all that waiting, and I was free associating about being bored, which led me to something like: "You know what's boring? A baby. For instance, having to read to the baby. If I have to say goodnight to the moon or pat that damn bunny one more time…"

But what did I want to look at instead? Cocktails, of course. Having just had a baby, I was ready for a drink. Thus was *Baby Mix Me a Drink* born. A book about a hangover breakfast was a logical next step.

The *Baby Fix My Car* book was an effort to cater to my son's obsessive love for vehicles. I knew nothing about the subject—I had to pick up a copy of *Auto Repair for Dummies* in order to give the book a whiff of authenticity. *Baby Do My Banking* was all Dave's idea. I don't mind going to the ATM, myself.

Some more books that are coming down the pipeline: *Baby Plan My Wedding* and *Baby Get Me Some Lovin'*. (Which I really wanted to call "Baby Get Me Laid," but some said that was far too skeezy. Jeez.) One happy result of writing these books is that my son, now 4½ years old, is well on his way to being a fairly decent little bartender. I am particularly proud of his work with the martini shaker.

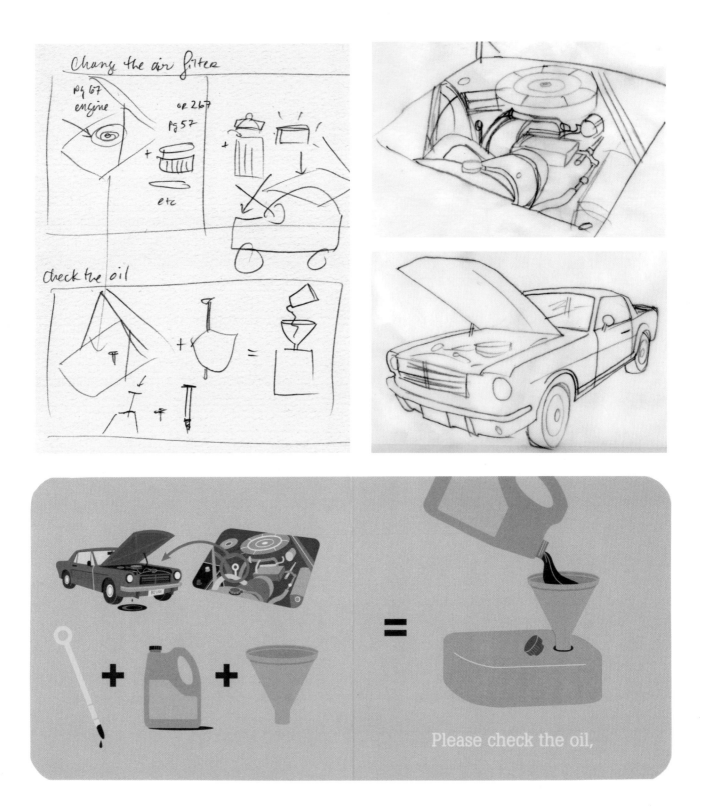

Please check the oil,

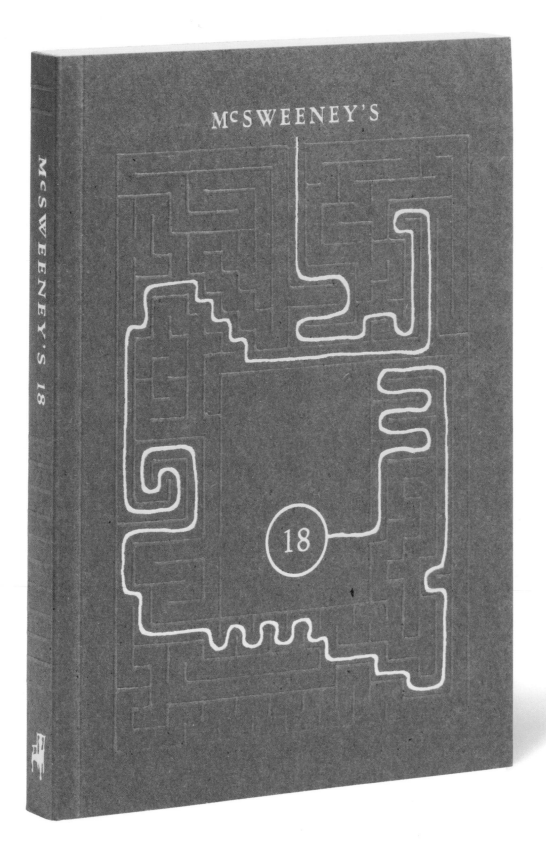

McSweeney's 18

(2006)

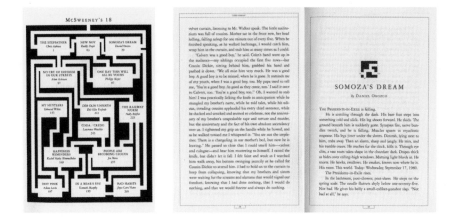

Issue 18's table of contents, and the first page of Daniel Orozco's "Somoza's Dream"; the maze-glyph above the title is attempting, in some small way, to indicate that the story can be pleasurably read before or after stories by Chris Adrian, Roddy Doyle, Nelly Reifler, or Philipp Meyer.

ELI HOROWITZ: I remember this issue had to be put together fairly quickly, and printed in North America, since Issue 17 had taken forever. The cover is kraft board. The beauty of this material is that it's always on hand, and it's cheap—it's a packing material.

CHRIS YING: I think some interns and I had to make sure that maze on the cover was solvable.

HEIDI MEREDITH: I remember seeing an image of the maze before the issue got printed, but you couldn't tell it was "raised," so when I saw it in real life I was really impressed. I am a huge fan of the movie *Labyrinth*, so maybe that has something to do with it.

ELI HOROWITZ: I think the cover maze might have been mostly a good vehicle for some of the production techniques I wanted to use—the emboss, the stamp. Jason Shiga drew the actual cover maze. He lives in the area and he loves mazes. I heard about him through Suzanne Kleid, an early intern, and I had also seen his neat comic-mazes somewhere.

We also printed the table of contents as a maze of sorts. And above each story, we printed details of the table-of-contents maze, suggesting connections between the stories in the volume. The interior maze was partly a way to extend the cover design into the issue. I did think carefully about where each story led. I guess I was interested in nonlinear paths through the issue. I've never read a collection of stories in order from front to back, so the cover was an attempt to suggest a variety of paths through the issue.

JOYCE CAROL OATES: I'd thought of the story "Bad Habits" as homage to younger generations of Americans eager to break free of the bad habits of their (parental, political) elders—it seemed an appropriate work of prose fiction for *McSweeney's,* which is a West Coast phenomenon of great interest in the East, especially in the New York City region—distant from the great plains, and from Washington, D.C.

RODDY DOYLE: Way back in the last century, somewhere between World War II and *Shakespeare in Love*, I was a school teacher. There was a knock on the classroom door one day. I went to the door and opened it. There was a small boy standing there. "I'm new," he said. I didn't use that line in "New Boy"—it wouldn't have fit—but it's the line that inspired the story, twenty years after I heard it.

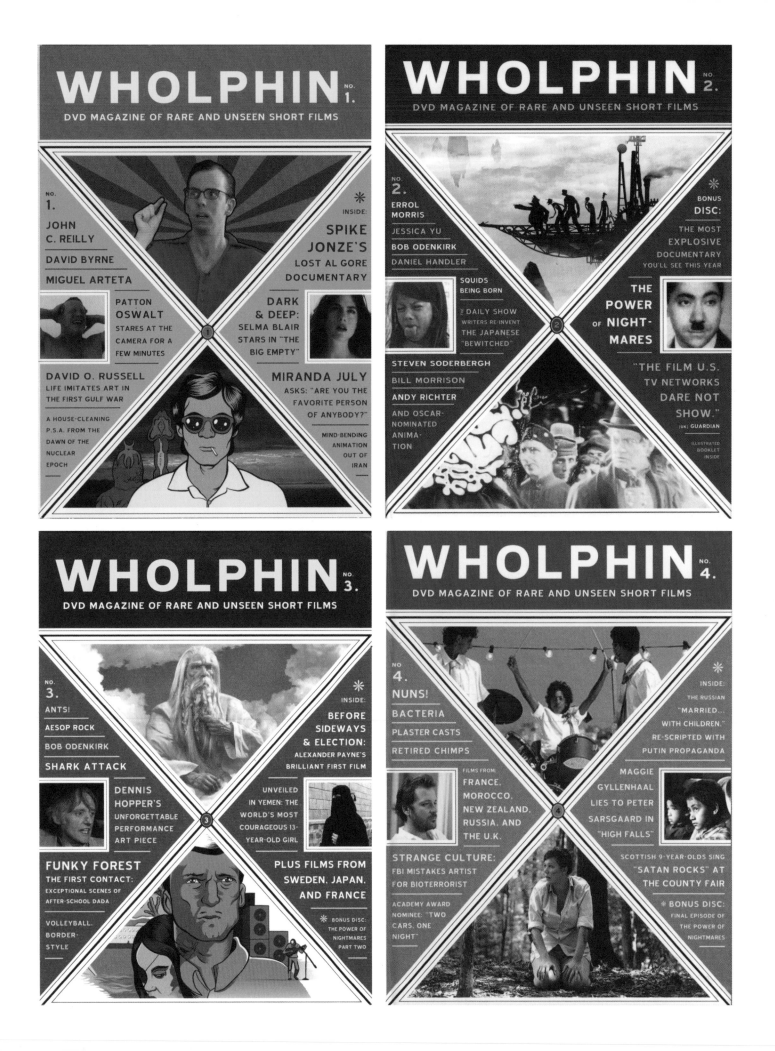

WHOLPHIN NO. 5.
DVD MAGAZINE OF RARE AND UNSEEN SHORT FILMS

NO. 5.

KUNG FU

DRUNK BEES

DRUMS AS TARGETS

GIANT PAPER AIRPLANES

"HOUSE HUNTING": STARRING PAUL RUDD & ZOOEY DESCHANEL

WORLD-RECORD-SETTING, ONE-HANDED, BLINDFOLDED RUBIK'S CUBE CHAMPS

TREE-HANGING: NO-FRILLS WORK-OUT, IMPROVES YOUR HEAD-LOCK

✳ INSIDE:

SPEND A DAY WITH THE SUDAN LIBERATION ARMY

U.S. GOV'T STEALING HORSES FROM SHOSHONE GRANNIES

ANIMATED FAKE ROCK STAR VS. HEROIN-ADDICTED CARNIVAL MONKEY

SPANISH SCI-FI: ALIENS HASSLE BOY, SPOIL ADOLES-CENCE

WHOLPHIN NO. 6.
DVD MAGAZINE OF RARE AND UNSEEN SHORT FILMS

NO. 6.

LIZARDS

JOHN CLEESE

LEE HARVEY OSWALD

GREAT WHITE SHARKS

RODDY DOYLE'S "NEW BOY": MAKING NICE ON THE FIRST DAY OF SCHOOL

SASQUATCH HUNTERS INTERDIMENSIONAL BIGFOOT APPEARS AT CONFERENCE

DANIEL HANDLER

COCKROACHES

INTOLERABLE GUY NEXT DOOR

✳ INSIDE:

RE-SCRIPTED SURREAL DATING WITH MICHAEL CERA

MINIATURE SEEING-EYE HORSE SEEKS SWEET KICKS FOR PROM

CHINESE THIRD GRADERS DABBLE IN AMERICAN-STYLE DEMOCRACY

SECRET TAPE IN THE EVENT OF PRESIDENTIAL ASSASSI-NATION

WHOLPHIN NO. 7.
DVD MAGAZINE OF RARE AND UNSEEN SHORT FILMS

NO. 7.

UFOs

BUBBLEWRAP

ROTOSCOPED ROLLERCOASTERS

FACE-OFF: AMERICAN GRAY SQUIRRELS VS. BRITISH RED SQUIRRELS

A HALLUCINOGENIC POST-KATRINA NEW ORLEANS MASTERPIECE

NACHO VIGALONDO

CARSON MELL

BUMPER CARS

✳ INSIDE:

WILLIAM BURROUGHS ADAPTED BY GUS VAN SANT

BRAND NEW SCENES FROM SIERRA LEONE'S REFUGEE ALL-STARS

✳ A BONUS DISC WITH:

A SCIENTIFIC EXPERIMENT IN RETROCAUSALITY

BE A PART OF THE VERY FIRST INTERACTIVE DVD STUDY

WHOLPHIN NO. 8.
DVD MAGAZINE OF RARE AND UNSEEN SHORT FILMS

NO. 8.

KIM JONG IL

CARLOS D. FROM INTERPOL

JAMES FRANCO

FILMS FROM SWEDEN, ENGLAND, N. KOREA, & SILVER LAKE

PATHOPHOBIA

MARIA BAMFORD

CREED BRATTON OF "THE OFFICE"

BUZZCOCKS

PATRICK MARBER

✳ INSIDE:

LAUREN GREENFIELD'S AWARD-WINNING DOCUMENTARY SHORT: KIDS + MONEY

SHORT TERM 12: "BEST SHORT" AT 2009 SUNDANCE FILM FESTIVAL

SAM TAYLOR-WOOD'S SHORT STORY ADAPTATION "LOVE YOU MORE"

AN ANIMATED DOCUMENTARY FOCUSED ON DISPLACED KIDS OF PERU

PIRATES OF DIOR

Wholphin

(2 0 0 5)

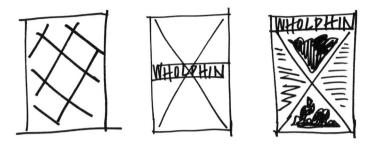

Three sketches by Dave Eggers for the "X" design of Wholphin's cover template.

DAVE EGGERS: *Wholphin* started as an idea back in 2003. I was working with Spike Jonze on *Where the Wild Things Are*, and one day he showed me his Al Gore documentary. I'd known about the film for a while; it had been commissioned by the Gore campaign as a way to humanize Gore. So Spike went down to Tennessee and spent a few days with Al and his family. The resulting movie revealed Al to be the guy who everyone who knows him knows: warm, funny, endearingly dorky, and loved by his family. In the movie, he even bodysurfs. When Spike showed me the movie, we both wondered aloud how this would ever get a wide audience, given it wasn't ever used—not really—by the Gore campaign.

So I talked to Spike about something like *Wholphin*, and really soon after that I started talking to Brent Hoff, who I'd known forever and knew film, TV, production, and screenwriting. Eventually all these conversations led to *Wholphin*, which included Spike's documentary, and a bunch of other great short films found and curated by Brent.

BRENT HOFF: I had just been to a film festival where by far the best films were these odd but perfectly crafted shorts. Dave asked me why, if there were all these amazing films out there, no one was successfully compiling and releasing them. I had no answer. We knew there had to be a reason why the idea wouldn't work, but since we couldn't think of one, we started crafting it up. First, we had to see if we could find enough films to fill a DVD. Then we had figure out how films smuggled out of Iran on PAL VCR tapes get transferred onto NTSC DVDs. Then Joe Garden from *The Onion* showed me a DVD of a guy singing "Stairway to Heaven" backwards. Then Dave filmed Patton Oswalt making faces for three minutes. Then a friend sent me a copy of the Turkish version of *The Jeffersons*. After that, all I had to do was choose a name that was impossible to pronounce, difficult to spell, and was completely meaningless to everyone but a few marine biologists in Hawaii. And by the way: Dave got to meet Al Gore.

DAVE EGGERS: I did get the chance to meet Gore a few years back, and when I mentioned that we'd put the documentary on *Wholphin*, he immediately said that had the American public seen it, he would have been elected. The film was that effective in telling people who he was and is. Think of the power of film! Think of what a different world we'd be living in had he been elected.

CARSON MELL: I was working in a studio in a basement under a Chinese restaurant when Brent Hoff called to tell me he wanted to put "The Writer" on the first issue of *Wholphin*. The night before, a tank of red sauce had leaked through their floor—my ceiling—onto a stack of a year's worth of drawings. And as I held them in my hands, the sound of bok choi–chopping knives filling my ears, the phone rang. Thanks to that phone call, I now work above ground.

EMILY DOE: At *Wholphin*, there hasn't been a single job I've done that I'm actually, technically, qualified to do. A few months after college, liberal-arts degree in hand, I found myself negotiating the terms of a contract with four of Steven Soderbergh's lawyers. I was producing short films like *Walleyball*, and when worse came to worst, performing in them, if you can call crying on camera performing. No one has broken my three-tears-in-twenty-five-seconds record. My mom is so proud.

BRENT HOFF: You can check out Emily's crying chops on *Wholphin* #2. I wanted to hold a crying competition as sort of a parting homage to reality television, because really what is most reality TV but a race to see who can cry first?

First time we tried it it was a miserable failure. Turned out that, unbeknownst to us, all the L.A. actors we cast were on a variety of antidepressants. They were as surprised as we were that the SSRI's so effectively prevented them from accessing their tear ducts, especially when, as they later revealed, they were thinking of things like their parents dying in horrible car crashes and things like that.

DAVE EGGERS: I designed the original packaging, thinking we wanted it to look very different from *McSweeney's*. That's why I went against my serif-only policy, and purposely tried to make it non-geometric, more modern and playful. But right after it was printed, I didn't like it. I thought it was amateurish. So I sat down to do a new template. And as with *The Believer*, I tried to think of an iconic and easy-to-maintain template. And after that it was kind of easy, maybe too easy, in that just as *The Believer* had been a nine-panel grid, and because *McSweeney's* was always given to a strict sort of geometry, I just started sketching other very simple designs. I just sat down and said, what form hasn't been used much?

And I knew we'd used every permutation of wheels and circles and rectangles, but we hadn't used triangles. So I just started drawing Xs on the page, and then got into Quark to see if it would work. And though it was tough on the images, it eventually did

work. And the design, I think, is durable, maintainable by anyone on staff, and is visible and recognizable across the room; these are always the goals of one of our cover templates.

CHRIS YING: I'm that staff member who updates the *Wholphin* cover template from issue to issue. Triangles aren't the ideal workspace for fitting text and images, but it's satisfying to finally settle on an adjective with the right number of letters for a given space. It's like a quarterly crossword puzzle.

If there are any real difficulties with the production of each issue, it's in procuring high-resolution images. Note to independent filmmakers: take more photos on your sets! Screen captures come out looking fuzzy and low-def. The triangular frames don't really make the image hunt any easier, either. There's a lot of space to fill at the widest parts of the triangles. To be honest, I've Photoshopped in more than my share of dirt, trees, and clouds.

BARB BERSCHE: Trying to sell the first issue of *Wholphin* was difficult and frustrating. Stores couldn't grasp the hybrid concept of a DVD magazine—was it a DVD, or was it a magazine? Where should it sit in the store—in the DVD section, or in the book section, or on the magazine rack?

One magazine buyer for a national chain was particularly bullish about the debut issue—he wanted to order 4,000 copies and place them in the magazine section in the front of the store. This felt fantastic! Oh, but he wanted to tear the covers off the copies that didn't sell, just like they do with all the normal magazines and periodicals.

We couldn't bear to let them destroy the unsold copies, so we were passed to their DVD buyer, who ordered 100 copies. I think that's when I gave up on trying to cold-sell the debut issue to new distributors. We opted instead to bundle *Wholphin* 1 with *McSweeney's* Issue 18 and also with a special "visual issue" of the *Believer*. And that was good. Stores began to order *Wholphin* as a DVD series after they became familiar with it through the bundling.

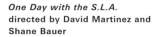

One Day with the S.L.A.
directed by David Martinez and Shane Bauer

About the film: A short documentary on the rebel movement in Darfur. After spending time candidly filming rebels in the Sudan Liberation Army, the directors smuggled themselves out of Sudan on a horse cart. (from *Wholphin* #5)

Cheeta
directed by *Wholphin*

About the film: The original star of *Tarzan* (Cheeta) has retired to Palm Springs where he spends his days painting and playing the piano. On his recent 75th birthday, he received a very special message from Jane Goodall, who sang him the birthday song in a hybrid English/chimpanzee. (from *Wholphin* #4)

Lucky
directed by Nash Edgerton

About the film: Australian actor/director/stuntman Nash Edgerton awakes to find himself tied up in the trunk of a car speeding down a dirt road. There is precious little time. (from *Wholphin* #6)

Site Specific_LAS VEGAS_05
directed by Olivo Barbieri

About the film: Olivo Barbieri's work explores the urban landscape and focuses on the ethereal sense of space. This film is an aerial study of Las Vegas and the surrounding desert landscape, including such landmarks as the Grand Canyon and Hoover Dam. (from *Wholphin* #4)

McSweeney's 19

(2 0 0 6)

JORDAN BASS: Dave, sometime in mid-'05, had gotten hold of some 18th-century pamphlets, one of them having something to do with witchcraft. That's how this started.

DAVE EGGERS: I go to antiquarian book fairs, and one day I went to one in San Francisco and bought an old abolitionist newsletter. It was beautiful, and it also told more, I think, about those times than almost any textbook could. There's something about a primary document that soaks you in a period or frame of mind better than something secondary or filtered. So I brought that pamphlet to Jordan and we started putting together a pile of strange old documents with the plan to reproduce them exactly.

ELI HOROWITZ: The ephemera came first. Then we had to figure out where to stick it all. That's where the cigar box came from.

The witchcraft pamphlet that inspired the issue.

DAVE EGGERS: I drove by this cigar shop one day, and they had a sign out front offering free cigar boxes. I took a bunch home, not really knowing what I would do with them. But about six months later we started collecting these pamphlets and postcards, and the cigar box seemed like the perfect place to put them. We wanted the issue to look like the sort of box someone who had lived through WWII would have kept under their bed. So then we asked Michael Kupperman to design the box. We were assigning everything to Kupperman at the time. He's capable of anything. He and Chris Ware are two guys you just know will take care of things.

MICHAEL KUPPERMAN: It was a great opportunity to experiment with patterning and military motifs.

DAVE EGGERS: By this point, we'd seen how Issue 4's box had aged. Not well. To this day, it's really hard to find even one copy of Issue 4 where the box isn't bent or torn. So with this cigar box, I kept obsessing about it being extremely sturdy. The whole idea with all of the *McSweeney's* packages is that they're sturdy and lasting—if the exterior is strong and worth owning and keeping, then the stories inside survive. So we paid extra for a very sturdy cigar box.

ELI HOROWITZ: The stuff in the box—the pamphlets and the letters and all—is all real. We just reprinted it. There wasn't even a temptation to make it fake.

JORDAN BASS: The idea was to put together an issue of all kinds of things—pamphlets, ledgers, letters, speeches, posters, pretty much anything with a compelling textual element, most of it political. EBay was great because you could look at a lot of things very quickly, and then, if you liked them, you could get the thing itself—you didn't have to wrangle them away from a librarian or an archivist, you just had to give some guy in Iowa $9. And having them on hand to scan and otherwise get a sense of was pretty much essential.

ELI HOROWITZ: I was against eBay.

JORDAN BASS: Eli thought I should have been going to antique stores instead. I disagreed with him, and did not go to any antique stores. He went to one,

Above: The cigar-box case for Issue 19, illustrated by Michael Kupperman.

Below: Among the ephemera included in the issue were a pocket guide to the Middle East (left) and an air-raid instruction card (center). The larger book (right) contained five short stories, with a cover adapted from a postcard Dave Eggers found on eBay.

A 1940s pamphlet on pre-war preparedness in the United Kingdom and a sales pitch for the U.S. Marines.

A series of letters concerning a man in jail for miscegenation.

A WWI-era pamphlet on soldiers' risk of gonorrhea.

A 1940 pamphlet decrying the trial of twelve Communist leaders in the United States.

and that's where the "Air Raid Instructions" card came from.

ELI HOROWITZ: I found the air raid instructions at the Alemany flea market, in San Francisco.

JORDAN BASS: Everything else, except for a couple of the government documents, came from eBay.

ELI HOROWITZ: Everything was printed by TWP in Singapore. We just tried to use as many different tweaks as possible, to give it that hodgepodge feel. Different papers, different tints. The storybook underneath everything else, the one object we invented ourselves so that the issue would have some fiction in there, was made to match the dimensions of the box. The idea was that one thing at the bottom would actually feel like it fit.

ANGELA PETRELLA: That makes it very hard to take the actual book out. You have to turn the box over and shake it, basically. At book fairs, no one can figure out how to do this.

ELI HOROWITZ: The stories themselves didn't come into play until pretty late in the process—initially, the issue was only going to be ephemera. As things started to take shape, though, we decided to do the book of quasi-historical fiction. The T. C. Boyle novella, which we already had on hand, sort of served as the anchor for that idea.

JORDAN BASS: The cover of the storybook also came from eBay; Dave had come across it and wanted to use it. Here's the email I got from him, under the subject "Urgent—eBay fun": "There's a postcard for sale from the McSweeney's castle in Ireland. I think we should buy the postcard and put it in the cigar box. Jordan, can you buy the card? It's for sale now, but

only for THREE MORE HOURS! So act fast. I think it'll make a nice addition. Go to McSweeney's on eBay." I paid four pounds ninety-nine pence for it.

SEAN CASEY: "The First Chapter" in Issue 19 was a distillation of my patriotism (2000–2006), and a first venture into "creative nonfiction." I had never done research for a piece of writing, let alone collected stool samples. One of my prized possessions is fruit of this research: a desiccated bowel movement Barbara Bush dropped behind the American Consulate in Port Au Prince, Haiti (1990). While the turd did not make it into "The First Chapter" or the cigar box, in its lines and creases I found an invaluable exposition of her slow son's compassion for the Third World. Email from Eli Horowitz, 5/22/05: "Sean: We've ruled out including a rubber replica of the Barbara turd in Issue 19. The price is prohibitive, and the sheer size of the monster would prevent our including anything else— literary fiction, say—in the box."

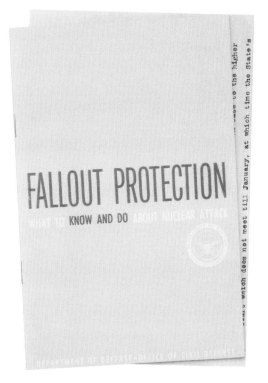

A WWII-era pamphlet, "Fallout Protection," detailing what to do in the event of a nuclear attack.

A photo from a Jewish summer camp in Winnipeg.

Next pages: Some of the material bought for good money on eBay that was ultimately not included in the issue. "Germany Invites you" was later deployed as an interstitial add-in in the McSweeney's Book of Lists.

CORNELL UNIVERSITY
DEPARTMENT OF AMERICAN HISTORY
CHARLES H. HULL

237 GOLDWIN SMITH HALL
ITHACA, NEW YORK

March 22, 1917

Professor J.N. Force, M.D.
Department of Hygeine,
University of California,
Berkeley, California.

My dear Professor Force.

      Your agreeable letter of the fifteenth of March
imputes to me an ingenuity of conjecture far exceeding anything
which I am capable of. Even if I were endeavoring to concoct
an old-fashioned detective story I should not have begun its a
plot which would land you in our Summer Session by a letter
from Dr. Anna Nivison about anything apparently so unrelated
as the original of the much repeated expression which Ezra
Cornell used at our opening exercises. How could anybody even
in a yarn or a play have conjectured that that was going to
make its way round through President Wheeler and Professor Burr
and come back to me through Miss Nivison? The very pleasing
correspondence which I had with her was not at any point marred
by the slightest suspicion in my mind of an ulterior motive.
I merely assumed that a friendly interest in her nephew such
as a lady of her evident animation would take had prompted her
to throw out a suggestion quite as much because she was pleased
with the prospect of possibly accomplishing something agreeable
both to you and to us as because she imagined it would actually
be accomplished. I wish there might have been some way to
accomplish it but under the circumstances there was not.

      My blunder about medical work was just the result
of writing off the top of my head and originated from a loose
inference that any M.D. must be a medical person, professionally
speaking. I really know better, and am much interested to
learn that the public health work in the University of California
is part of the work of the College of Arts.

      When you visit Ithaca I am promising myself the
pleasure of introducing you to my friend and former pupil (but
not, however, in public health or medicine) Dr. H.H. Crum who
is district health officer here and has had a varied and interesting and on the whole a useful experience as officer of the
local Board of Health for some years. Crum is a farmery person
of great confidence in his own judgment, but on the whole not
without some warrant for it in a sufficient portion of emergent

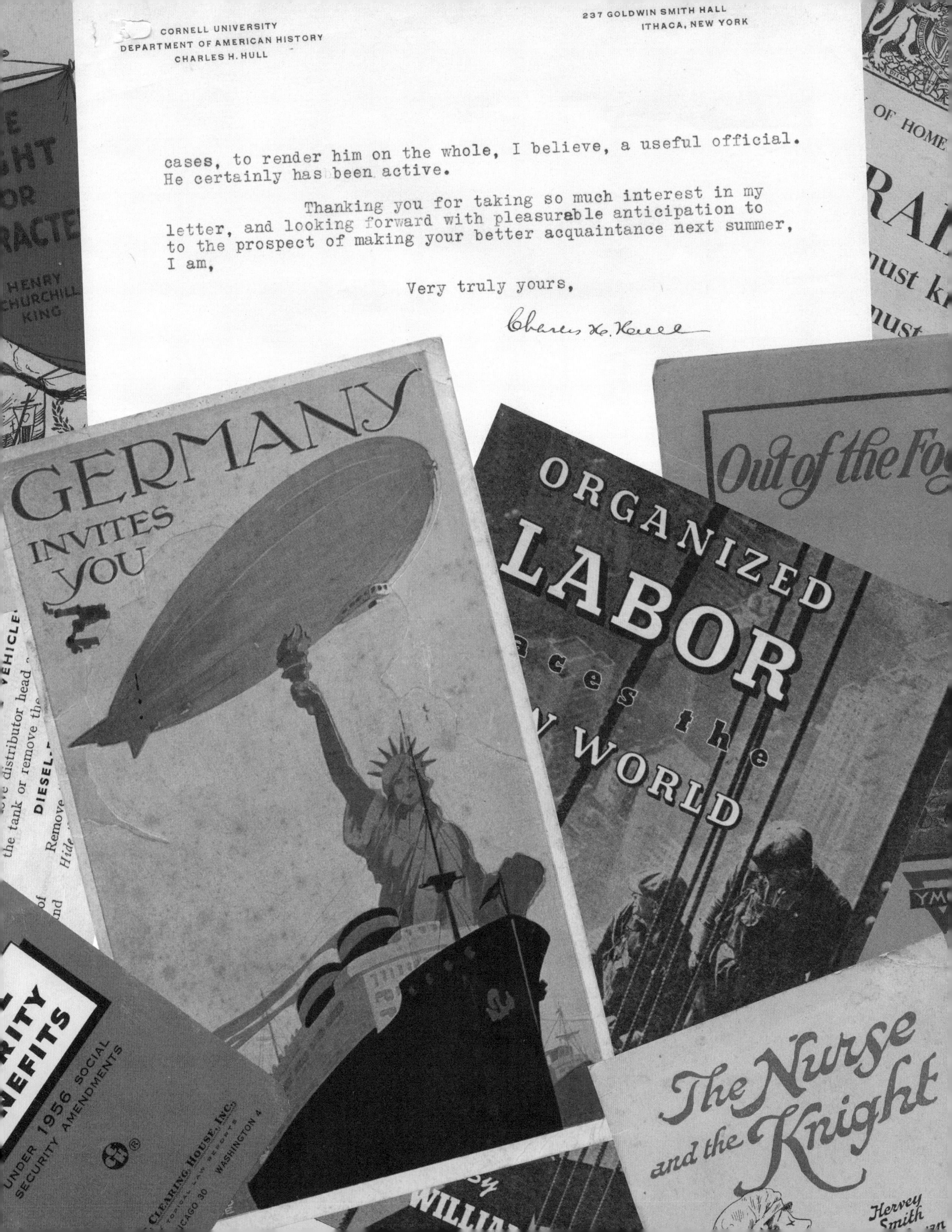

cases, to render him on the whole, I believe, a useful official.
He certainly has been active.

Thanking you for taking so much interest in my
letter, and looking forward with pleasurable anticipation to
to the prospect of making your better acquaintance next summer,
I am,

Very truly yours,

Charles H. Hull

GERMANY INVITES YOU

ORGANIZED LABOR faces the NEW WORLD

Out of the Fog

The Nurse and the Knight

1956 SOCIAL SECURITY AMENDMENTS

CHICAGO 30 — WASHINGTON 4

This page: Two photos by John Glassie from his book Bicycles Locked to Poles (2005). The book presents a hundred or so—ten percent—of Glassie's photos of the subject.

Opposite: Four pages from The Secret Language of Sleep: A Couple's Guide to the Thirty-Nine Positions by Evany Thomas, illustrated by Amelia Bauer (2006). Urban Outfitters agreed to carry this book on one condition: the title had to get shortened to The Secret Language of Sleep: A Couple's Guide. Thus, a retitled editon was made.

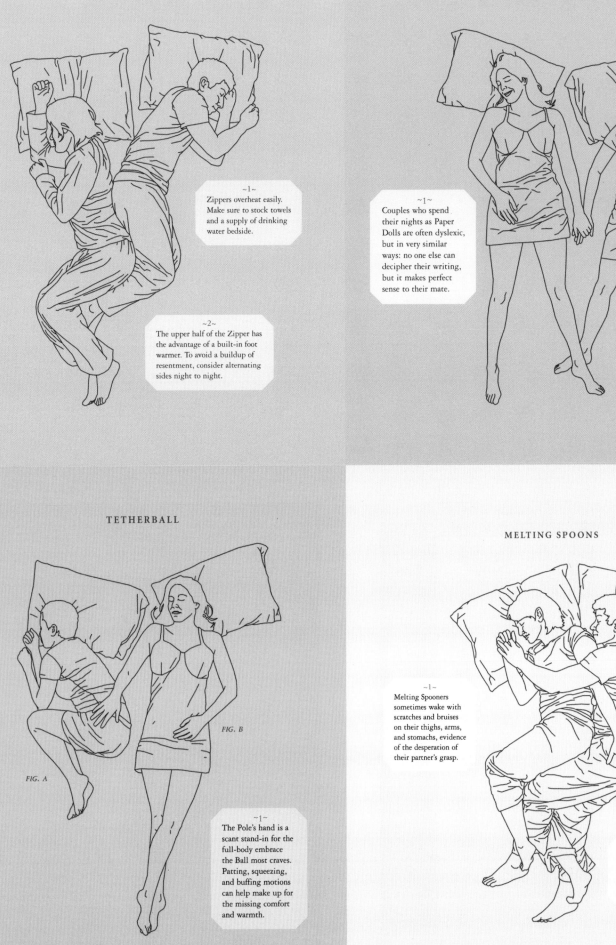

THE ZIPPER

~1~
Zippers overheat easily. Make sure to stock towels and a supply of drinking water bedside.

~2~
The upper half of the Zipper has the advantage of a built-in foot warmer. To avoid a buildup of resentment, consider alternating sides night to night.

PAPER DOLLS

~1~
Couples who spend their nights as Paper Dolls are often dyslexic, but in very similar ways: no one else can decipher their writing, but it makes perfect sense to their mate.

TETHERBALL

FIG. B

FIG. A

~1~
The Pole's hand is a scant stand-in for the full-body embrace the Ball most craves. Patting, squeezing, and buffing motions can help make up for the missing comfort and warmth.

MELTING SPOONS

~1~
Melting Spooners sometimes wake with scratches and bruises on their thighs, arms, and stomachs, evidence of the desperation of their partner's grasp.

~2~
A mark of over-intimacy: note the inner Spoon's toes, which are clothespinned onto both the outer Spoon's Achilles tendons.

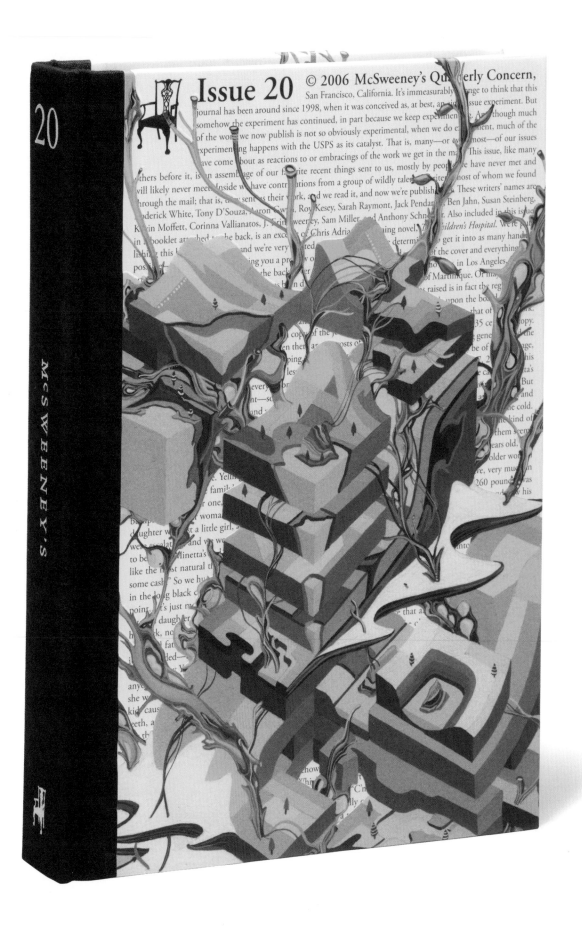

McSweeney's 20

(2 0 0 6)

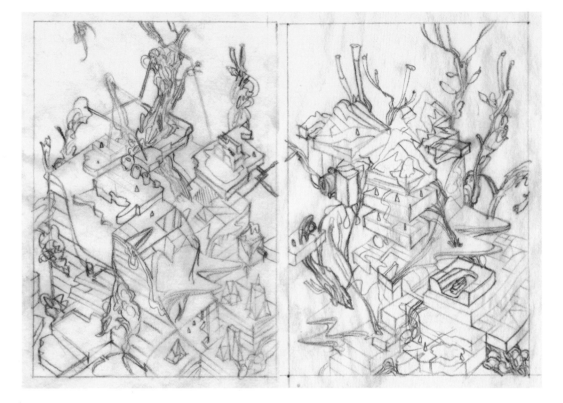

*Opposite and above: The front cover of Issue 20, with an illustration by Jacob Magraw-Mickelson
and text by Dave Eggers; two of Magraw-Mickelson's initial sketches.*

ELI HOROWITZ: After issues 17 and 19, which were both sort of chaotic, I wanted to do something simpler, sturdier, handsome, immediate—just a nice book.

JORDAN BASS: We wanted to include an image every four pages, a full-color, full-page painting, and before we even began to get the stories together Eli had been setting stuff aside for a while. It was quite a search.

ELI HOROWITZ: I felt like I was in way over my head, way too ignorant, so I just looked at as much as I could—books, Web sites, galleries, artists that other artists mentioned to me. I had a particular aesthetic in mind, but I never knew how to describe it. The two initial touchstones were Henri Rousseau and Chris Duncan, a painter out here in Oakland. Jacob Magraw-Mickelson, the cover artist, was a former student of Lisa Wagner, who had worked with us on *Dear New Girl*, and she had included him in there. His weirdo landscapes were exactly what I was looking for, I think, even though I never could have ever pictured anything like the stuff he did before I saw it.

JACOB MAGRAW-MICKELSON: Eli contacted me to say he'd seen a piece I'd done for a gallery and asked if I wanted it included in Issue 20. I said yes and forgot about it. Then he wrote and said that they still hadn't received the image file and actually it would be better if I did a cover, too. Oh, and that it should wrap around and maybe connect on the top and bottom. So I said yes and forgot all about it.

ELI HOROWITZ: The plan was that the vines and whatnot would wrap around on all four sides, not just

Issue 20

It's immeasurably strange to think that this journal has been around since 1998, when it was conceived as, at best, an eight-issue experiment. But somehow the experiment has continued, in part because we keep experimenting. And though much of the work we now publish is not so obviously experimental, when we do experiment, much of the experimenting happens with the USPS as its catalyst. That is, many—or even most—of our issues have come about as reactions to or embracings of the work we get in the mail. This issue, like many others before it, is an assemblage of our favorite recent things sent to us, mostly by people we have never met and will likely never meet. Inside we have contributions from a group of wildly talented writers, most of whom we found through the mail; that is, they sent us their work, and we read it, and now we're publishing it. These writers' names are Roderick White, Tony D'Souza, Aaron Gwyn, Roy Kesey, Sarah Raymont, Jack Pendarvis, Ben Jahn, Susan Steinberg, Kevin Moffett, Corinna Vallianatos, J. Erin Sweeney, Sam Miller, and Anthony Schneider. Also included in this issue, in a booklet attached to the back, is an excerpt of Chris Adrian's upcoming novel, *The Children's Hospital*. We're publishing this book in October, and we're very excited about it, and so we're determined to get it into as many hands as possible—so much that we're giving you a preview of it, with an approximated version of the cover and everything. The artwork on this front cover and on the back cover is by Jacob Magraw-Mickelson, who lives in Los Angeles, has lustrous medium-length brown hair, and was born during a thunderstorm on the island of Martinique. Or maybe Boston. The technique utilized on these cover is called debossing, wherein the area that seems raised is in fact the regular elevation, but the area on which this type occurs is depressed. That is, a heavy stamp descends upon the board—this type of board is called 3mm chipboard —and this stamp squashes all the areas that are now lower than that of the artwork. This debossing costs about 11 cents for each copy of the journal. The printing of the artwork costs 35 cents per copy. The cloth spine costs 15 cents per copy. Then there are the costs of the paper inside, and the printing generally, and the binding and wrapping and boxing and shipping. It's interesting to break up a fight. It's strange to be of a certain age, and to have never broken up a fight, much less a fight on 6th Avenue in New York City, on March 7, 2006. But this happened. The conflict unfolded, every second of it, before our eyes, as we were lost en route to a place called Minetta's Tavern, or Minetta Lane Restaurant—something like that. Good Italian food, dim lighting, odd-behaving waiters. But before we got there, we were lost, and were calling the other party, named Miguel, who would be met at Minetta's, and we saw a very nice family pass by—father, mother, daughter about five years old—all bunded heavily against the cold. The cold that dark night was the sort of cold that was debatable, something between forty and fifty-five, the kind of weather that brings out joggers in shorts and also families still wearing parkas. So this trio passed by, all of them seeming cheerful, heading home. Seconds later, they passed by a woman, thin, in a long dark coat, about sixty years old, tall. And all hell broke loose. Yelling. Barking. Pointing and arms waving wilding. Something about how the older woman had bumped into the family's young daughter and had not apologized. The father was livid, explosive, very much in the face of the other one, who seemed unable to form words. The man, who was about 5'6" and 260 pounds, was bumping the older woman, and pointing in her face, and screaming about how she needed to apologize, and how his daughter was just a little girl, and how the older woman was sick and awful and needed to be taught a lesson. Things were escalating, and we were closest to the conflict, and we were on the phone. We were on the phone with the party to be met at Minetta's and we said, "Hold on Miguel, I think I gotta break up a fight," and it was so strange—it seemed like the most natural thing, as if we were saying, as we had a few minutes earlier, "I gotta go into the ATM and get some cash." So we hung up on Miguel and we stepped in. We stepped right in between the man and the older woman in the long black coat. And we thought the man was taking things far too far. We said, "Hey, okay, you made your point, let's just move on." And the man repeated his claims, now directed to us, about how the woman had bumped into his daughter and had not apologized. And we said, "Well, fine, she bumped into your daughter and you bumped her back, now let's all calm down, move on, it's over." We said something like that and it almost seemed to calm the red-faced father, and things were almost diffused, until everything changed. The older woman, with whom we had initially sided—because first of all, she might have not even known she had bumped the child and more importantly, this was New York, stuffed silly with people everywhere, where people, including children, are jostled at all hours by anyone and everyone—started screaming. The woman was screaming utter terrifying madness. "You got knocked up!" she wailed, in the voice of a melting witch. Oh god it was a wretched voice! And then: "It's your problem! She's your kid 'cause you got knocked up!" On and on like this. It was then we turned and got a good look at her. She had no teeth, and her scarf was made of burlap. There was something broken in her eyes, her lipstick had been applied with her thumbs, and she was clearly altogether batshit crazy. And what she was saying had now enflamed the mother of the bumped child, and the mother was now hitting the old batshit woman, over our shoulder, and landing her gloved hand right in the old woman's big toothless mouth. Meanwhile, over our other shoulder, the melting batshit witch was hitting the father with her purse, big and square and ringing with the weight of coins and knicknacks. And we were there in the middle of it all! Nuts! But we still somehow felt like we belonged there, in between the angry and the mad, and that we were still able to solve this problem. Which we did, sort of, by now appealing to the less-insane of the two warring parties, the family of three. "She's not worth it," we said. "C'mon. Look at her." And after the man and woman protested a few more times about the lack of an apology, it finally occurred to them that they weren't dealing with a reasonable person who wouldn't acknowledge a mistake, but a twisted person, quite ill, whose crazy switch had been flicked. So when the family finally moved on, turned and walked up 6th Avenue, the old woman in the coat and burlap scarf continued screaming, "You got knocked up! She's your kid!" until the family was two blocks away. And then we went to get some dinner with Miguel.

east/west, but also north/south—something I don't think I'd ever really seen before. But it got really complicated, partly because of how the casewrap folds and partly because of bleeds and partly—I don't know. It was complicated.

JORDAN BASS: The cover references the typical wordy copyright page, but with the pure joy/fury of art/nature busting through and running wild. I remember talking to Eli one day about how to approach it, and suggesting that I'd always liked *A Humument*, the artist book by Tom Phillips, the one he made by painting over every page of a novel he picked up from a discount bin, and how it felt a little akin to the image/text mixture Eli had engineered. It felt like a similar impulse, putting all this art within the stories. Dave wrote the text that went under the image, which I think was the last time he did a copyright page. And you can't even read it.

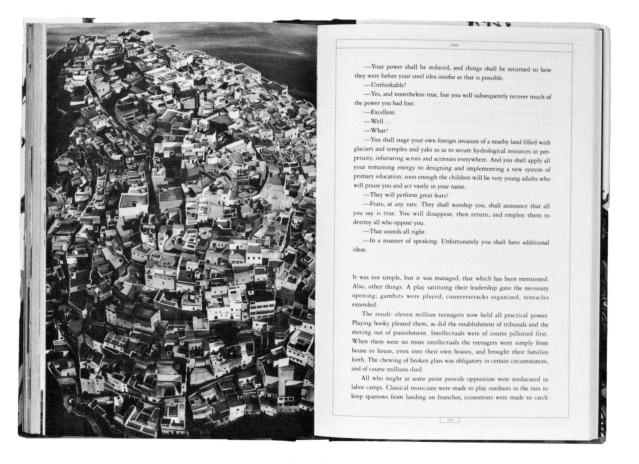

Above: Pages 128 and 129, with a painting by Jodie Mohr.
Opposite: Page 96, a painting by Kevin Christy.

KEVIN MOFFETT: Five paintings are interspersed throughout my story and, when I would read this story aloud to people while promoting the story collection in which it appeared, I would read from Issue 20 instead of the story collection because of the fourth picture, a painting of a man in gray camouflage holding up a silvery fish. The man, I think, has no right arm, or the fish has obscured it. He is surrounded by pink roses, he smiles grudgingly. There's something profoundly comforting about him.

JACK PENDARVIS: I remember Eli Horowitz was more protective of my main character than I was. In the original draft, I had a whole page listing the character's problems with each and every part of his body. Eli felt I was "piling on" and "creating a monster." I didn't have the heart to tell them that the list was almost one hundred percent true and gathered from my own physiognomy. But I incorporated nearly all of Eli's edits (including the deletion of the list of ailments) in the version of the story published in my second collection, though I had previously considered it "finished" and had even turned it in with a smug smile on my face. Like, "That's that!" Like, "Can't improve on perfection!" Much later I discovered by chance that F. Scott Fitzgerald had written up a list of his own physical problems (a small sample: "Alcoholism, Infected Nose, Insomnia, Ruined Nerves, Chronic Cough, Aching Teeth, Shortness of Breath, Falling Hair, Cramps In Feet…") that was much better than mine. So I was thankful to Eli for saving me from seeming to imitate Fitzgerald in the poorest way imaginable. Still later, I met Eli. He seemed extremely young and healthy, and I understood at once his optimistic attitude about the human body. I ate a burrito in front of him and let it tumble and slop all over me, so that he undoubtedly had his own revelation: that I was indeed the pitiful character he had championed.

Next spread:
The panoramic 360-degree wraparound
cover of Issue 21, a paperback edition
which is not described in this book.

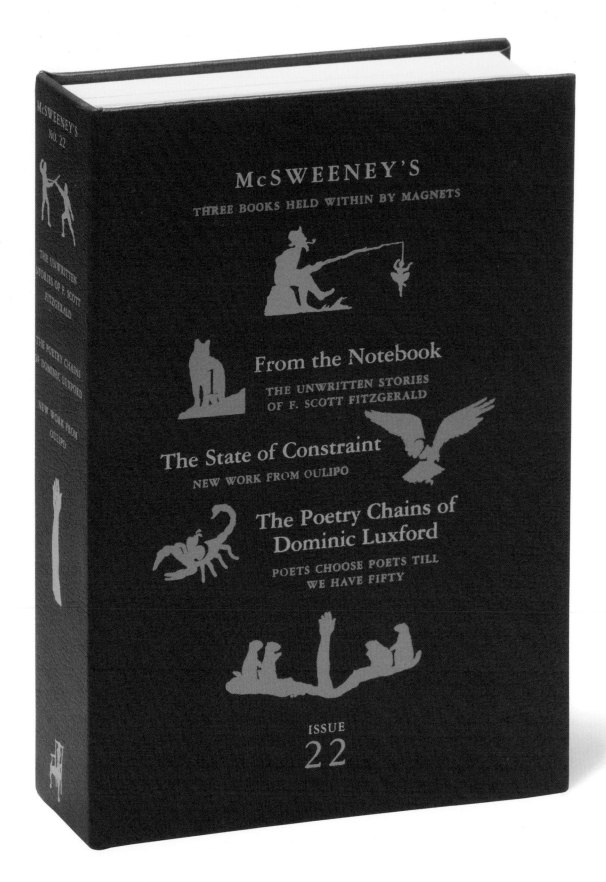

McSWEENEY'S

THREE BOOKS HELD WITHIN BY MAGNETS

From the Notebook
THE UNWRITTEN STORIES
OF F. SCOTT FITZGERALD

The State of Constraint
NEW WORK FROM OULIPO

The Poetry Chains of
Dominic Luxford
POETS CHOOSE POETS TILL
WE HAVE FIFTY

ISSUE
22

McSweeney's 22

(2 0 0 7)

Opposite and above: The magnetic outer shell and the three booklets of Issue 22, designed by Dave Eggers.

DAVE EGGERS: I forget where the idea came from, but it had been gestating for a while. It probably had its source with Elizabeth Kairys.

ELI HOROWITZ: Elizabeth showed Dave and me a double-CD set—it might have been *A String Cheese Incident-Live!* Or maybe Phish. The case was kept shut by a nice little magnetic strip. Nothing so wild, but satisfying. This was 2003, I think. So for the next three years magnets were in the backs of our minds. I had a dummy book made in 2004—pretty different from the ultimate design—but we never quite had a reason, a magnetic need.

DAVE EGGERS: It seemed interesting in theory. We had no idea how hard it would be to make effective, and how heavy it would be.

ELI HOROWITZ: The finished issue was really heavy—due to the large hunks of metal, I guess—which made shipping bills enormous. We didn't consider that before we went to press.

HEIDI MEREDITH: Shipping it out to international subscribers really ate up some money. It costs $4.25 per pound—rounded up to the nearest pound—to ship overseas from our warehouse. We had to pay the three-pound rate, even though the issue is just seven-tenths of an ounce over two pounds.

JORDAN BASS: Eli has a good story about the meeting with our distributor where the issue was presented. After Eli explained how the books would snap into the case, a cranky old sales guy said something like, "You should put the magnets in the other way around, so when you open the thing the books hit you in the face." It was maybe also at that meeting that someone raised the worry that this issue, with its magnet, would wipe out credit-card paraphernalia and anti-theft devices in bookstores across the nation, leading to the demise of all brick-and-mortar book sales and the collapse of the industry.

DAVE EGGERS: The final cover design wasn't what I had in mind. I had been fiddling with other designs, and they didn't look so great, and I did the silhouettes at the last minute. I really don't love how they turned out. I feel like I mucked up the cover on what was a great issue from a content and engineering perspective. I feel terrible about that.

JORDAN BASS: I really like the Oulipo section in 22. Oulipo's been around since the 1960s—the basic idea, as I understand it, is that interesting writing can come out of imposing rules and constraints on the writer.

ELI HOROWITZ: The Oulipo section was inspired by a visit from Paul Fournel, their current president. I don't know how it happened that he came to our office. It was a Sunday, and I was on a paddleboat in Golden Gate Park, and I got a call from Dave saying this guy was stopping by at 4:00, could I make it in? So I paddled back to shore.

DAVE EGGERS: Paul Fournel got in touch with us from Paris, and then visited San Francisco and came to the office. I think he was pretty shocked to see we were operating out of a one-bedroom apartment attached to a tutoring center. We didn't have anywhere for him to sit. That was, I think, when we realized there wasn't a place for a guest to sit.

JORDAN BASS: I tried to make almost everything in the Oulipo book break midway and continue on a later page, as the Paul Fournel story does, but no one liked that idea. They didn't like it when I did it in Issue 26, either, with Uzodinma Iweala and Ismet Prcic's pieces, but that time I did it anyway.

DAVE EGGERS: The Oulipo booklet juxtaposed nicely with another semi-freelance project we had going on. Michelle Orange had pitched the idea of finishing a bunch of story ideas F. Scott Fitzgerald had jotted down in a notebook. She said she'd curate the whole thing, and there's nothing better than knowing a smart person will be doing your job for an issue.

MICHELLE ORANGE: I was having drinks with two writers after seeing *Kill Bill 2* in the early spring of 2004. We were all new acquaintances, when one of them turned to me and said, "And what are you working on?" I forewent the truth ("my second g&t") and told them about turning my F. Scott Fizgerald daydreams into a story collection. I was carrying "The Crack-Up" around with me in those days and pulled it out of my bag, mage-style. The writers got very excited. I asked if they would contribute to a collection and they swore—they swore, reader—that they would.

JORDAN BASS: One of the nice things about the Fitzgerald book is that no one really attempted to write like F. Scott Fitzgerald—they took the ideas on their own terms, instead of trying to complete them on his behalf.

MICHELLE ORANGE: As the deadline for the F. Scott Fitzgerald section loomed, I had a couple crack-ups. One writer broke an elbow, another got chronic fatigue, some pieces came in thousands of words too long, two writers took on the same idea.

DAVE EGGERS: This issue was, aside from a page or two in Issues 3 and 6, the first time we published poetry. Early on, in an effort to differentiate the journal from other journals, we made a swap: instead of publishing poetry, we decided we'd publish interviews with scientists. So that was the tradeoff, and I think it gave readers something unexpected amid the fiction and experiments. But friends were always bugging us to run poetry. There was actually a time, when we were located in Brooklyn, when a woman jumped out from behind a tree and yelled at me about not running poetry. I was walking down Seventh Avenue and she was actually hiding behind the tree waiting for me, so she could advocate for our publishing poetry. That's an absolutely true story. But we didn't want to just step on the toes of other journals. It wasn't until Dominic came along that there was an idea to publish poetry in a way that felt right.

DOMINIC LUXFORD: My first proposal was a hodge-podge of various elements, including a collaboration between poets and visual artists, a booklet containing a colloquium on poetry, a CD of the poets reading

McSWEENEY'S
NO. 22

THE UNWRITTEN
STORIES OF F. SCOTT
FITZGERALD

THE POETRY CHAINS
OF DOMINIC LUXFORD

NEW WORK FROM
OULIPO

McSWEENEY'S 22   3 BOOKS & MAGNETS

An earlier version of the cover, which fell victim to the inefficiencies of foil-stamping technology.

their works, and a reader haiku contest. In retrospect, I realize it would have cost tens of thousands of dollars and taken several years to pull off. Eli politely suggested other, more manageable, avenues of approach, the dialogue continued, and somewhere along the way the idea for poetry chains was born.

Here's how the chains worked: we invited ten poets to contribute poems. And then each of those poets invited another poet to submit poems. And it went on like that, until we had fifty poets involved.

MICHAEL BURKARD: I was surprised and flattered that Denis Johnson chose me to participate; I had a hard time deciding on who to ask next. Because of my love of Gogol's stories, I was pleased that the recent poem I had written then—as if there were a way of sensing what unwritten stories Gogol might have wondered about—was accepted.

THOMAS KANE: I think that perhaps the most lasting memory generated from my participation in Issue 22 came through a handing down of the volume. I'd had an ongoing information exchange with this olympic-ally foul-mouthed Russian icon painter who walked his dogs in the alley behind my apartment in Pittsburgh. More than anyone in town, he was insistent on my adhering to a rigorous writing schedule (almost all of our conversations began with him asking if I had written yet that day), and I gave him a copy of the issue as proof of my commitment to the poetry cause. I ran into him before I left town, and he assured me that the poems sat on a shelf with his "cherished" literature. He admitted not being able to fully internalize all of the work, but wanted me to know that he still found an intrinsic value in the project. It was such a hopeful response, a validation that this idea of the chain could continue on into infinity.

What Is the What

by DAVE EGGERS

(2006)

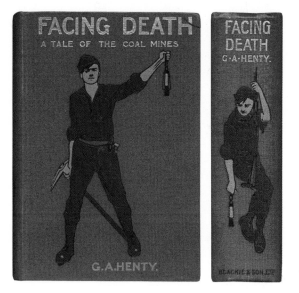

Illustrations on the cover and spine of an adventure novel published in 1895.
The artwork is printed directly on the cover. There is no dustjacket.

DAVE EGGERS: Here I wanted to revive some of the illustration styles that were used anywhere from the turn of the century to the fifties—with the illustration printed not on a jacket, but directly on the cloth or faux-cloth. These are the main sorts of older books I collect, so I'd been thinking of using something like that technique for this book. We called Rachell pretty early on—maybe six months before press (which is a long time where we come from). I knew it would be complicated.

RACHELL SUMPTER: Eli called and asked if I could come down to the office. He didn't give any details other than that there was a project going on that he thought I might like to be involved in. When I got there Dave talked with me about this book he was in the process of writing.

DAVE EGGERS: I tend to come up with the cover of a book somewhere in the middle of working on it. In this case, years before I finished the book, I had the idea of just having Valentino's face on the cover. The main thing I thought was crucial, because the book was being told in first person, was that the reader have Valentino's face in their mind—a face to connect the voice with. Without his face, there was a danger, because I was writing it in first person, that a reader would be thinking of me and my voice.

RACHELL SUMPTER: The challenge was how to pull something cover-worthy out of a manifold epic. Something singular, and iconic, without becoming too specific. I'd send Dave a sketch, he'd tweak it a little and send it back.

DAVE EGGERS: Rachell did a bunch of sketches from photos I'd sent her—pictures of Valentino, and some of his friends and family, whom we'd met in Sudan in 2003. In the end, because the book was called a novel, she didn't try to do an exact likeness of Valentino. He

Left: Some signs from Southern Sudan that influenced the type style and colors of the cover of What Is the What.
Right: Early cover sketches by Dave Eggers.

wasn't sure he wanted to be recognized everywhere on the street, so she altered it so it wasn't Valentino.

ELI HOROWITZ: The printer we used for this one, because we needed it in a hurry, was in Canada, and they'd never done a book like this. It was a pretty expensive job, because of the size and the materials. We got them back from the printer, and they looked fine, but the blue stamp was spotty and smudged. Turns out that blue inks take longer to dry, or something, and this was a rush-job, so the books had to be shipped as soon as they got off press and so the foil

would get rubbed before it was sealed. Or something. In any case, we weren't thrilled with the beige leatherette, so we tried something else for the next edition.

DAVE EGGERS: As far as I was concerned, it was a good problem to have, because it gave us a chance to play with a different color scheme on the second printing. I played with the Photoshop file for a while, and Rachell and Eli did, and finally we decided on the orange background, partly because it reminded me of a sign I'd seen in Sudan, dominated by that same orange.

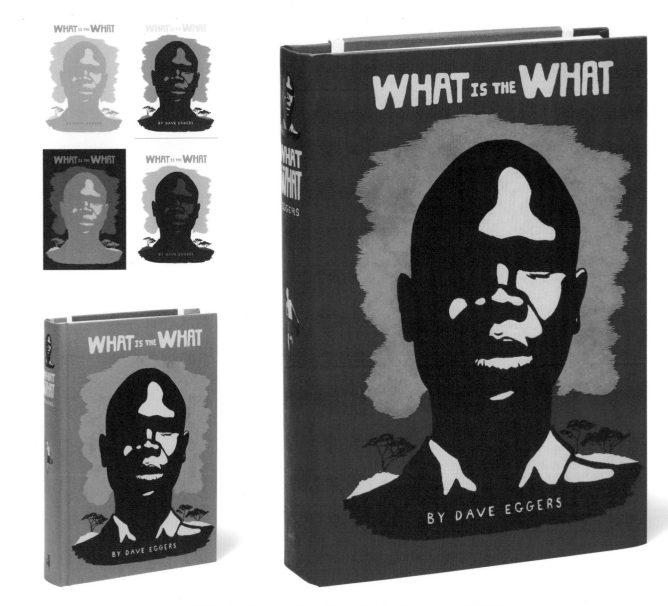

Upper left: Four of countless unused color combinations sketched out by the cover artist, Rachell Sumpter.
Also: Pictures of the orange-colored second-edition hardcover and red-colored third edition.

ELI HOROWITZ: The orange faux-cloth—actually a paper called Rainbow—was a better deal than the leatherette, and I think it looked nicer too, but the foil still didn't hold well. We probably never should have stamped this art in the first place. Printing or silkscreen would have looked as good, and would have been much more affordable. We were pursuing a certain bygone aesthetic, but bygones are bygones, I guess.

DAVE EGGERS: It's been strange, because every book Valentino and I sign looks so damaged, as if it's been attacked by generations of mice. The readers don't seem to mind, but I'm always apologizing for the toll even one read seems to take on the covers.

ELI HOROWITZ: For the third printing, we went with red just because we could—Dave was getting tired of seeing the orange one, so I tried a deep red. That was for the last 10,000 copies or so. Ohio State had assigned the book to their entire incoming freshman class, so the red worked out pretty well. Most of that print run actually went to the Buckeyes.

McSweeney's 23

(2007)

One of a few drawings by jacket artist Andrea Dezsö that didn't quite fit anywhere in the issue.

ELI HOROWITZ: We first knew Andrea Dezsö as a writer, when she contributed a story to Issue 12—her first published English-language fiction. It turned out she was also an incredible artist and bookmaker.

ANDREA DEZSÖ: Eli asked if I'd like to make some art for the upcoming issue—the one going to press in three weeks. The project started out small but kept growing. I ended up making front and back covers for all ten stories in the volume—as if each story were its own little book—plus the jacket. I used drawing, painting, paper cutouts, shadow puppets, and embroidery. I did everything by hand— it felt like I worked every minute of every day for nearly a month. I slept two or three hours a night, calling Eli at the wee hours or on weekends. Amazingly, he always picked up the phone. Afterward, one of my tech-savvy undergraduate students asked me, "What kind of program did you use to make this?" pointing at the repeating lattice pattern. I explained that I drew it by hand. "So you used a digital tablet," she said, nodding. "No," I answered, "I used a pencil and paper." She looked confused. "Was it the drawing tool in Photoshop or a third party plug-in?" she asked. "I made it like this," I said, grabbing pencil and paper, demonstrating the process of drawing. "Oh," she said after a little while. "I didn't know people still do that."

DAVE EGGERS: The poster on the flip-side of the fold-out dust jacket was something I think I'd been trying to do for years. I had done a bunch of sketches, trying to extend the radial design of Issue 3's cover to its logical conclusion. It was only when Brian McMullen got roped into the project that it started to come together. I sent him the stories, and a sketch of how I saw the poster in my mind. I knew it would require a more powerful computer than I have, and I didn't know how to curve the type. On Issue 3, I had done it all by hand, tilting each letter in Quark.

BRIAN MCMULLEN: Dave emailed me a 120-page Quark document containing about forty-five short-short stories and said, "Let's turn this into a poster, with drawings." The stories ranged in length from a few sentences to a few hundred words. Turning it all into a poster was pretty fun work until about two-thirds of the way through, when it became a technical nightmare. The layout software started to crash every hour or so under the weight of all the layers and all the curved text. It got to the point where, when I made a change, I could count to five before the

Above: Some of Andrea Dezsö's colored-pencil sketches for an unrealized full-color jacket framework. The complete sketch has been lost.
Below: The Technicolor-Dreamcoatless cover of Issue 23; front and back "covers" for Deb Olin Unferth's story, featuring honest-to-god embroidery by Andrea Dezsö.

Below: Eli Horowitz asked Andrea Dezsö to complete this 27"-square jacket in three days, but it ended up taking a little longer.
Opposite: An actual-size detail from one of Andrea Dezsö's sketches for the jacket.

change showed up on the screen. Totally ridiculous. Meanwhile, Eli's impractical deadline loomed.

ELI HOROWITZ: The original idea was to package and distribute the poster as its own stand-alone thing but not long before Brian finished, it all changed. We decided that the poster would be the "B-side" of the dustjacket, which was about to go to press. Hence the big hurry.

BRIAN MCMULLEN: We shrunk the poster from a 37-inch square to a 27-inch square to make it fit the jacket. So the dense structure got even denser, and then it got buried—like treasure, or a map to buried treasure—where only a very curious reader would find it. When it was done I hoped people would see it and enjoy it, but mostly I was relieved.

JORDAN BASS: We got an email later on saying "I don't know which I enjoyed more: discovering the underside of the dust jacket on Issue 23 or the astonished look on the face of the girl that worked at the bookstore as I unfolded it." That seemed like the perfect reception to me.

WELLS TOWER: My story "Retreat" was a feat of literary midwifery on the part of Eli, whom I kept trying to convince that it would be impossible for me to write the thing. But he kept clamoring at me with all sorts of editorial forceps and dilators, and after much sweat and grunting, together we sprung the tale.

CAREN BEILIN: I think one thing a writer wants is to be out of her league, to be with writers who are astounding to be included with. I was very excited to be in the same issue with everyone, particularly Deb Olin Unferth, who I think is the best.

DEB OLIN UNFERTH: You have this image in your mind of who you could be and it's just sad because you could be lovely but look at you, you're a mess. You work so hard and most of the time the effect is Sisyphean (who cares, this is dumb, you are a fuckup). Then here comes Issue 23 in the mail. You open it and it's this incredible mosaic of stories and pictures, and hardback, mind you. It's elegant and celebratory and full of moving stories,

and all your favorite people are huddled in there with you (Clancy Martin, Caren Beilin...).

CAREN BEILIN: I was really amazed to be included. April Wilder's story (the meat, the tooth) blew me away. I just used Chris Bachelder's story about the masturbating son on the first day of my Intro to Fiction class.

SHAWN VESTAL: One day in 2006, I got an email from Jordan saying that the editors had liked a story of mine. Was it still available? Yes. Ultimately, that story didn't make it into *McSweeney's*. But, in a rejection note written just for me, Jordan encouraged me to send something else. I did so, 17 seconds later. He wrote back in November 2006 to accept it—the email, still saved, starts, "Shawn, so I think we're sold on..." I got the message in the newsroom where I work as a reporter. I jumped up and did a little fist-pumpy dance that should have been profoundly embarrassing but was not. I was forty years old. I had been writing short stories for twenty years. When the issue came out—complete with amazing artwork and one astonishing story after another and my name actually in there, and the story actually in there, right between Roddy Doyle and Ann freakin Beattie!—it displaced the personal rejection and the initial acceptance of the story as the highlight of my life as a writer. I've had other stories published since then, and it's always a thrill. But the publication of that first one remains a singular experience.

JORDAN BASS: I try not ever to lose sight of the fact that getting published here or in any journal is a big deal. And the act of sending one's work out there to strangers is a big deal. We try to make sure people know that just as they're laboring alone hoping to connect with someone, we're also laboring, semi-alone, very happy to be connected with.

Opposite: Outtake drawings from Andrea Dezsö, provided by the artist at the last second, in case any holes needed to be plugged. (Thankfully, but also sadly, there were no holes.)

Two views of an unfolded Issue 24, with panoramic cover and endpaper art by Rachell Sumpter.
The two-part issue includes two front covers and two spines—twice the number of front covers and spines found on normal books.

McSweeney's 24

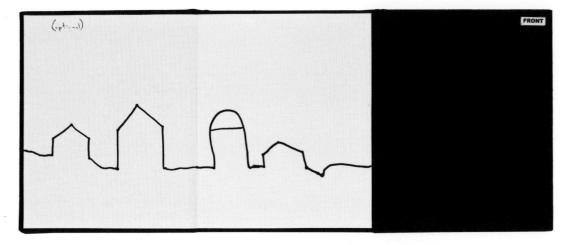

An early, vaguely phallic sketch of the cover concept by Eli Horowitz on a printer's dummy.

ELI HOROWITZ: Jordan mentioned a Z-shaped binding at one idea meeting, and then Dave lit up.

DAVE EGGERS: I'd been wanting to do an S-shaped binding for as long as I can remember. I guess it's very similar to a Z-shaped binding.

RACHELL SUMPTER: There was a phone call, followed by some riddled talk of a Z-binding. I tried to to visualize it, both covers unfolding, covers connect, interiors connect to covers, covers to interiors.

ELI HOROWITZ: None of us had ever seen something like that—but I guess TWP, our printer in Singapore, had, because I just described it to them over the phone and when the very first dummy book arrived it was perfect. Usually those first dummies are not perfect.

DAVE EGGERS: Sometimes we come up with a concept and then, sometime later, try to marry it to some content that's in the works. At the time the Z-shaped binding was in the works, we got a proposal from Justin Taylor, a graduate student whom we'd never met, to do a symposium on Donald Barthelme. We're all sort of obsessive Barthelme fans, so we just said

"Sure, you've got a hundred pages to work with. Let us know when it's done."

JUSTIN TAYLOR: I turned in the manuscript for "Come Back, Donald Barthelme"—a symposium on the author's life and work, as told by his friends, colleagues, and disciples—in late December 2006, after about a year spent putting it together. Dave found that term, symposium, a bit pretentious, and sort of half-winced whenever he had to say it. Looking back, he was right, but at the time I was absolutely married to the word. In the end, he let me keep it, so I guess I better go ahead and keep using it.

RACHELL SUMPTER: The content was to celebrate a revered writer whom I'd never read, Donald Barthelme. Looking for an inroad to the art, I read all the Barthelme fiction I could find. His works left me feeling, oh, postmodern? Filled and contented but lonely. I thought about how his presence and subsequent absence seemed to affect the contributing writers in a similar fashion. The art had to convey those things too, a cryptic lonesomeness, a lost presence, countered by dark celebratory bursts of fiction.

Rachell Sumpter's better sketches of the cover concept.

JORDAN BASS: The only hitch on the Barthelme side, design-wise, came from Robert Coover. His entire contribution to the symposium was three words: "Donald was laconic." When we asked our contributors for their bios, Robert asked Eli "Will your Barthelme segment have the usual brief descriptions of the several authors?" Eli confirmed it would. Robert then submitted his bio: a story about an event he organized where Barthelme gave one of his last public readings. In short, the bio was the piece. We talked for a while about whether that meant the bio needed to be closer to his "contribution" within the text, but there didn't seem to be a good way to do it. So we kept Robert's bio at the end, with the others. Hopefully people noticed.

ELI HOROWITZ: Once we had Justin's symposium, our basic thinking was just: okay, we've got two separate parts here—there's a section dedicated to Donald Barthelme and a set of six stories in there—what can we do about it? We don't like it when there's one main feature and then, oh, here's some other stories—it feels too loose. (That was the structure of Issue 15 and it pains me to this day.)

DAVE EGGERS: So the Z-shaped binding came into play. We had the dummybook, and we had Justin's stuff, so we just stuck the two together. Then we had to find someone to illustrate the whole thing. There were a bunch of surfaces to work with, and we wanted it to wrap around, so any way you unfolded it the image would be continuous.

ELI HOROWITZ: We weren't planning to have Rachell draw this cover. We've used her a lot, so I was just calling her to see if she had any artist suggestions. But she pulled a Dick Cheney; she nominated herself.

RACHELL SUMPTER: Dick Cheney? I'd never touched an issue cover before this. Friends had, and friends of friends, but not me. What was I supposed to say? Yaks? Besides, it sounded exciting.

ELI HOROWITZ: I think I suggested doing a landscape, but Rachell came up with the actual subject matter. It had been a while since we'd used cloth on a quarterly—Issue 16, I guess. Cloth needs to be ordered early in the production process—in this case, before we knew anything about the art. So actually, Rachell's work was partly inspired by the blue background, which Dave had picked out early on.

JORDAN BASS: Rachell's got some references to a few of the stories on the back, which is always nice—the pickup truck from Aaron Gwyn's piece, the tank from Chris Howard's. And the fireworks are Barthelme. For the story side, the interior artwork came from Eric Hoffman, one of the guys who wrote *Comedy by the Numbers*. He used to be a radioman in the army and had an old army-radio manual that we used originally as a template for the look of *Comedy*. When this issue came around, we went back to it for the art. The schematics in there felt like they fit with the stories, which are all more or less conflict-oriented—a lot of gunshots, guys in bad spots.

AARON GWYN: Seems guys these days are always walking into public places armed to the teeth and butchering folks. Afterwards, you'll sometimes hear people ask, "Why didn't somebody do something?" I started thinking about that, about the kind of person who actually could "do something," and what I ended up with was the short story that appeared in 24. My friend Stephen Elliott read and liked it well enough to show it to Eli. Eli thought the story was doing some things, but wasn't quite sure it fit the mode of literary fiction, wasn't quite sure it didn't. I felt the same way. In the end, Eli thought, whatever else it might be, it certainly was Trouble, and I was excited about the issue and the writers I'd be grouped with. I've sometimes wanted to present the story at a reading, but always end up feeling it'd be too much. Not sure I know what I mean by that other than it might seem like a massacre in its own right. You hope you've seen the last of those. It doesn't hurt to hope.

JOE MENO: I wrote a story for Issue 24, "Stockholm, 1973," based on a historical event, a Swedish bank robbery, weaving in facts and interview statements from some of the actual participants. Right before the piece ran, I emailed Eli in a panic asking him if I was going to be sued for not citing my sources. He told me not to sweat it: that a piece of fiction does not need to list its sources. Is this true? I'm still not sure.

DAVE EGGERS: Why would someone sue Joe or us for that? Joe is from Chicago, where there are too many lawyers. I don't know if we've ever put much thought into getting sued. We sort of imagine ourselves to live in a world where no one would sue a little literary journal. If anyone ever got mad at us we figure we could find a way to work it out. I have to say, every aspiring publisher or editor I know worries a lot about getting sued—sued for using a photo they found somewhere, sued for reprinting a few lines of Elizabethan poetry. My strong advice to everyone is this: Most people are sane. Most people don't sue people. So even if someone gets perturbed about something, you will find a way to work it out. Just do your best, try to be fair, and expect the best out of people.

A test run on red cloth of the "Come Back, Donald Barthelme" section cover. No one knows why it was done on red cloth. By this point, blue cloth was the plan.

McSweeney's 25

(2007)

LEAH HAYES: Eli asked me to do drawings—to "use them in whatever manner"—for the front and back of this hardcover issue. I tried for a long time to do something amazing, but it wasn't working. I was nervously trying too hard to make something that looked like a cover, and the drawings ended up looking contrived. Finally one night—extremely close to the deadline, maybe the night before?—Eli told me to do another try, and I freaked out. To get my mind off drawing the cover, I started copying a Garbage Pail Kid card that was sitting on my desk. I wrote "McSweeney's" in snot-font with garbage cans all around it. After I finished, I sent it to Eli sort of as a joke. He called me immediately and told me that it was exactly what they were looking for.

ELI HOROWITZ: I was excited to see how Leah's hand-drawn, doodly style would look in foil stamp. I really like loose-lined foil stamps, the contrast between the handmade and the mechanized. I'm not sure we explored it to its full potential here, but someday. I don't want to talk about the tri-color case. This issue gets on my nerves. A few decisions were made quickly and out of context, and then the rest of the design was trying to paste it all together. I'm really happy with the way Amy Jean Porter's horses came out, though.

AMY JEAN PORTER: I was having a memorably crummy day when I got an email from Eli asking if I would like to contribute to the next issue of *McSweeney's*. I did a kind of double take because it was like the cosmic cheer-up crew had landed in my inbox. We talked on the phone and settled on some horse drawings I had done that year. I started this series of gouache-and-ink drawings "Tiny Horses Say What" because I wanted to draw horses and think about places that were interesting or important to me. And, for me, all of them are saying "what"—like that joke you mumble under your breath in second grade to make your friend say "what"—but I also like that "what" can be

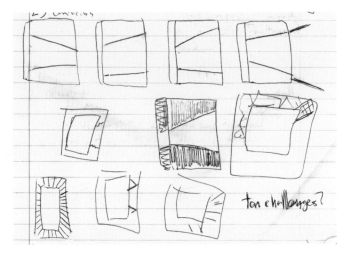

Ten alternate casewrap possibilities, sketched by Eli Horowitz. Note the similarity of the top-row drawings to men's briefs.

Three early casewrap layouts, using Leah Hayes's original drawing, white rather than black cloth, and red or uncolored board. A chilling glimpse of what could have been.

Leah Hayes's two final drawings, with extra legs and sans text. As with all McSweeney's covers, the pedagogical message is clear.

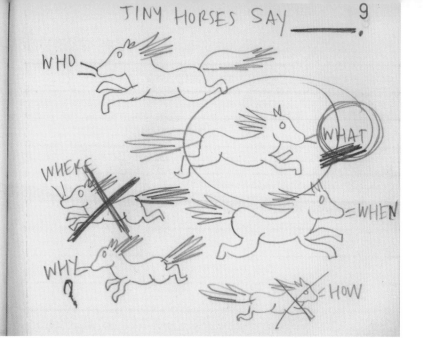

WHO

WHAT

WHERE

=WHEN

WHY?

=HOW

*A fake sketch by Amy Jean Porter, which does not show the process
by which she chose her signature interrogative.*

BOLA

LOVE,
THE
FRONTIER
EMILY ANDERSON

Peggy's
Li'l Darlins

what

PEACE-
KEEPERS,
1995
KENNETH BONERT

*Above: The title pages for two Issue 25 stories. As can be seen from the illustrations,
"Love, the Frontier" is a series of metafictional journal entries written by a
woman on a wagon train, and "Peacekeepers, 1995" is a 15,000-word account of a
Canadian journalist in Bosnia who is forced by a terrorist to smoke opium.*

*Opposite: The original frontispiece for the 1877 Fun magazine omnibus.
The rest of the omnibus was dedicated mainly to racist puns.*

a declaration about where you stand. If a horse could only say one word, I think it would say "what." Most of the backgrounds are based on photographs I've taken in the last couple of years in places like Oklahoma City, Phoenix, New Orleans, Honolulu, Brooklyn, Coney Island, Chicago, etc. When the drawings were paired with the *McSweeney's* stories, there was some great serendipity. For example, the Morab was perfect for the story "The Tower." The towers in the drawing are based on Founders Tower in Oklahoma City. Most of the horses have little stories in the background, but they're secret stories for me, mainly.

JORDAN BASS: I dream that, one day, Amy will tell me her secret horse stories. The illustration facing the title page (the frontispiece) came from an 1877 *Fun* magazine omnibus I found at a used bookstore in Plymouth, Massachusetts. (*Fun* was kind of a *Cracked* to *Punch*'s *Mad*.) There's a numerical and allegorical significance to the text—it's an introduction, written in a time of war, to the 25th volume of a magazine. So it came together in a really nice way, and our contributors were great. I remember in particular one interesting conversation I had with Emily Anderson.

EMILY ANDERSON: Jordan emailed me to say, "I really like your pioneer story, 'Love, the Frontier.' Let's change the ending. You want to?" We talked wagon wheels and musket balls until everyone was satisfied.

CONNOR KILPATRICK: When I got published in Issue 25 I had to stop pretending to hate *McSweeney's*.

THE war had been going on for some time.

Every day brought news of a great battle with victory for both sides, which, as all will admit, is an entirely new phase of the oldest art in the world.

The Emperor of Russia sat in his ivory car, and encouraged his soldiers. The Sultan of Turkey could be seen in the distance, bivouacking on pipes and coffee, inferiors in rank being only permitted pipes and tabors.

Fiercely went on the fighting for several hours, with slight intervals for refreshment, and when time was called for the day victory was once again claimed by both.

The night expired, and many soldiers both Turkish and Russian followed suit, but again the position was unchanged, and again both claimed to have won. It was the first time in the history of sport that a dead-heat had been so appropriately discovered.

The Emperor of Russia got out of his ivory car, and placed his fevered hand upon his erewhile placid brow. "What will they say in England?" murmured he, and an echoing breeze seemed to him to catch up the words and whisper, "What indeed!"

The Sultan of Turkey laid down his pipe, and swore at his principal backer. "What is the good of my winning while yonder Tartar horde knows not that it has been defeated?" The backer backed out of the Imperial presence, and the only answer that even the Sultan could obtain was the same as that vouchsafed the Cæsar, "What indeed!"

A truce was called and a consultation held that very evening, and it was decided—first, that no London daily paper should be admitted into either camp, as it was chiefly through them that both sides believed they never could be beaten; and second, that an Umpire should be properly appointed to decide who had won and who lost on all future occasions. These resolutions having been properly proposed by the Emperor, and seconded by the Sultan, were put to the meeting, and everyone signified "the same" in the usual way. A cold collation followed, after which and the recognised loyal and patriotic toasts the war proceedings were resumed de novo.

Just then a fresh arrival appeared on the scene, and all knew that a change was at hand. The new-comer was a mild and pensive gentleman, clad in a picturesque garb, and his visiting card bore on it the famous address: "No. 153, Fleet-street, London, E.C." There was a lurking devil in his deep blue eye, and his bullets were made of lead. He was at once, by acclamation and the Imperial ukase specially prepared for this ukasion, appointed sole Umpire, his decision to be final and free from any appeal to a court of law whatsoever.

In the dead watches of the night he was known to be hard at work solving the knotty problem. When morning dawned the halo of joy and peace which illumined his happy face was a thing to see. "I have hit on an expedient," he whispered to the rivals, "and War shall be no more. You see yon target and this gun"—producing both from his waistcoat-pocket, and proceeding to place the former in position—"you see them both? No one can hit that target with this gun while he is in the wrong. You shall both fire at it, and he who has right on his side will be at once victorious, while he who is wrong will be utterly confounded. Thus will Peace again reign triumphant on earth, and the reign of Wretchedness be over.—Tum-tum."

Even as he spoke a blessed balm seemed to suffuse the air, the sun burst forth from a bank of clouds where it had been deposited, the birds began to sing, the rivers ran babbling as of peace and plenty, and all nature smiled when it was seen that the target of truth and virtue, of wisdom and of wit, was none other than

The Twenty-fifth Volume of the Second Series of Fun.

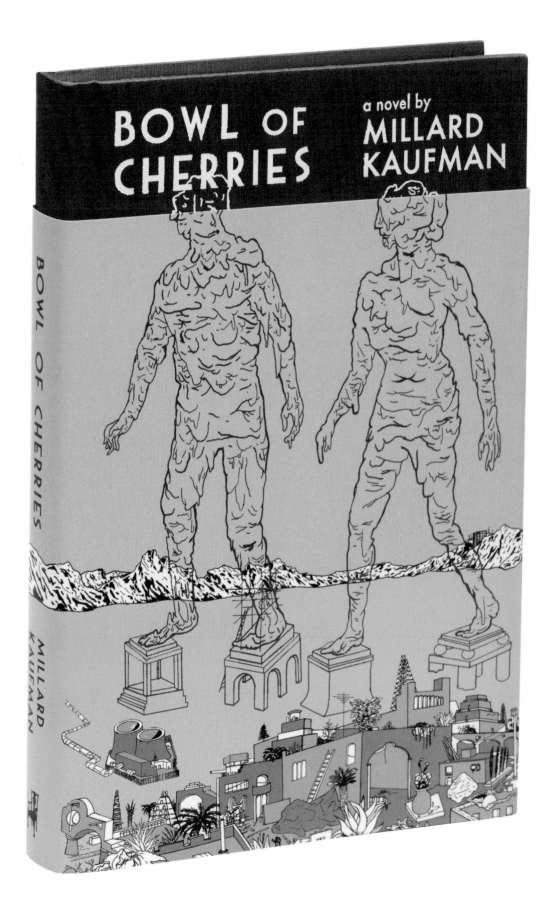

Bowl of Cherries

by MILLARD KAUFMAN

(2007)

ANGELA PETRELLA: Eli came into the office and said, "You are really going to like this next guy. He's right up your alley." And holy shit, he was. The man was nominated for two screenwriting Oscars in the 1950s, worked with the likes of Elizabeth Taylor, Spencer Tracy, Montgomery Clift, and co-created Mr. Magoo. And he's ninety years old.

ELI HOROWITZ: Millard's book came to us through Laura Howard—she helps us with the *Believer*—who is friends with a woman named Nina Wiener, who knew Millard from a book they had worked on together years before. I heard this manuscript was coming my way, and I think I heard the author was old or something, but none of it really registered— we get plenty of manuscripts from unusual sources. So the manuscript arrived, in an enormous box, many pages long. I started reading and realized: Hold on, this might be something. Just the amount of energy and intellect and obvious glee on every page. At some point I took a break, and then I googled Millard's name and it got weird. Mr. Magoo? What? *Bad Day at Black Rock*? Born when? And so on.

MILLARD KAUFMAN: What actually happened, and it certainly is nothing to be terribly proud of, it was inevitable: When I hit eighty-six I realized that I had just done my last picture. Nobody was going to hire

SHIT-BROWN-STATUE-PEOPLE SEEN through the mouth of A CAVE

Cover sketch by Jason Holley. More sketches on the next spread.

me, I was just in their eyes much too old; as a matter of fact, I was much too old, I suppose, in everybody's eyes. So I decided to launch something else. I had always been interested in the novel as a reader, and I thought, what the hell, why not try it. Now I remember having gone to a lecture at UCLA where the speaker was Somerset Maugham, and some kid in the audience got up and rather nastily said to him, rather gruffly too, "How do you write a novel?" And without hesitation Maugham said, "There are three rules for writing a novel. Unfortunately nobody knows what they are." And having said that and my listening to it, I thought, what the hell, I can try that. If nobody knows the rules I can either conform to what nobody knows or make up my own. And that's how it started.

ELI HOROWITZ: I read the whole thing, liked it, and decided to call Millard. We always talk to the author before accepting anything, to make sure we all get along and the writer is still willing to work. So I called Millard—I remember I was walking along a bike path around dusk, and there were some bells ringing, for real—and we talked, and after we hung up I called Jordan and said, "We are definitely doing this book." The writing was great in itself, but talking to Millard was so much fun—I couldn't pass up a year of conversations like that.

DAVIA NELSON (MILLARD'S NIECE): I could listen to Millard Kaufman tell stories all night. War stories, Hollywood stories, life stories. As a little girl I was mesmerized by the worlds he lived in and described. He used words like "gams." As in, "Davi, your mother was a helluva broad with a great set of gams." I wanted to go to the set with him and meet Monty and Liz and Spencer, and Dalton Trumbo, whom Millard helped out during the blacklist. It's not just Millard's stories, it's his questions when you sit down around the table. Jabbing, probing, curious, wanting to know everything about everybody. A kind heart nestled in a salty dog. One day he asked me if I knew this "outfit" up in San Francisco, where I live. Had I heard of McSweeney's?

MILLARD KAUFMAN: I had heard about you guys from my son, Fredrick Kaufman, who is a hell of a good writer; he just turned out a book on the American diet called *The Short History of the American Stomach*, which is very good, very funny, and very authentic. He had mentioned that he thought you guys were great. Out of that my friend Nina Wiener, who was the editor of the first book I wrote, a nonfiction thing about screenwriting, she, too, thought you guys were pretty spiffy. I didn't have an agent at the time, my agent died, Darce Halsey. She was a little younger than I but she nevertheless decided to die before me. At that age it was almost impossible to get an agent. You know, who the hell wanted to hire anybody my age to write a movie? When Nina told me

RENDERED LANDSCAPE
With GRAPHIC SNIT-STATUES
AND FLOATING CAVE BITS

about you guys she said that if I liked she'd send it to you, which she did and you more or less immediately took it, which knocked me out, I thought it was great.

ELI HOROWITZ: Editing was fun. A little slow, because Millard doesn't use email or a computer—he writes everything longhand, which he then gives to a man named Ron, who was crucial to this project. Ron is a carpenter by profession, but also a fan of Millard's, and so he typed up all Millard's handwritten revisions. Problem was, sometimes Ron was on a job building sets in Las Vegas, so we'd have to just freeze, marinate for a while. One time I had Millard just send me his writing directly—how hard could it be, I thought. It was hard. After that we always waited for Ron. Because the revisions took a little longer than expected, we didn't have time to print this in Asia—we did it at a very large printer in Virginia, who wasn't really suited to our usual nonsense. So the trick was to find a way to do something interesting using very normal specs. A stamped line drawing is easy, and cutting the jacket a little short is easy, and so I was pleased with this one.

MILLARD KAUFMAN: The only eccentricities I encountered were my own. I'm rather, at times—maybe more that at times—rather peculiar, and the only thing I like to do really after all this time is write. So I sat down and I started to write and it just kind of rolled out, this *Bowl of Cherries* thing. Precisely why, I don't know. I had a vague idea, a lot of vague ideas. One of them, of course, having been in the marine corps in World War II and what was going on in Iraq, I thought I wanted to do on the one hand a novel about warfare, and the other I thought, that's been done so many times; it's been done well so many times that I didn't want to get into any competition about that. So what I decided to do was let the war sit there in the background and go on with the individuality of the various people I'm playing with, none of whom are actually in combat.

ELI HOROWITZ: For the cover art, my goal was some sort of skewed Tintin. The story is kind of like a Tintin adventure gone bad—precocious lad in foreign land, but just making a mess of things. For a while the title was actually in the *Tintin* font, but that looked a little cute. But the colors are taken directly from a Tintin book I had by my bed growing up—I think it was *The Land of Black Gold*. The artist was Jason Holley, who had actually been the teacher of some of our earlier artists: Rachell Sumpter, Josh Cochran, Jacob Magraw-Mickelson.

mountain/shit climbers

For each printing—there were three—the copyright page didn't change, but we used a slightly different texture of paper for the casewrap. I was excessively pleased by that.

MILLARD KAUFMAN: I was speaking, I don't know where it was. Because of this book I was speaking, as you know, in a lot of places. And a woman got up and asked me about how all this started, just as you're doing. And I think it kind of started because there were certain things apparently I obviously wanted to get off my chest, and this was, I thought, a way to do it. What was curious was my reaction, because the question she actually asked is what was kind of a high point in the book's coming out. And the curious thing, and this is true, is the thing that I felt is that, my god, I am actually going to have piece of fiction in the Library of Congress! I don't know why that so impressed me because that's what happens to books if they're any good at all. But it certainly crossed my mind.

I didn't at the time, and I still don't understand, what's being conveyed on the cover. I don't know what that means, I don't know what it is. But I rather like it. I never even mentioned it to Eli. But look, they could have written a goddamn thing in Yiddish and I would have said, "My god, that's wonderful!" The idea of doing a book seems to me to be a kind of accomplishment that I never really felt about pictures or short stories. A novel is something that Charles Dickens did, and the idea, while not the same class, at least I have the same outlet. And that I find very pleasant.

ANGELA PETRELLA: Millard, he tells the most gorgeous, outrageous stories. A reporter from Minnesota asked for his hand in marriage after the interview. He is a snake charmer with a wicked wink. I'm convinced he's going to live forever as there is something suspiciously supernatural about that Baltimore boy.

McSweeney's 26

(2 0 0 8)

DAVE EGGERS: This one started about a year before we actually published it. I'd been thinking about how seemingly easy it was for the Bush administration to sell the war in Iraq—even to the liberal segment of the country—and I thought we could publish an issue that basically laid out equally compelling reasons to topple the governments of a handful of other sovereign nations.

STEPHEN ELLIOTT: Basically, *Where To Invade Next* makes the case to invade seven different countries including North Korea, Syria, Iran, Sudan, Pakistan, Valenzuela, and Uzbekistan. General Wesley Clark had been quoted as saying that there was a memo in Rumsfeld's office detailing seven countries we were going to roll over in the next five years.

Top: The original cover sketch for Issue 26.
Below: U.S. serviceman John Grodin
reading a copy of Issue 26 in Iraq.

it would encourage people to vote for John McCain.

JORDAN BASS: The best response I received was from a veterinary entomologist in North Carolina. He wrote in with "Am I to accept this add-on to my usually enjoyable *McSweeney's* parcel as journalism? Or is it a kind of Jello Biafra version of current historical ramblings culled extensively from pulp media and the Internet?"

ELI HOROWITZ: The best strategy with *Where To Invade Next* is to let it speak for itself.

STEPHEN ELLIOTT: I hope that people read *Where To Invade Next* and understand how easy it is to make the case for war in seven countries. All you need is two months, three novelists, and eight college kids on summer break to fact-check and research.

DAVE EGGERS: And the key thing was that the book would be entirely factual, and even persuasive. The arguments made would, on the surface, seem rational and convincing enough to the average liberal, well-informed person.

STEPHEN ELLIOTT: Some people freaked out because they thought the book might actually help people who wanted to invade these countries. They thought

CHRIS YING: The most time-consuming part of the production phase was finding relevant, useful images for each chapter. We wanted to be really careful about finding images in the public domain, which isn't easy if you're also confined by resolution restrictions and a budget of zero dollars. Flickr turned out to be a wonderful resource. There's a serious citizen-journalist movement happening there.

JORDAN BASS: The two little paperbacks that come with *Where To Invade Next* arose from a need to include the issue's short fiction in a not-entirely-arbitrary manner. We initially discussed making the invasion book the entire issue. But that didn't feel right. So we added the two storybooks and titled them, "New Stories from Overseas" and "New Stories from Home." These two are pretty much the only covers I can claim to have designed. And even then Chris Ying did a lot of the bolt tightening.

CHRIS YING: It was a struggle making the mini-books depicted on the covers look realistic. The original Armed Services Editions all had that inclined image of the books they were based on. We spent a lot of time tilting things different ways in Photoshop, then holding up actual books and tilting them around, then trying to recreate that in Photoshop again, so that it looks like the books are being hurled right at you.

JORDAN BASS: I think it helped that our paperbacks were very small, and simple, and more or less exactly like the World War II–era Armed Services Editions that we based those books on. There were all kinds of interesting aspects to the backstory of those Armed Services Edition books, claims that they'd basically invented mainstream paperback publishing, things like that. Back then they were running them off on pulp-magazine presses, printing them one on top of the other and then slicing them apart. That kind of thrifty creativity is something we're always aspiring to, and I liked that you could recall that method by packaging them the way we did—by making the two booklets look like one normally proportioned book, and then having the reader divide them. So really I didn't even design these; someone in the War Department designed them in the early 1940s.

ELI HOROWITZ: I really wanted the three pieces to fit together perfectly. I thought this would help move the issue from "hodge-podge" to "enigmatic bundle." Jordan and I bickered a lot about the suitability of the Armed Services Editions, and especially the soldier-illustrations used throughout. He won.

JORDAN BASS: I won. Eli had no argument. One of the neatest things about the original ASEs was the eclectic spectrum of titles they chose. They had poetry, ghost stories, Dickens, Fitzgerald, and Virginia Woolf. We'd just done a combat-heavy set of stories in Issue 24, so I didn't want to repeat that, and I guess I thought, if you were actually out there at war, would you just want to read stories about war? So we ended up with a book of stories set in the U.S. and a book of stories set overseas, with things like Dana Mazur's amazing account of a trip to the Kazakh afterlife in there.

DANA MAZUR: I had given up on my novel and resolved to send out a chapter as a short story. I titled the chapter "Black Shaman," as the final adieu to my writing. Lacking a better plan, I selected five or six literary journals; *McSweeney's* turned out to be the only one accepting email submissions. I emailed my story since I was too broke to pay for the postage to the other four. The rest was even eerier—the check from

The two booklets included in Issue 26. Stories were split up based on whether they were set in America or elsewhere, which required two stories to be broken in half and serialized across both booklets.

McSweeney's was the exact amount I needed to enroll in my writing class. In Kazakhstan there is a tradition called Koremdyk: You reward someone who shows you something new and important (a new baby, for example). When I visited my family in Kazakhstan, I ended up making a fat buck by showing off Issue 26.

Maps and Legends

by MICHAEL CHABON (2008)

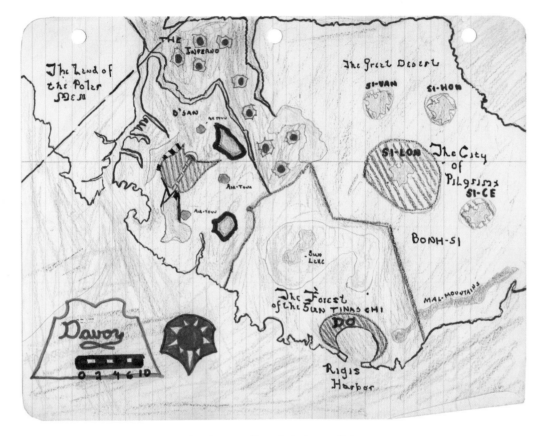

An early cartographic exercise by the young Chabon.

MICHAEL CHABON: Here is how the cover of *Maps and Legends* got designed: I came up with about 283 lame-ass design ideas. I showed them to Dave. He praised them warmly. Then he ripped a piece of paper out of a notebook or turned a phone bill upside down and took out his pen. "I was kinda thinking maybe something like this," he said. His pen went *zip zup zip*. "Like, we have three separate belly bands." *Zip.* "This one is the mountains." *Zup.* "This one is the land." *Zip.* "This one is the water, the ocean, right? Then maybe we put in a bunch of the characters you talk about in the book, we kind of have them hiding in there, all over the place. Then there's a keyhole, and it goes all the way through all three belly bands to the

stamped design on the cover." *Zip. Zup. Zip.* "Like that." "Awesome," I said. I didn't really understand it, to be honest. But you would be crazy not to trust Dave's design sense. A few days later some samples of brilliant work by Jordan Crane showed up in my inbox. I was awed. "I want this guy," I said. "We got him," I was told.

JORDAN CRANE: I'm idealistic about books, so that probably sets me up for suffering. But making the *Maps and Legends* cover was a pleasure. Eli called me and told me what he was thinking about the cover, the size it needed to be, and that was it. And then, when I had another idea, and another, he actually encouraged

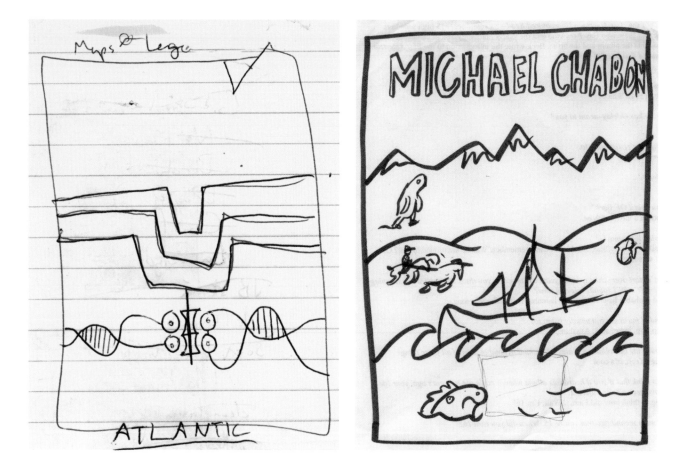

Above: Preliminary sketches: Mythic landscapes (Eggers, right) and overlapping jackets (Horowitz, left).
Opposite: Early drafts of the cover art by Jordan Crane, involving three overlapping dust jackets and an illustrated case.

it! Editors have a pervasive need to put their "stamp" on a design, this always wrecks the design, cripples it, flaws it, impairs the artist's vision of it. Did you ever wonder why so many book covers absolutely suck? It's because of the book editors of the world! They're idiots! Worse, they're idiots in love with their own fifth-generation, watered-down ideas of good design! Not Eli. If Eli has a "stamp," that stamp is quality. He encourages ideas, nurtures them. When I first turned in the final files for the covers, they were sensibly separated as an economical 4-color CMYK print job. Eli thought the colors looked lackluster when compared to my color mockups. So did I, but I was thinking of his budget, trying to be practical. But Eli, he puts the book first. Use more colors, he says! So I turned in the covers, each with its own pantone colors, 9 in all. Still he thought the colors were lacking in luster. He was right, of course. He asked me how we could

make it better. I told him that if each cover printed in 5 pantones, we could get the depth and resonance of color that we were looking for. So I turned in the final version. It's got 5 different pantone colors per jacket, quite a few varying in tone by hardly a shade. It's a 15-color cover. Because that's what it needed to be a good cover, to be the cover that I first envisioned. And it was like this right down the line. He helped me by clearing the way for my ideas. Every idea I had for the cover, unless it was actually physically impossible for the printer to do, and unless I actually cut the idea myself, made it unmolested to the final version of the book. Every idea. Compare this to other books I've done, where, if I have 12 ideas, I'm lucky if 2 of them make it to the final unmolested. And I do mean lucky. Frequently all of the ideas I have are molested in one way or another before the book gets printed. But not with Eli. Every single idea made it. What freedom!

I could make the cover as I saw it, and this made it a better cover.

ELI HOROWITZ: What made me think of Jordan Crane was stumbling upon a sea-monster drawing he did for a book called *Beasts!*. He had just the right balance of draftmanship and playfulness and intensity. What I didn't know then is that he's also an absolute coloring genius—he knows more about printing than anyone I've ever worked with.

Tien Wah did a terrific job on this book—they were totally unfazed by the design, and executed it perfectly, and didn't even charge much. I guess three jackets doesn't need to cost much more than one—it's still just a few pieces of paper.

JORDAN CRANE: Eli makes a good book, and he is a good editor because he picks good artists and designers, and he lets them do their job. And really, is that such a novel idea? Perhaps Eli is exceptionally gifted with this insight because he is first a good designer, and he knows the level of personal investment that good work takes. Thus he is able to stand back and let artists and designers invest themselves in the work they do for him. That's the big secret. Book editors of the world, what do you do best? If you're honest with yourselves, you coordinate projects, you answer email, you take calls. You do not design books well. If you designed books well, you would have to take a substantial pay cut. So, book editors of the world, stop trying to design the books. Just stop it.

The Three-Piece Dust Jacket of Maps and Legends

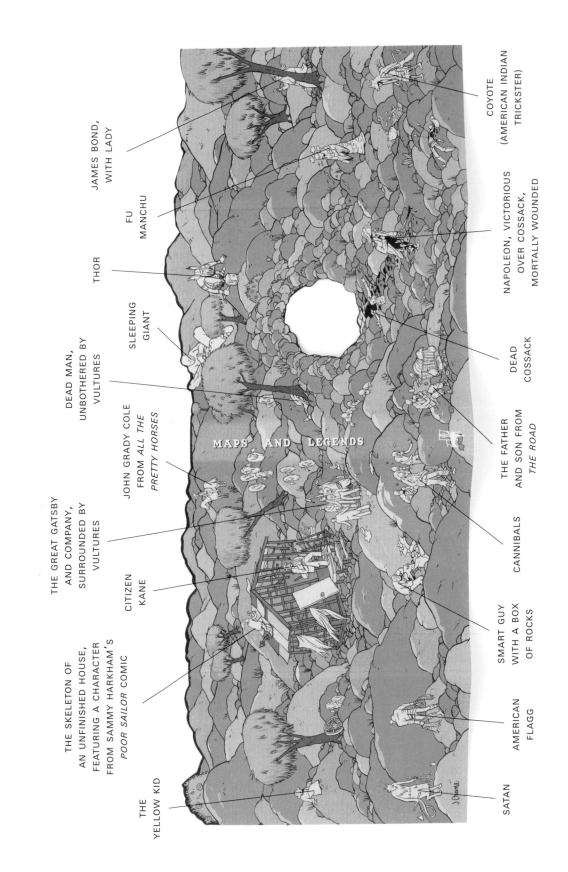

THE SKELETON OF
AN UNFINISHED HOUSE,
FEATURING A CHARACTER
FROM SAMMY HARKHAM'S
POOR SAILOR COMIC

THE GREAT GATSBY
AND COMPANY,
SURROUNDED BY
VULTURES

DEAD MAN,
UNBOTHERED BY
VULTURES

JAMES BOND,
WITH LADY

COYOTE
(AMERICAN INDIAN
TRICKSTER)

FU
MANCHU

THOR

SLEEPING
GIANT

NAPOLEON, VICTORIOUS
OVER COSSACK,
MORTALLY WOUNDED

JOHN GRADY COLE
FROM *ALL THE
PRETTY HORSES*

DEAD
COSSACK

CITIZEN
KANE

THE FATHER
AND SON FROM
THE ROAD

CANNIBALS

SMART GUY
WITH A BOX
OF ROCKS

THE
YELLOW KID

AMERICAN
FLAGG

SATAN

MAPS AND LEGENDS

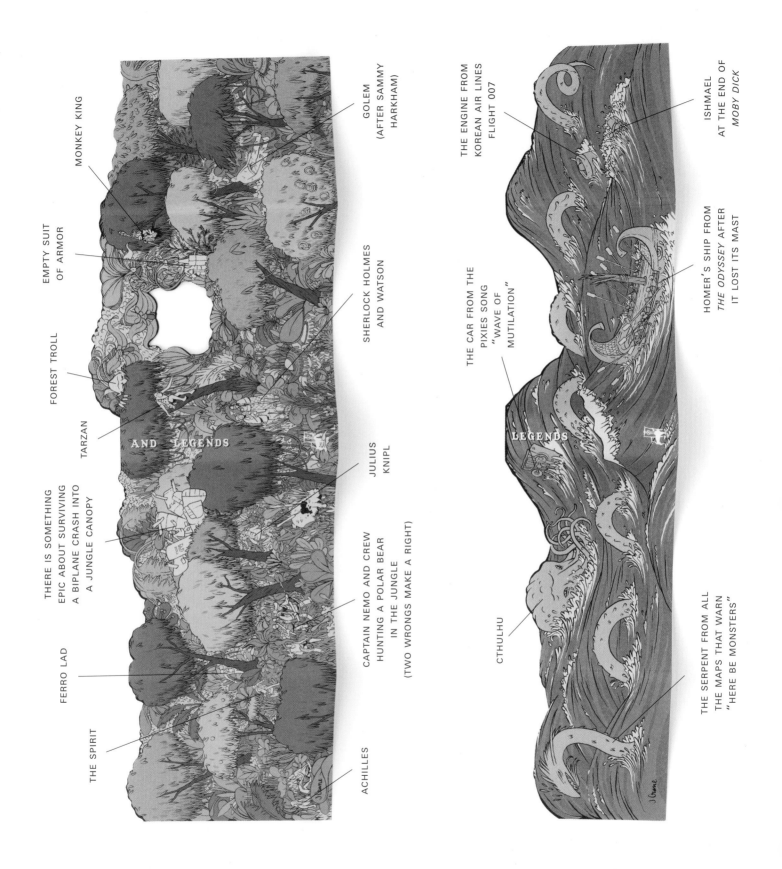

MONKEY KING

GOLEM
(AFTER SAMMY
HARKHAM)

EMPTY SUIT
OF ARMOR

FOREST TROLL

SHERLOCK HOLMES
AND WATSON

TARZAN

AND LEGENDS

JULIUS
KNIPL

THERE IS SOMETHING
EPIC ABOUT SURVIVING
A BIPLANE CRASH INTO
A JUNGLE CANOPY

FERRO LAD

CAPTAIN NEMO AND CREW
HUNTING A POLAR BEAR
IN THE JUNGLE
(TWO WRONGS MAKE A RIGHT)

THE SPIRIT

ACHILLES

THE ENGINE FROM
KOREAN AIR LINES
FLIGHT 007

ISHMAEL
AT THE END OF
MOBY DICK

THE CAR FROM THE
PIXIES SONG
"WAVE OF
MUTILATION"

HOMER'S SHIP FROM
THE ODYSSEY AFTER
IT LOST ITS MAST

LEGENDS

CTHULHU

THE SERPENT FROM ALL
THE MAPS THAT WARN
"HERE BE MONSTERS"

McSweeney's 27

(2008)

Opposite and above: The slipcase of Issue 27, with a photo by Irving Underhill, and the three booklets it contained, with covers (from left to right) by Scott Teplin, Tucker Nichols, and Art Spiegelman.

JORDAN BASS: This issue ended up as three books: an art catalog and an Art Spiegelman sketchbook and a book of stories. This design didn't get sorted out until fairly far in.

ELI HOROWITZ: What was that odd idea you had for this one, Jordan?

JORDAN BASS: I had high hopes for a hardcover with a hinged spine, with the art on the top half and the stories on the bottom part of each page, and a cut all the way through the middle, so you could look at both sections together or flip the whole thing open like a lighter and go through one segment at a time. But just when we were about to start hashing out that design, we found out that Spiegelman was giving us seventy-two pages, and that he wanted to present them as their own little notebook, like the book he'd drawn in originally. So the hinge-book went back to the bench.

ART SPIEGELMAN: Over dinner with Dave Eggers a while back, I'd started bitching about another

literary journal that had agreed to publish "BREAK-DOWNS: Portrait of the Artist as a Young !@#$!!" as a serialized work-in-progress. But a year or so into it, they started balking when they got to the section that included sexually explicit visual content. Dave looked at the offending pages and shrugged, saying, "Well, we're not funded by a university; we can publish anything you like—is it okay if we put a photo of donkeys fucking on the cover?" Instead, I offered a very private sketchbook that became a rather public component of this issue.

DAVE EGGERS: Like the Spiegelman notebook, the art catalog also started out as an offer from someone else. Apexart, a gallery in New York City, asked me to curate a show, and the first thought I had was to do something to feature the work of people like David Shrigley, Tucker Nichols, Raymond Pettibon, and Maira Kalman—artists who used text and art in a way that straddled comics, fine art, illustration, scribbles. So I employed Jesse Nathan, a recent intern, to help put the show, and the Issue 27 booklet, together. Every day he would either research names and pieces

An early sketch by Scott Teplin, showing the raw lettering for the story-booklet cover.

I remembered, or, more often, he would venture off on his own, finding examples of the genre. He ended up finding stuff by Shel Silverstein, David Mamet, Leonard Cohen—so many unexpected people, in addition to folks like Philip Guston and Ralph Steadman, whom we wanted to include from the start.

JESSE NATHAN: I have no formal art education, so it was a whirlwind to educate myself and at the same time track down all this artwork. I spent a few months combing through stacks and stacks of art books from the Berkeley and San Francisco public libraries, and from SFMOMA, which had a well-hidden contemporary-art library you could get into for research purposes. I was living in Berkeley at the time, and using a messenger bag to haul everything from my house to the McSweeney's office to these various libraries. My back started to hurt, so I had

to switch back to my old Jansport pack. Then that started to fill up, so I had to lug books around in a cardboard box. One day just after I got there, Tucker Nichols walked in with a portfolio of drawings. I was sweaty and flustered looking, I'm sure, from hauling an armful of art tomes across San Francisco. I wiped my forehead and we got down to business.

TUCKER NICHOLS: I brought some drawings to Mc-Sweeney's to be scanned. I parked on 20th Street and as I turned the corner onto Valencia Street, a mighty wind came up and the big pad I was using to store the drawings turned uncooperative. I had a cup of tea as well and the combination seemed like more than my arms could handle. A passerby offered to help me but I felt ashamed and assured her that I had the situation under control. I was committed to not letting the drawings blow all about the street and lost sight

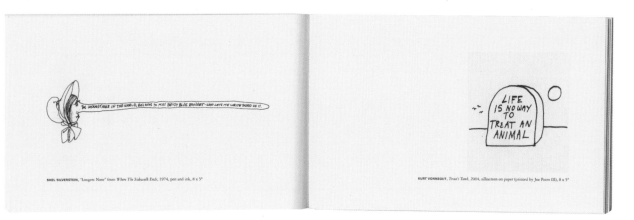

A spread from "Lots of Things Like This," with drawings by Shel Silverstein and Kurt Vonnegut.

of the tea and then it was falling in slow motion and superfast the way bad things tend to and then it was exploded on the sidewalk. Totally undrinkable.

PAUL HORNSCHEMEIER: When I was contacted to have my cartoon, revolving around two kids consuming ice cream and making crass mom jokes, included in a Dave Eggers–curated show and subsequently in the Issue 27 booklet, I naturally said yes. The more mom jokes the better. But when I later saw the cast I was joining (Vonnegut, Basquiat, Mamet, Duchamp), I blanched, demoralized by inferiority. I happened to be in New York the day of the opening and stopped by. I examined the work on the walls of the gallery, breathing a sigh of relief: they were all, more or less, mom jokes (or dick jokes, or orphan jokes). It was good, classless company.

JORDAN BASS: The cover artist for the story book, Scott Teplin—he was actually suggested first as a guy for the art show. Brian McMullen had seen his drawings of cross-sectioned buildings with each floor shaped like a different letter. And that's the kind of work he did for us, after Eli and I stole him away.

ELI HOROWITZ: The covers of the individual books were all hand-drawn and kind of wild-looking, so I wanted the slipcase to be quiet. I had come upon that old photo of New York buildings at least a year before. There's nothing so distinctive about it, but I liked it. And then it just seemed to fit, especially with

Teplin's architectural letter drawings. We actually had Teplin match his drawing to that picture, so his structures have the same dimensions as the buildings on the slipcase, as viewed from the opposite side.

SCOTT TEPLIN: I don't illustrate, I just draw what interests me at that moment. But the cover sounded like a fun opportunity to try and work within the parameters set by someone else, knowing the results would be much different (less stale?) than when I work inside my own head. Eli gave me a list of objects that appear in each of the six stories and I got to design the rooms around those objects. That, and I'd never pass up drawing a gigantic steaming pile of poop in a school classroom.

ELI HOROWITZ: I'd been a big fan of metallic ink on brown board for a while but I didn't know how to get it done for the case. So I called Jordan Crane, who had just drawn the jacket for Chabon's *Maps and Legends*. His understanding of printing mechanics was amazing. We brainstormed a variety of approaches, using overprinting, different shades of silver, multiple passes. The final box uses two passes of one silver ink and four passes of another. It's confusing and expensive to get this right, just for the proofing costs alone, so we made some guesses and hoped for the best.

Next pages: Artwork from Marcel Dzama's book
The Berliner Ensemble Thanks You All *(2008)*.

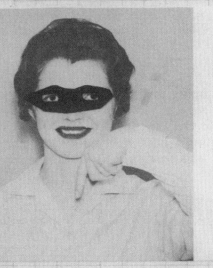

A tale of marginalized characters hardened by war and overpowering Hollywood stereotypes and role-playing.

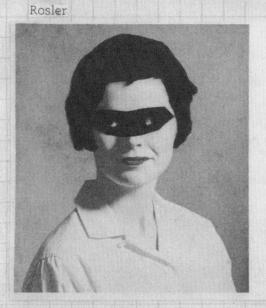 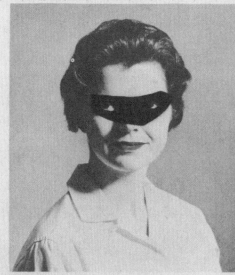 

Rosler

Carole

Laurie

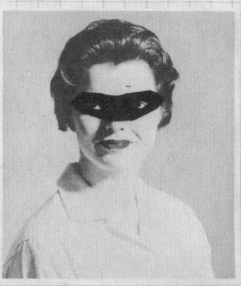

Sadie

Nereida

Giulietta

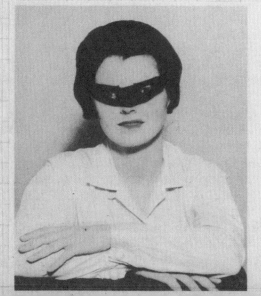 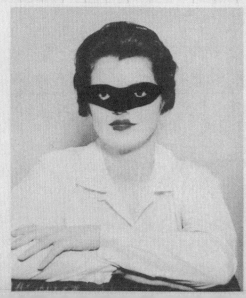 

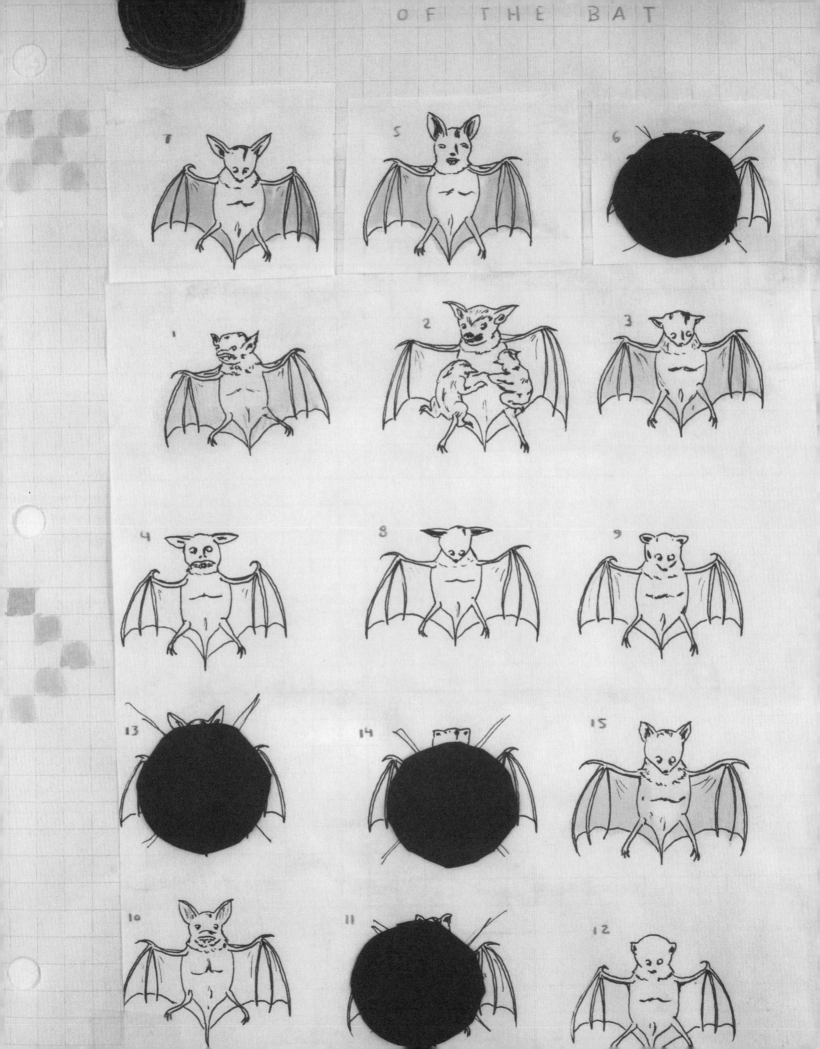

McSweeney's 28

(2 0 0 8)

JESS BENJAMIN: I'd been kicking around a proto-idea for the fables issue before I pitched it at an intern meeting one fine summer afternoon in San Francisco, circa 2006. Originally I'd been thinking that it would be fun to create a children's book for adults, a sort of simplified, big-picture version of a novel. After talking it over with Dave, the whole thing morphed itself into the present fables concept, and the rest was two-years-in-the-making. Even still, it was exciting to see the idea take off so quickly—before I left to go back to college we'd already come up with a list of potential authors and had begun sending out solicitations. After graduating, I hightailed it to Tibet and spent the rest of the year traveling around South Asia with a big backpack. It was during the transition from Nepal to India that Dave contacted me about writing the Introduction. At that time it was snowing and freezing in Northern India, and I spent most of my time in cramped Internet cafes blowing on my fingers and trying to shake my feet awake through the three pairs of socks I was wearing. I'd like to think that a lot of blood, sweat, and tears went into writing that Introduction, but it was probably more like chai, daal, and long johns. Skip ahead six months and this stunning book arrives at my door. What an unbelievable process.

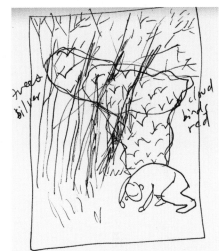

Opposite and above: The face of Issue 28, with a four-part illustration by Danica Novgorodoff, and two of Novgorodoff's early sketches.

DAVE EGGERS: Jess went back to college, and we got started on the issue. Right away we assumed that the fables would be their own individual books, and figured that each would be illustrated by a different artist. So it was seeming, from the outset, like a lot of work, and follow-up work, so I called Elizabeth up. She's great with illustrators, and I knew she'd be into the format. Or what we had figured out so far about the format, which was only that the stories would be bound individually. Beyond that, we didn't know much.

ELIZABETH KAIRYS: When I set out to design this issue, what kept coming to mind was my favorite collection of stories as a child: Maurice Sendak's *Nutshell Library*, a box filled with four stories, each its own little book. I always loved taking the books out of the box and then re-arranging them and reading them over and over again. I wanted this issue to have that same feel of interactivity, so I chose to package them in a way that would encourage people to play with them in addition to reading them: two layers of books unified by two paintings across their covers.

DANICA NOVGORODOFF: I was asked to make a pair of paintings for the cover of the McSweeney's book of fables. Elizabeth said they were looking for something based on the themes of light and dark, above

and underground, so I decided to do one painting of a tree growing in brilliant light, a boy listening to the ground, and a flock of birds flying out of him in awe at what he's hearing below. And below the ground, miners excavating something luminous, with a curtain of bats and the tree's roots draped above them. Elizabeth asked me for a sketch before I started the paintings, but I was afraid to show it to her: (see below).

ELIZABETH KAIRYS: Dave and I thought it would be exciting to have each book illustrated by a different artist to give each book its own identity. All of the interior illustrations are two-color and borrow from the palette of the cover art. We had lots of ideas for how to keep the books secure in the box, but ended up liking the elastic straps the best.

JORDAN BASS: Elizabeth actually had all the illustrators lined up before we had all the fables in—I think we had seven of 'em all set, and Dave was trying to decide who to bring in for the last spot. And then, at a meeting about exactly that, I remembered that Sarah Manguso had said something to me months before about how much trouble she'd been having finishing off her fable. It turned out we had eight authors after all—we'd actually forgotten that she was working on one.

DAVE EGGERS: It was kind of surprisingly difficult to get all the writers to write morals into their stories. It had been part of the task from the outset, and the sample stories mentioned all contained morals, and I'd chosen writers who I thought weren't averse to some clear and powerful messages in their work.

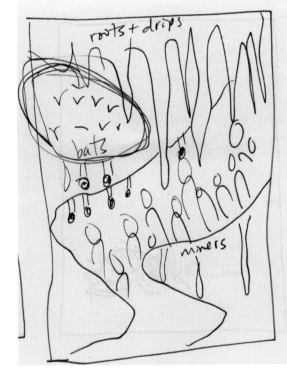

Opposite and above: The inner layer of Issue 28, with another four-part illustration by Danica Novgorodoff, and another early sketch.

But still, it was hard. It's difficult to both make a point in a fable and make the story interesting all the way through. Either you're telegraphing the message from the first sentence, or you're sending a too-obvious or pat message or... there are so many pitfalls. But still, I was surprised at how much these guys resisted coming out and saying what the point of the stories were.

SARAH MANGUSO: Draft after draft, the moral of my fable stayed ambiguous. I kept trying to hide it. I didn't know I would do that. Charles Simic says, "Be brief and tell us everything." Easy. The shorter the better! I kept trying to make my fable shorter. It was an irrational urge.

BRIAN EVENSON: Between the Fables issue and the fake Turkish sitcom subtitles that *Wholphin* had me do, McSweeney's has a good record for hitting me up for projects I never could've seen coming! I wanted to see if I could keep my story close to the pattern of *The Giving Tree* (which was the model suggested to us) while letting it become thematically infected by my own odd concerns.

TAYARI JONES: When I got the invitation to participate, I was too shy to tell Dave I had never read *The Giving Tree*. I don't know why I hadn't heard of it. I promise that my parents read to me when I was little, but this just wasn't in their reportoire. I was at MacDowell at the time and I found out that every other child in America had read this book. I went to the nearest bookstore and read the book while standing in the aisle. The funny thing is that fables are supposed to have a clear message or moral, but I thought

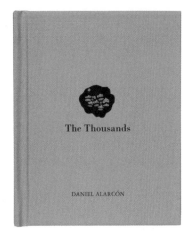

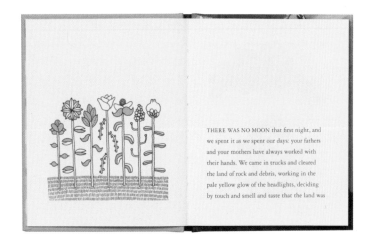

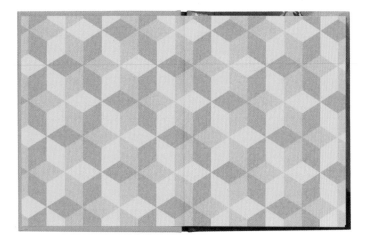

The Giving Tree was really ambiguous. I felt like it meant something, but I didn't know what. I mean, was the message "Give Give Give" or "Take Take Take"? Or was the message that people want what they want and you shouldn't judge desire? I couldn't figure it out.

ARTHUR BRADFORD: I'd just become a father so I was interested in the idea of some kind of kid's story. The thing was Dave later explained these aren't supposed to be kid's stories, they are fables, with morals. I've often thought that morals in stories make me want to puke and the other thing about fables is they are so clearly fake, like they never could have happened in real life. Even though my stories have talking animals and mutant couplings I like to imagine that they are real. So anyway I was resistant to the fable idea but then Dave explained the concept more and he wrote to all the writers for the issue and told us we were missing the point, all of us except Sheila Heti, who'd gotten it right on the first try. It felt a little like being back in school. So I must have given Dave six or seven drafts of that story and in the end I'm not sure if it has much of a moral, but that's because I can't imagine coming up with a moral first and then writing the story around it, which is what I think I was supposed to do. I don't even have any morals to impart on anyone, except maybe to wash your hands thoroughly whenever possible.

DAVE EGGERS: We were all having a lot of trouble with it. We'd gone through about six drafts with each author. One author had honestly gone through twelve drafts and we weren't getting much closer. Then Sheila Heti's story came in, and we had a breakthrough. It was for adults, and it moved briskly along, giving just enough to the audience until the end, when it takes an unexpected turn and hits us smack between the eyes. In my mind it's the definitive story of any length written about the relationship between a self-destructive person and the unwitting enablers around them.

RYAN BOUDINOT: I was happy to have a story in the fables issue. I could go on and on about the design and illustrations, but if I may be candid I'd like to mention the mid-production smackdown Mr. Eggers laid

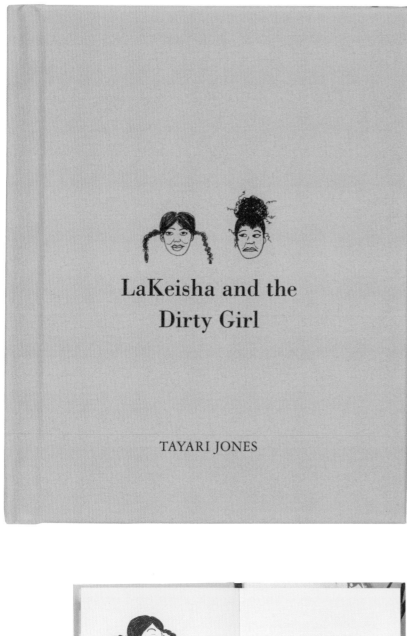

The cover and an interior spread from Tayari Jones's "LaKeisha and the Dirty Girl," with illustrations by Morgan Elliott.

on most of us contributors. He basically said, "Listen, fuckers, what you wrote aren't fables. They're pansy-assed contemporary stories of ennui in fables drag. For an example of a superb fable, look what Sheila Heti wrote. Now that is a fucking fable. The rest of you people make me sick. Come on, Sheila, let's go get Indian food, just you and me."

TAYARI JONES: Actually, we all got to go get Indian food. Everyone but Ryan. It was delicious. Anyway, despite my brief *Giving Tree* problem, I was jazzed about the project. I knew I wanted to write about a girl like LaKeisha. As a girl named Tayari, I always wanted to see a story with names like the names I grew up with. And from them I just sort of branched out. Partly, I lampooned my own personality. I do love myself some external trappings. The hard part was writing the ending. Dave kept saying we need to up the "whoa" factor. Once I let go of the idea that a fable has to be let the good guys win, I was able to get more whoa in my ending. When I saw the issue, the artists gave the whoa factor right back. So gorgeous. I have it right here in a little stand.

MORGAN ELLIOTT: I loved Tayari's story immediately; I found it both insightful and funny. Tayari really captured one of the hardest things about being a little girl, which is weathering the selfishness of other little girls. I really identified with the Dirty Girl. I feel like I've had to deal with LaKeishas my whole life.

NATHAN ENGLANDER: How I got involved in Issue 28 goes like this: There's this hotel in Amsterdam, the Ambassade, where everyone on book tour in Holland ends up staying. It's kind of like writers' camp. Dave and I were there at the same time, which was great fun. During that trip, Dave made two requests of me: Would I write a fable-for-adults for Issue 28, and would I please, please stop using product in my hair. We have very similar curls—and yet Mr. Eggers has been product-free for years. I took both requests under advisement, and now, a year later, the most stunning issue of *McSweeney's* arrives at my door, though my hair remains waxed up like a well-loved surfboard.

McSWEENEY'S 29

McSweeney's 29

(2008)

ELI HOROWITZ: I was happy with this one. The cover was inspired by a book called *Art Deco Bookbindings* that I borrowed from Heidi Meredith and haven't given back. Tons of great stuff. Meanwhile, for years I had been carrying vague ideas of overlapping die-cut casewraps. When I began working on the design, I had a clear sense of the features— the varying cuts, the geometric feel—but I didn't know what it should actually look like, what this would all add up to. My circles eventually turned into planets, but still I didn't really have any specific motivation. Then I sat down with Brian McMullen, and within thirty minutes we were pretty close to the moon-phase design you see today. There are exactly twenty-nine stars on the spine. That's all Brian. There are three different colors for this issue: gray, blue, and red. No real reason—it was easy and free and so . . . The red is the most rare, by far—we thought it was a wacky goof, but actually I think it turned out the best.

BLAZE GINSBERG: I wrote my piece about my crush on Hilary Duff. This was part of my memoir I started

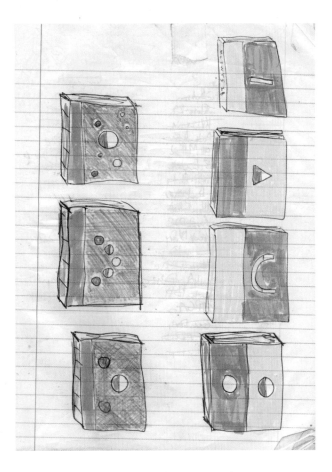

Opposite and above: The cover of Issue 29, designed by Eli Horowitz and Brian McMullen, and some early sketches of less-good cover ideas. (Candy corn?)

writing about my school issues and things that were bothering me. Writing is something that I really enjoy doing and want to be my career. When I heard that my piece was going to be in *McSweeney's* I was really, really excited even though I did not know then that *McSweeney's* was a magazine people bust their asses to be mentioned in. I also was with Joyce Carol Oates in this issue. I had just read her in my college English 100 class. That was the class where my professor failed me because she did not believe that I was doing my own writing.

RODDY DOYLE: I worked as a road sweeper in London in 1978. It was summer work, and in early October I went back to Dublin, to "do" my final year in college. More than 20 years later I met a man I'd worked with that summer, who was now an artist. He told me a story. He'd asked a woman, a barmaid, if he could paint her. She'd said yeah, as long as he did a copy of the portrait for her too. He did, but when he went to the pub where she worked to give it to her—and what a great excuse for going to the pub—she'd gone. She stayed gone for quite a while—two years. The next

251

Above: A loose and ruffled solar system sketch by Eli Horowitz (left) and two versions of the final cover (right).
Opposite: The opening endpapers, at top, and the first three spreads from the issue's second story, Dawn Ryan's "The Strauss House."
All the illustrations come from Jane McDevitt's collection of Eastern European matchbook labels.

time he saw her, he saw more of her—she'd put on quite a lot of weight. She asked where her painting was. He said he'd give it to her the next day—and he stayed up all night painting her additional weight. He delivered the portrait, and she was delighted. That's where "The Painting" comes from.

NELLY REIFLER: I don't usually write with specific readers in mind; actually, I never do. But somewhere in the middle of writing "History Lesson," when I realized I was doing something really strange, I began to think of McSweeney's editors—Eli, Jordan—as the people who would read it. In spite of the fact that I had imagined McSweeney's as the ideal place for my story, I really didn't assume that it would wind up there. I was delighted and honored to have the chance to work with these fine folks again. I was equally delighted when I was sent some images of the strangely pretty, blocky Russian graphics that adorn the title (and other) pages of the stories. With every issue of *McSweeney's* it's a pleasure to feel how the tendrils of certain pieces curl out toward others;

reading stories like Laura Hendrix's, John Thorson's, and J. Erin Sweeney's, I find it touching to think of our imaginations paddling around in similar ponds.

J. ERIN SWEENEY: That summer while I was going back and forth with Jordan about "Augury," I had just been laid off, so I had this bewildering overload of free time. I dedicated myself to the art of obsessive over-thinking and over-thought that story like it was my job, since it was. I was honored to share pages with all the writers in this issue, but my favorite story was one that put a lid on some of my learning that summer about over-thinking and the art of covering my tracks. Laura Hendrix's sentences in "A Record of Our Debts" is so human and organic that the story comes off as a calm retelling of events that really happened. I believed it. It provided—for me—a fine example of the connection between believability, simplicity, and really, really good story writing.

PETER ORNER: Regarding my story, "Pampkin's Lament": In my family, politics—especially being on the losing end of politics—runs in the blood. My father, in 1972, ran for the Illinois State Senate against a popular incumbent. He got crushed in the Democratic primary. I remember nothing about the race itself but for many years we kept a life-size cardboard cutout of my father smiling and waving. Under my father's feet, the still inexplicable slogan: ORNER FOR THE NEW INTEGRITY. Mike Pampkin, a losing candidate for governor of Illinois, is my pale contribution to a long line of heroes. I hope he speaks up a little for failure. In politics, yes, but also for the mightiest losses of all—defeats in love.

DAWN RYAN: When I got Jordan Bass' email asking me if the story I'd sent McSweeney's about nine months earlier was still available, I didn't know what he meant. Of course it was available. Every time I have one-too-many drinks, I start bragging. Even when sober though, I've been insufferable. When I finally got my copy, and had the thing in my hand, I was quickly humbled. McSweeney's always compiles a good collection, but Issue 29 is, as the cover suggests, stellar. I felt a true sense of honor after reading the other pieces in this issue. These pieces are loud and deep. These are exactly the kinds of stories we're discouraged from writing in school.

YANNICK MURPHY: When Dave asked me if I wanted to contribute to the Sci-Fi issue, I had been thinking about the next book I would write. I read tons of sci-fi as a kid, but as an adult it has never occurred to me to write a sci-fi story. There are probably certain rules for writing sci-fi (alien must appear by page 20, etc.) but the only thing that came to my mind was "spacecraft." I decided I'd cheat and write the story the way I wanted to, without investigating or thinking about what the rules were for writing a sci-fi story, but I would also include a spacecraft. The funny part is, after Dave accepted the story for publication, he said McSweeney's had changed its mind, it wasn't going to be a sci-fi issue after all, but I liked my new character, "the spacecraft," that sometimes hovers around us so intimately that it became a big part of the novel that I just finished, and which is based on the story that appears in Issue 29.

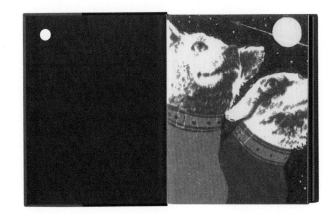

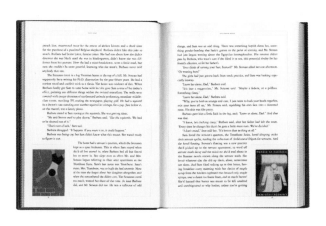

Zeitoun

by DAVE EGGERS (2009)

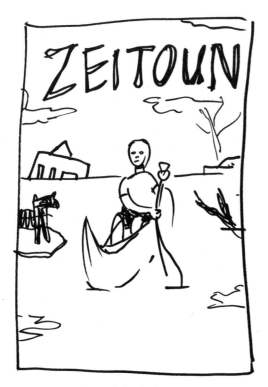

Step 1: Dave's first sketch — so crude.

DAVE EGGERS: From the start, I had the thought that we'd have Zeitoun paddling toward the viewer, and that the image should show the devastation after Katrina, but that there would also be a heroic sort of feel to Abdulrahman in his canoe. And given the subject matter, the work required the artist to step back a bit and avoid overstylization. So I called Rachell Sumpter and asked if she'd be interested, warning her that it would be a bit limiting. She's so good at everything, and had no fear of the job. I gave her my crude sketch, some photos of New Orleans I'd taken after the storm, and some photos of Abdulrahman—including his prison ID. Her first drawing was 94% there. After that, we went through a bunch of small variations, making sure that the cover remained about Zeitoun, and not the color, or the style, or anything tangential. Again Rachell nailed it.

Step 2: Rachell takes the first stab. The paddle shape and position is a bit off, and his hair is too dark. But otherwise we're on our way.

Step 3: Dave gives Rachell more photos of Zeitoun, and she zeroes in on his face. She removes the line of kudzu that was infringing too much on the sky. Dave asks that there be some scope and volume to the sky—clouds that might indicate a connection to the heavens.

Step 4: First inked version.

Step 5: First color version. A bit too colorful, too festive.
Dave suggests maybe using a more limited palette.

Step 6: First experiment with three-color look.
Getting so close!

Step 7: Near-final artwork (with byline shrunk).
Final cover has silver foil for reflections in
the rain, and a burgundy spine.

McSweeney's 30

(2 0 0 9)

BILL COTTER: Say, I have a question about the cover. A friend noticed that the first and last three letters of the title of Issue 30 could serve as a cunning acrostic for that issue's venerated place of printing. Was that intentional? If so, that's pretty swell.

DAVE EGGERS: For months—years, really—we'd been feeling that it was high time to print another issue of the Quarterly in Iceland. And we did. We called this the "forge ahead/throwback" issue.

BILL COTTER: I love Jason Polan's illustrations—how they come in pairs, each drawing parked tidily into a five-line indent at the outer edges of text. It would be neat if all books were illustrated like this, pertinent little grotesques that demand their own separate readings, once before and once after all the stories are consumed.

ELI HOROWITZ: There was once a full story inspired by Jason's illustrations for the other stories—a sort of parallel narrative. A few sentences of this story appeared at the bottom of each page. Could have been neat.

CATHERINE BUSSINGER: I was curious to see what other stories woule chosen for the issue; I didn't see how my story could fit within a theme or mesh into any kind of collection. But after reading the other stories I caught a glimpse of a subtext: Most of the pieces detail some kind of slow-motion grudge match in progress; they reveal the ugly underpinnings that drive human interaction and which prevent life from becoming what we hope it might be. J. Malcolm Garcia's "Cuts" is a perfect example of that; the story aptly shows how someone operating with the most laudable of intentions ends up entangled in a back-stabbing competition with a coworker. Nick Ekkizogloy's "Stowaways" also shows two coworkers embroiled in a complex psychic wrestling match; Kevin Moffett's story—same deal but with a father and son this time; Wells Tower matches brother against brother. Sometimes the adversary is not a person but a circumstance that is dangerous, bizarre, or compromising, and which warps the protagonist in ways that are unflattering and undesirable, and that's when the story gets really interesting.

NICK EKKIZOGLOY: I really liked how the "It's too late to screw it up, right?" pretext/note from God echoed through all the stories. Even down to the last line of "Retreat" when Tower's narrator eats the "leper moose," you get the sensation that Issue 30 is about taking chances. For better or worse all the motley guys and gals in these pages are doing something and making interesting decisions.

SHELLY ORIA: When I opened the email from Jordan Bass inquiring if "The Beginning of a Plan" was still available, my husband and I were on the phone with good friends of ours, telling them we were likely moving back to Tel Aviv. In the following month, sorting through closets and sorting through sentences became synonymous. In both cases I mainly asked myself what was necessary and what I could do without. In both cases a man was part of the dialogue— my husband when it came to books, clothes, and furniture, Jordan when it came to sentences, scenes, and characters. I'm good at all kinds of things (peeling cucumbers really fast, helping people understand their feelings) but letting go isn't one of them. Which means that I usually find that last bit of editing difficult; when it's done there's nothing left to do but let go. That day, letting go felt natural. Maybe that's what happens when you know your story's headed to a place where it will be happy.

The Wild Things

by DAVE EGGERS (2009)

DAVE EGGERS: While Spike [Jonze] and I were working on *Where the Wild Things Are*, Maurice Sendak called one day and asked if I'd write a novel based on the book/screenplay. And I think as soon as I was thinking about the book, I was thinking about a fur cover. We'd talked about fur in the office for years, and so Eli contacted TWP, the printer in Singapore.

ELI HOROWITZ: They sent us a bunch of fur samples. The one we chose is usually used to fix fur coats. Like if you burn your fur coat or someone throws red paint on you, you use this fur to fix it.

DAVE EGGERS: It's really soft. So then I called a friend of mine, Natasha Boas, whose son was about the age of Max in the book. I took some pictures of him looking fierce, and then painted the eyes in acrylic. The other cover was done by Rachell Sumpter, because she's just such a versatile and gifted artist. I didn't give her much direction, outside of showing her the book and asking that the cover be a bit creepy and dark in tone. She came up with that silhouette, with that weird red foliage. It was instantly the right thing. I just asked that we put the same silhouette on the back, too, albeit with the crown on Max's head. We added the gold-stamped title and that was that.

Left top: Photo of Dave's young friend Jack Boas, used as a reference for the cover painting.

Left middle: Acrylic on canvas painting by Dave Eggers for the fur-covered edition of The Wild Things.

Left bottom: Faux-fur samples from Tien Wah Press in Singapore. Option 2 was the winner.

Below: The faux-fur edition of The Wild Things.

Above and left: Rachell Sumpter's early sketches for the hardcover edition of The Wild Things.

Below: The final sketch for the front and back covers of the hardcover edition, and the finished book.

McSweeney's 31

(2 0 0 9)

Opposite and above: The front cover of Issue 31, with an illustration by Scott Teplin, and, from left to right, a binding and a frontispiece that helped inspire the design, and an early mock-up of the cover.

GRAHAM WEATHERLY: One of the first issues I ever read was 22, the magnetic one. When I picked it up, I was already going to be an intern at McSweeney's, so I was just brushing up on the latest stuff so as not to look like an idiot. I read the issue's introduction, which described how Dominic Luxford pitched an idea, "Poets Picking Poets," which ultimately became part of the issue, and later its own book. The idea that a low-level intern could pitch something that would end up in an issue... Well, being a low-level intern I made that my goal.

DARREN FRANICH: A few weeks into the internship, Andrew Leland came over to the intern table and announced an upcoming pitch session, where Dave would sit down with all the interns and let them pitch ideas for stories, books, music, anything. Since all great business deals come off the golf course, Graham and I went out to Golden Gate Park, drank a few Coors, threw some frisbees, and started talking about the environment.

GRAHAM WEATHERLY: For content, one idea we had was recycled fiction: somebody would take a masterwork like *Moby Dick*, extract lines from it, and reconstitute those lines into a new story. I still think it's a cool idea. Unfortunately, that was pretty much the only clear idea we had, which became very apparent at the meeting.

DARREN FRANICH: Because Dave hated it. Actually, pretty much everyone hated our pitch. There were about fourteen other interns, and everyone had their own brilliant pitch, and the crowd tended to be very supportive of every new pitch—"That's a great idea!" From the moment we said the words "green issue," the crowd turned hostile. Suffice it to say, Dave did not go for the roof shingles.

GRAHAM WEATHERLY: But he liked our energy and said, "I don't like it, but I like where it could possibly go." He told us to rework it and present it again the following week. We were totally emboldened by

261

having our idea soundly rejected. We retreated to Darren's apartment late one night, and we were literally just going through Wikipedia trying to narrow down "environmentalism" and one of us just said "Endangered Species." It was this notion that there were all these old forms of literature that were dying or already extinct, and why couldn't we put them in a zoo and repropagate the species?

DARREN FRANICH: It was definitely an "Aha!" moment for both of us. "Endangered species" seemed to be an easily digestible way to explore writing from different societies across the world. The more we talked about it, the more genres we found.

GRAHAM WEATHERLY: For the next meeting with Dave, we came up with a solid list of thirty genres.

DARREN FRANICH: I seriously don't think it was thirty. Probably twelve.

GRAHAM WEATHERLY: Twenty-five, conservatively.

DARREN FRANICH: Dave immediately slashed half of them. No penny dreadfuls, no picaresques, no patericons.

GRAHAM WEATHERLY: But he liked the endangered species idea, and he wanted us to come up with a list of potential authors for each genre. We put together a list of about fifty writers, musicians, critics, and poets.

DARREN FRANICH: With our list of potential writers in hand, we composed a generic letter, explaining the project, asking writers if they would be interested. We passed the letter over to Dave, who tore it apart. He sent us to letter-writing boot camp.

GRAHAM WEATHERLY: But we were seeing our project take on a life of its own. Every new writer who said "yes," every new submission we received, was like watching our infant roll over for the first time. I was always ridiculously optimistic, and I didn't think there was any way we could fail.

Most consuetudinaries were not illustrated—but wax is an important and symbolic commodity in the genre. Different varieties of candles and tapers were used on specific occasions and in a particular manner, and several monks would often be charged with requisitioning them. Consuetudinaries specified precise weights and dimensions in each case.

It wasn't unusual for a consuetudinary to contain a prefatory note like this one, explaining the origins of the text and of the sect. *The Testament of John of Rila* begins:

This testament of our holy father John, citizen of the Rila wilderness, which he delivered to his disciples before he died, was rewritten from a parchment with great preciseness by the most honorable and reverend among priests, lord Demetian, a man of erudition and intelligence, who was a disciple of the reverend hermit Varlaam, who lived nine years on the Cherna mountain... [The testament] was rewritten for easier reading and for commemoration by all monks in that monastery, because the parchment on which the testament was written originally was hidden carefully together with the other objects of the monastery because of the great fear which was reigning in that time from the impious sons of Agar. In the year of the creation of the world 6893 and from the Nativity of Christ 1385, on the twelfth day of the month of February, on the memorial day of St. Meletios of Antioch.

conclusive event was the discovery on her damp pillow, after a restless night some months later, of a peculiar waxen object, which she recognized to be a word in an as-yet-untranslated language of the dead. The subsequent day, she closed herself in her study, allowing only her chamber pot and thrice-daily tray of graham crackers and milk to cross the threshold, and reemerged nine months later with mild anemia and a new cosmology. The land of the dead is made of language, she taught; we make a world whenever we speak. The dead inhabit it, and speak in turn, and die; the world they speak is ours. Gravity is a form of grammar. The planets obey the rules of rhetoric. "Death is the mouth from which we crawl, the ear to which we fly," she remarked, as she severed the blood-red ribbon draped across the tall, narrow doors of the Word Church.

Since that day, everyone associated with the Vocational School (faculty, students, employees, visiting aunts) has been obliged to gather on those hard wooden seats every Friday and indenture themselves to death—or, as the students say, "die." The Alphabetical Stutterers expertly halt speech-time, three hundred mouths backtalk furiously, and in every throat the dead rise up. The chapel fills with the ambiguous air of the Mouthlands, in which fleeting notions have the presence of two-thousand-year-old megaliths, and material things look at you like distant cousins, and nothing you have ever done is what you thought it was. The Thanatomaths pitch themselves through their own mouths, showing the whole congregation their "red" or "tonsil" faces, and strike out into death. Outside, the cries of birds rise up like a wall of thorns.

In theory, the Word Church needs no consuetudinary, since in it, every day is the same day—namely, the first day the Founder led the congregation in hailing the dead. Its time-reversal techniques are meant to transport every mouth back to the previous service, when another mouth stood open in its place, so that it can transmit what that mouth said without alteration. That mouth which was itself channeling a previous speaker, who was channeling another, who was channeling another, and so on, all these mouths tunneling backward through history forming a sort of ear trumpet through which resonates the very first of the series: the voice of the dead Clive Matty, speaking through the Founder at that reverberant first service.

132

DARREN FRANICH: I was ridiculously pessimistic and constantly expected to fail. Graham and I made a great team. Eli told us early on, "If you guys drop the ball on this, nobody else is going to pick it up." That sounds cold-blooded, but it was actually the most inspirational thing anyone ever told us.

WILL SHEFF: I was on tour in Australia with my band, Okkervil River, and I got an email from Graham Weatherly. He told me about the "endangered species" issue of *McSweeney's* and asked if I wanted to contribute a song or something. Because I'm the kind

In practice, of course, minor differences in the embouchure of speakers—a lisp here, an overbite there—add up. The ear trumpet gets a kink in it, and then another, until nothing can be heard at all. In such cases, the following procedures will recalibrate the faulty instrument.

The original of this text, laboriously handwritten on thirty-seven pages of an otherwise empty notebook and starting, by accident or design, at its intended end (thus the words COMPOSITION BOOK appear on the back cover, upside down), was until now the sole existing copy, since the SJVS chose never to set it into type, out of simple negligence or a superstitious conviction that to do so would only remove it further from its source. Some effort was expended, however, on making it *appear* machine-printed: the letters are minute and bristle with serifs like little hooks (inducing a half-conscious discomfort in the throat-clearing reader). The pretense is carried so far as the travesty of an "engraving"—really, pen and ink—on the title page, depicting an open mouth, very clumsily rendered, with more teeth than is typical in *Homo sapiens sapiens*.

CONSUETUDINARY OF THE WORD CHURCH.

I. *Of the structure of the Church, disposition of its Congregation, etc.*

II. *Of the several Bodies of the Congregation.*

III. *Of the manner in which the Vocation is to be practiced day and night throughout the year.*

IV. *Of the manner in which the Friday office shall fittingly be carried out; with the rituals, their order, and their occasions.*

V. *Of the Liturgies.*

VI. *Of the Readings.*

VII. *Of the use of Sacramental Ink, Saliva, and Chewed Paper.*

VIII. *Of the use of Gags, Prosthetic Mouths, etc.*

IX. *Of Signs that may be used during the Offices.*

X. *Of the Services that the Pupils shall render to the Community.*

XI. *Of the Manner in which a dead Pupil shall be sent into the Mouthlands.*

In his introduction to *A Consuetudinary of the Fourteenth Century for the Refectory of the House of St. Swithun in Winchester*, G. W. Kitchin writes,

The document, which is written on two skins of fine white parchment, and is 3 feet 4 inches long and 11 inches broad, is by no means easy to read. For it not only belongs to a time when the general handwriting was becoming much contracted, but it has also suffered much from careless usage. It probably lay about in the Refectory, was taken up and thumbed by the Monks, curious to learn their own, and, still more, their neighbours' duties, until in some parts the parchment has grown brown, and the writing is here and there almost obliterated; nor has the difficulty of reading it been diminished by the carelessness of some good Brother, who spilt his beer on the back of it.

A partial table of contents from the House of St. Swithun in Winchester consuetudinary:

XX. Of Maundry-Bread.
XXI. Of the Curtarian. Of the customs to be allowed in the Refectorarian's Account-Roll before the Curtarian.
XXII. Of the four Sergeants of the Church. Of the four Sergeants of the City.
XXIII. Of the Refectorarian's Valet.
XXIV. Of the Usher.

A spread from Shelley Jackson's consuetudinary, "Consuetudinary of the Word Church, or the Church of the Dead Letter."

of person that never takes the easy route when there's also an impossible route, I told Graham I'd love to write an actual prose piece. Graham suggested the *fornaldarsaga*—legendary tales from Norway and Iceland. I'd had absolutely no exposure to a fornaldarsaga at all, but I said sure, took a trip to the bookstore, and dove headfirst into such accessible titles as *Ragnars saga loðbrókar* and *Hervarar saga ok Heiðreks*. The sagas that I read told supernatural tales of death and violence, but almost all of them purported to recount the lives of actual historical figures. I figured the most "natural" way to compose a new fornaldarsaga would be to just update one of these legendary tales into a modern setting. But then I decided it would be harder, stupider, and more fun to attempt the opposite—to describe modern events in my version of an awkwardly translated thirteenth-century Icelandic style.

GRAHAM WEATHERLY: I can remember how in the fourth-to-last week we had a few things to do every day. The next week, a couple things to do. Then the next week, just one thing to do. In the final week, we had two tasks total. And then it just stopped. It was like watching the Big Bang peter out.

ELI HOROWITZ: It seemed like something old-ish might be appropriate for the cover. But we do old-ish all the time, and we didn't want to repeat ourselves. So we decided to aim for vaguely medieval rather than vaguely Victorian. In the end, it turned out vaguely yearbookish—I'm not sure how. The coloring is inspired by an old copy of *Tales from Shakespeare* by Charles and Mary Lamb that I got at the Whitlock Farm Book Barn in Bethany, Connecticut—one of my favorite bookstores anywhere. That book has a gold leafy pattern stamped on a white spine, but over the past hundred years, the gold tarnished and the white yellowed, so the artifact has a nice low-contrast effect. Our cover art is a magnified detail of a Scott Teplin drawing of a million waves—the full piece can be seen on the endpapers. Jordan did a really nice job with the interior design.

JORDAN BASS: Our copy editor's father sent us an email the other day saying, among other things, "But I have to tell you, I was quite unable to read the sidebars, both because of the type size and the color of the typesetting. I do hope you will rethink your policy about type size. I admit I am 75 years old and my eyes are not those of a younger person. But I tried out this article on several youthful weekend guests and they all agreed the sidebars were unreadable. One must guard against the wayward instincts of designers. Your journal is far too valuable to be torpedoed in this way."

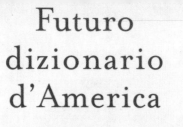

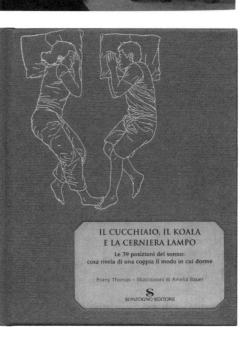

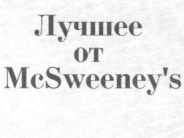